SPANISH POLITICS
DEMOCRACY AFTER
DICTATORSHIP

OMAR G. ENCARNACIÓN

polity

First published in 2008 by Polity Press

Polity Press
65 Bridge Street
Cambridge CB2 1UR, UK

Polity Press
350 Main Street
Malden, MA 02148, USA

ISBN-13: 978-07456-3992-5
ISBN-13: 978-07456-3993-2 (pb)

A catalogue record for this book is available from the British Library.

Typeset in 10 on 12pt Sabon
by SNP Best-set Typesetter Ltd., Hong Kong
Printed and bound in Great Britain by MPG Books Ltd, Bodmin, Cornwall

The publisher has used its best endeavours to ensure that the URLs for external websites referred to in this book are correct and active at the time of going to press. However, the publisher has no responsibility for the websites and can make no guarantee that a site will remain live or that the content is or will remain appropriate.

Every effort has been made to trace all copyright holders, but if any have been inadvertently overlooked the publishers will be pleased to include any necessary credits in any subsequent reprint or edition.

For further information on Polity, visit our website: www.polity.co.uk

CONTENTS

FIGURES

TABLES

Acknowledgments

Books are seldom the product of a single person's labor, and this one is certainly no exception. Since my days as a graduate student at the department of politics of Princeton University in the early 1990s, when my interest in Spanish politics matured, I have been very fortunate to have benefited from the generous financial support of numerous research institutions, grants, and fellowships, including the Princeton University's Council on Regional Studies and Center for International Studies, the Council for European Studies, the Fulbright–Hays program, the Ford Foundation, and the National Research Council. Two grants in particular, from the Bard College Research Council and the Program for Cooperation between United States' Universities and Spain's Ministry of Culture, contributed significantly to the development of this project by supporting research stays in Spain during 2005–7. While in Spain, I have always benefited from the hospitality and resources of the Center for Advanced Study in the Social Sciences (CEACS) of the Juan March Institute.

Many individuals contributed to this book in both direct and indirect ways. Nancy Bermeo and Juan J. Linz, my academic mentors at Princeton and Yale respectively, continue to be a source of intellectual inspiration in helping me understand both Spanish politics and the process of democratization. Robert Fishman served as an informal advisor to the project by reviewing the entire manuscript and providing invaluable analytical guidance. Sebastián Royo carefully reviewed the economic analysis contained in chapter 7. Aránzazu Borrachero served as useful reference for the analysis on the "return" of the past provided in chapter 8. In two different stages in the development of the manuscript, several anonymous reviewers from Polity Press provided useful advice on how to organize the book. Towards the completion of the project I was fortunate to have participated in the conference on "New Perspectives on the Spanish Transition to Democracy," held at King's College London (May 18–19, 2007), which provided a very productive forum for assessing thirty years of Spanish democracy with numerous colleagues, including Richard Gunther, Paul Heywood, Daniele Conversi, José Ramón Montero, Diego Muro, Monica Threlfall, José M. Magone, Sebastian Balfour, Charles Powell, Felipe Agüero, and Irene Martín-Cortés.

My students at Bard College are mainly responsible for my decision to undertake the writing of a general text on Spanish politics. It was at their request that I agreed to teach for the first time in spring 2006 a course on "Contemporary Spanish Politics," which provided the inspiration for the book. It was a treat to test the material upon such an eager and challenging audience. I am especially thankful to Owen Thompson, Joanna Klonsky, Rachel Meyer, and Risa Grais-Targow for their research assistance and thoughtful criticisms. While assembling the manuscript I relied generously upon my previously published research on Spanish politics that over the years has appeared in *Comparative Politics*, *Comparative Political Studies*, *Political Science Quarterly*, *West European Politics*, *Mediterranean Quarterly*, *World Policy Journal*, and *Human Rights Quarterly*. I thank the editors of these journals for publishing my work in the first place and for allowing me to reprint portions of it in this book.

As always, John and Amos provided much needed emotional support.

ABBREVIATIONS

ABI	Acuerdo Básico Interconfederal (Basic Interconfederate Agreement)
ACNP	Asociación Católica Nacional de Propagandistas (National Catholic Association of Propagandists)
AES	Acuerdo Económico y Social (Social and Economic Accord)
ANE	Acuerdo Nacional del Empleo (National Employment Agreement)
AP	Alianza Popular (Popular Alliance)
ARMH	Asociación para la Recuperación de la Memoria Histórica (Association for the Recuperation of Historical Memory)
CCOO	Comisiones Obreras (Workers' Commissions)
CEDA	Confederación Española de Derechas Autónomas (National Confederation of Autonomous Right-wing Groups)
CEOE	Confederación Española de Organizaciones Empresariales (Spanish Confederation of Business Organizations)
CIFESA	Compañía Industrial de Film Español (Industrial Company of Spanish Film)
CIS	Centro de Investigaciones Sociológicas (Center for Sociological Investigations)
CiU	Convergència i Unió (Convergence and Union)
CNEP	Comparative National Elections Project
CNT	Confederación Nacional del Trabajo (National Confederation of Labor)
CSC	Convergència Socialista de Catalunya (Socialist Convergence of Catalonia)
EEC	European Economic Community
EMU	European Monetary Union
ERC	Esquerra Republicana de Catalunya (Republican Left of Catalonia)
ETA	Euskadi Ta Askatasuna (Basque Homeland and Freedom)
EU	European Union
FAI	Federación Anarquista Ibérica (Iberian Anarquist Federation)
FN	Fuerza Nueva (New Force)
GAL	Grupos Anti-terroristas de Liberación (Anti-terrorist Liberation Groups)

GRAPO	Grupos de Resistencia Anti-fascista Primero de Octubre (First of October Anti-Fascist Resistance Groups)
HB	Herri Batasuna (Popular Unity)
HOAC	Hermandades Obreras de Acción Católica (Workers' Brotherhoods for Catholic Action)
IMF	International Monetary Fund
INE	Instituto Nacional de Estadísticas (National Institute of Statistics)
INI	Instituto Nacional de Industria (National Institute of Industry)
IU	Izquierda Unida (United Left)
JCO	Juventudes Católica Obrera (Catholic Workers' Youth)
LOAPA	Ley Orgánica para la Armonización del Proceso Autonómico (Organic Law for the Harmonization of the Autonomy Process)
NATO	North Atlantic Treaty Organization
NODO	Noticiarios y Documentales Cinematográficos (Newscasts and Cinematography Documentaries)
OECD	Organization for Economic Cooperation and Development
OSE	Organización Sindical Española (Spanish Syndical Organization)
PCE	Partido Comunista de España (Spanish Communist Party)
PNV	Partido Nacionalista Vasco (Basque Nationalist Party)
PP	Partido Popular (Popular Party)
PSC	Partit dels Socialistes de Catalunya (Socialist Party of Catalonia)
PSOE	Partido Socialista Obrero Español (Spanish Workers' Socialist Party)
PSP	Partido Socialista Popular (Socialist Popular Party)
SEU	Sindicato Español Universitario (Spanish University Syndicate)
UCD	Unión de Centro Democrático (Union of the Democratic Center)
UGT	Unión General de Trabajadores (General Union of Workers)
UNE	Unión Nacional Económica (National Economic Union)
VCO	Vanguardias Católicas Obreras (Catholic Workers' Vanguards)
WVS	World Values Survey

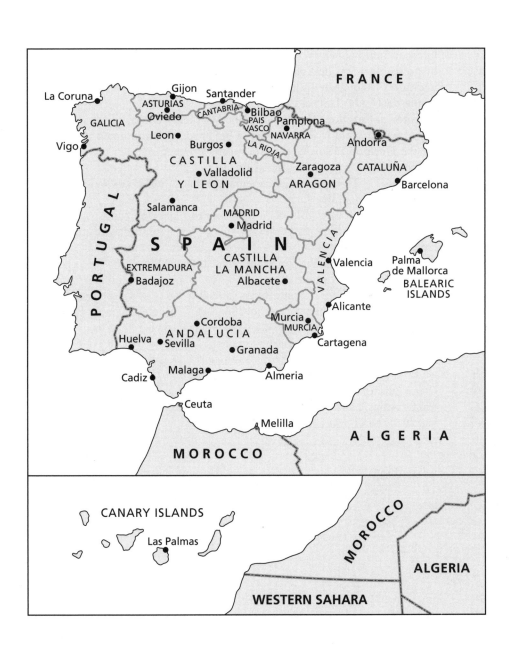

A POST-TRANSITION SETTLEMENT

A great paradox of politics in Spain is that this celebrated example of a successful transition to democratic rule seems, in some respects, surprisingly reluctant to let go of its authoritarian past. Visitors to the country are often startled to encounter numerous monuments to the memory of General Francisco Franco, who governed with an iron hand from 1939 until his death of natural causes on November 20, 1975. Undoubtedly, the most conspicuous material symbol of Francoist Spain is *El Valle de los Caídos* (The Valley of the Fallen), the monument that houses Franco's tomb alongside that of José Antonio Primo de Rivera, the founder of the Falange, a fascist organization. This gargantuan artifice on the outskirts of Madrid – built by Franco as a memorial to the victims of the Spanish Civil War, a conflict that he himself triggered with a military uprising in 1936 – features an underground basilica larger than the main one at the Vatican, topped by a 500-foot stone cross, the tallest in the world, that is visible from a distance of 30 miles. Virtually unaltered since Franco's body was deposited there in 1975, and impeccably maintained at taxpayers' expense, *El Valle* plays host to the hundreds of Spaniards who visit the site on the occasion of the anniversary of the dictator's death. The contrast with the fate of Franco's World War II de facto allies, Germany's Adolf Hitler and Italy's Benito Mussolini, is striking. Hitler committed suicide in his bunker; Mussolini was hung from a gas station awning in Milan. Understandably, for many Spaniards the "preserved" state of *El Valle* as a shrine to Francoism is an affront to the victims of Franco's repression and the country's new democracy.

Tellingly, the case of *El Valle* is not an aberration. Until 2005, a statue of Franco in full equestrian mode stood at Nuevos Ministerios, an area of central Madrid noted for its heavy concentration of government offices, embassies, and multinational corporations; and until the summer of 2006, another statue of Franco could be found in front of the national military academy in the city of Zaragoza.[1] Spanish currency bearing Franco's effigy remained in circulation until the disappearance of the peseta in the late 1990s with the introduction of the euro. Francoist symbols, such as the coat of arms of the dictatorship, are a common sight at churches, convents and monasteries, a vivid reminder of the prominent role played by the Catholic Church in the old regime.[2] It is in the names of the streets of Spanish cities and towns, however, that Franco's memory is most prominently evoked. Madrid alone is home to some 360 streets bearing the names of people or acts associated with the Franco regime.[3] Across the countryside, the once ubiquitous Avenida del Generalíssimo and Calle de José Antonio, the obligatory names of the main commercial streets in all cities and towns under Franco, can still be found.

Spain is a compelling reminder that transitions to democracy, even highly successful ones, seldom draw an unambiguous line between the past and the present. They are, in fact, quite messy; and unpleasant legacies of the old regime always manage to survive. But the disturbing persistence of Franco's material endowment is no accidental happenstance; ironically, it is intimately intertwined with how Spain became a democratic society. When the Spaniards undertook to democratize in 1975, following the end of nearly four decades of Francoism, they studiously avoided anything that could potentially delay, encumber, or inconvenience the path toward a consolidated democracy. This behavior was in keeping with the country's "post-transition settlement," a set of compromises forged by the political class in the wake of Franco's death, which in both content and spirit sought nothing short of creating a political environment that could sustain democratic government in Spain once and for all. It provides one of the most compelling and complex explanations for why Spain would be so successful at reinventing itself as a democratic society following the dismantling of the Franco regime, and shedding its well-earned reputation as the paradigmatic "authoritarian" state (Linz 1970).[4]

Three premises anchor Spain's post-transition settlement. The first and best known is the understanding to let bygones be bygones, an attempt to bring closure to the country's tumultuous past. After Franco's death in 1975, the Spaniards basically chose to turn the page of history and look to the future. This approach for dealing with a difficult and painful past by choosing not to deal with it was institutionalized with the *Pacto del Olvido* (Pact of Forgetting), also known as the *Pacto del Silencio* (Pact of Silence), an unwritten but explicit agreement that aimed for nothing short of collective amnesia about past political excesses.[5] Ensuring the survival of much of the material legacy of the old regime is one of the legacies of the pact, since the government, seeking to avoid an eruption of political passions, left it to the individual provinces to dispose of Francoist monuments as they saw fit.[6] More importantly, the deliberate attempt to bury the past guaranteed the absence of "transitional justice" in Spain's passage from dictatorship to democracy, a virtual anomaly in contemporary processes of democratization. No military trials of the kind that took place in Latin America in the wake of the collapse of military rule were staged in Spain. Nor did the Spaniards see fit to convene a truth commission to account for the human rights violations of the old regime, as was done in South Africa after the end of apartheid, or to engage in bureaucratic purges (so-called lustration) of the kind that accompanied the dismantling of communism in central and eastern Europe, intended to cleanse the political system of the vestiges of the old regime.

Spain's post-transition settlement also calls for a commitment to inter-party collaboration in the making of public policy, especially in the areas of the economy, national security, foreign affairs, and relations between the central administration in Madrid and autonomous regional governments. This compromise seeks to avert political conflict by essentially requiring that the party in control of the government does not act unilaterally on any major issue confronting the nation without consulting the opposition. It was inaugurated with great fanfare with the 1977 Pacts of Moncloa, a set of agreements signed by all the major political parties represented in the national parliament, and supported by the labor movement and the business community, with the intention of forging a coordinated approach to solving economic problems. This and subsequent agreements explain characterizations of Spanish policy making in the post-Franco era as "corporatist" or "neo-corporatist" (see Pérez-Díaz 1986; Foweraker 1987; Bermeo 1994; Encarnación 1997), for the extent to which cooperation is part of the national economic decision-making process, and the degree to which organized economic interests (e.g. unions and employers' groups) are granted an official role in influencing policy matters such as wages, inflation, unemployment, and social security.

A consensus on the identity of Spain as a "nation of nations" is the final and most complex component of Spain's post-transition settlement. As enshrined in the 1978 constitution, it recognizes Spain as an indivisible state that comprises within its geographic boundaries several "nationalities" and distinct cultures. This ambiguous compromise has resulted in the partition of the Spanish national territory into 17 autonomous regional governments (the so-called *autonomías*), each with its own elected president and legislative body, while allowing the country to retain the overall structure of a unitary state. The principal aim of the architects of this compromise was to reconcile a longstanding, contentious debate about "nation and state" in Spain. On one side are those who view Spain as a nation unified by a common history, the Spanish language, and institutions such as the monarchy and the Catholic Church. They have historically favored a highly centralized state and resisted any attempt to federalize the country. On the other side are those who challenge the very notion of a Spanish nation in light of the existence of important regional languages and sub-nationalist movements across the Spanish territory. They have historically advocated autonomy rights for Spain's ethnic minority communities and the creation of a federal state.

Negotiated by individuals representing the Franco regime and its democratic opposition, who met in secret, far away from the prying eyes of the media and the general public, Spain's post-transition settlement is the ultimate elite political production. This point is underscored in conceptualizations of Spanish democratization as a case of "transition by transaction" (Share 1986), an example of "political crafting of democratic consolidation" (Linz and Stepan 1989), "the very model of the modern elite settlement" (Gunther 1992), and a "pacted democracy" (Encarnación 2001a). The general public, however, was not irrelevant to the rise of the post-transition settlement, and much less to its maintenance. It is questionable that the political class would have emerged from the Franco era so willing to enter into political compromises without the implicit support of the public. As will be seen throughout this analysis, the agreements of the post-transition settlement enjoyed the broad support of the Spanish public, including, most surprisingly perhaps, the accord to repress the memory of the past. Thus, the democracy that was created by the post-transition settlement was by and large the one desired by the Spanish people.

A COMPLEX LEGACY .

The exuberant international press coverage that greeted the thirtieth anniversary of the passing of General Franco attests to the success of Spain's democratic transition, and by extension of the post-transition settlement. "Pass the Cava," declared the *International Herald Tribune* (December 6, 2006), in an article that celebrated Spain's "embrace of modernization after decades of stagnation under Franco" as "one of Europe's great success stories."[7] No less effusive was the normally staid *Economist* (June 26, 2004), which could hardly contain its enthusiasm for Spain's political and economic accomplishments in the post-Franco era. "In under 30 years Spain has emerged from dictatorship and international isolation, built a successful economy and established an effective democracy. Perhaps no other European country has achieved so much, on so many fronts, so quickly." A cover story in *Newsweek International* (February 2, 2004) proclaimed Spain "the new princely peacock, after being looked down on by the northern Europeans as a poor Mediterranean country."

Media acclaim about Spain echoes a broadly based scholarly consensus about the success of democracy in the post-Franco era. No other new democracy launched between the years 1974 and 1990, a period recognized as "the greatest period of democratic ferment in the history of modern civilization" (Diamond and Platter 1996: ix), has generated more lavish and sustained praise by the academic community.[8] Just a few years after Franco's death, Spain was heralded as "the principal success story of the 1970s" (Payne 1986a: 3) for the orderly manner in which democracy was installed in the country. Throughout the 1980s, Spain's skillful management of many of the challenges that have bedeviled other newly democratic states – such as economic reform, modernization of the military, and decentralization of the state – inspired references to the country as "a miracle" and "a model" for emerging democracies in Latin America, Asia, and central and eastern Europe (Przeworski 1991: 8). By the mid-1990s and early 2000s, when many new democracies were earning the labels of "delegative" (O'Donnell 1996) and "illiberal" (Zakaria 2003) – for the disturbing ease with which a democratic constitution and routine elections co-existed hand in hand with widespread corruption, large-scale human rights violations, a total lack of governmental transparency and accountability, and a head of state who behaves more like a monarch than a democratically elected leader – Spain was being hailed as an exemplary case of democratization. According to Juan Linz and Alfred Stepan (1996: 108), the deans of the democratization literature, Spain is "the paradigmatic case for the study of democratic consolidation much as the Weimar Republic became paradigmatic for the study of democratic breakdown."

Given all this praise, it is hardly surprising that the Spanish experience has become a central empirical reference in reshaping the theoretical understanding of what makes democracy possible. Traditionally, the scholarship on democratization has emphasized so-called "democratic prerequisites"; namely, a relatively advanced level of social and economic development (Lipset 1959; Rostow 1960), and a "civic culture" that embodies such values as tolerance, reciprocity, and trust (Almond and Verba 1963). These prerequisites are believed to advance democratization by promoting education, industrialization, and urbanization, among other signs of "modernity," and by creating a citizenry that cares about upholding democratic principles and institutions. At the present time, however, the conventional wisdom is to acknowledge the agency that political actors exert upon the process of democratization (O'Donnell and Schmitter 1986; Linz and Stepan 1989; Di Palma 1990). Special attention is given to the political strategies and institutional choices made by the political class during the juncture of regime change in determining whether democracy succeeds or fails. Democracies are created and not born, a point convincingly demonstrated by the Spanish experience, is the new mantra of democratization scholars.

From "different" to "normal"

Among the many contributions of the post-transition settlement to the success of Spanish democracy, the most obvious is to have assisted the political class in organizing a transition out of authoritarian rule in as non-confrontational a manner as possible. This is hardly an insignificant accomplishment considering the nearly four decades of highly institutionalized authoritarian rule endured by Spain, which meant starting democracy from scratch and with very high expectations on the part of the general public. Another easily appreciated contribution of the post-transition settlement is to have facilitated a string of moderate and very successful governments by underwriting a new political culture based on consensus and compromise. It is worth noting that the political regime inaugurated in 1977 is the first stable democracy in Spanish history, a fact that gives a good sense of the extraordinary nature of the process of democratization in Spain and the post-transition settlement itself. All other attempts at democratization since the nineteenth century had ended in chaos and violence.

Less apparent but no less important is the extraordinary degree of cooperation between political forces from the left and the right, as well as from the state and civil society, made possible by the post-transition settlement on matters as varied as coping with ethnopolitical conflict, modernizing the outmoded economic structures inherited from the Franco regime, and ending Spain's international isolation by securing admission into the North Atlantic Treaty Organization (NATO) and the European Economic Community (EEC), the predecessor to the European Union (EU). Encouraging and sustaining this cooperation is a set of institutions created directly or indirectly by the politics of consensus of the post-transition settlement, such as the process of "social concertation," formalized bargaining among the government, employers' associations, and the unions, and the "state of the autonomies," the system of regional governments that resulted from the decentralization of the state.

Notwithstanding the obvious importance of the post-transition settlement to democratic stability in the post-Franco era, its special significance rests in the radical departure that it represents in the evolution of politics in Spain. It is hard to overstate the extent to which the post-transition settlement has transformed the very essence of Spanish politics. Confrontation rather than compromise has been the dominant mode of political interaction in Spain, a point tellingly captured in the popular notion of *Las dos Españas* (the two Spains). This conception of Spain as a land tragically split into two irreconcilable halves has been a reliable explanation for the nation's inability to comport itself under the rules of democracy.[9] "Traditional" Spain – which represents the historical social and political order embodied in the Spanish monarchy, the military, the Catholic Church, and the rural oligarchy – promotes the mythic view of Spain as a culturally homogeneous land and sees the country's identity rooted in its once vast colonial empire in the Americas, North Africa, and Asia, and in its historic role in spreading the Catholic faith around the world. "Modern" Spain represents the liberal ideas that swept Europe, the United States, and Latin America during the eighteenth and nineteenth centuries, such as egalitarianism, republicanism, and federalism, together with the Spaniards' reputation for individualism, rebellion, and revolution. Its standard-bearers are secular republicans, intellectuals, anarchists, regionalists, the socialist and communist parties, and an often-revolutionary labor movement.

Beginning in the late nineteenth century, when the phenomenon of the two Spains became fully crystallized, Traditional Spain and Modern Spain began to confront each other with devastating consequences. Their ideological battles climaxed during the interwar years, which witnessed the collapse of the Second Republic (1931–6), Spain's first real attempt at democratization, and the country's descent into civil war (1936–9). During this barbaric conflict each side sought nothing short of the annihilation of the other, resulting in the bloodiest of the many civil conflicts that erupted in Europe during the interwar period, with a tally of casualties exceeding more than half a million people. The chaos and devastation of the war, paired with the longevity of Franco's authoritarian regime (1939–75), solidified longstanding and deeply entrenched negative stereotypes about Spain and its people that today are all but forgotten, eclipsed by the success of democracy since the mid-1970s.

"Spain is different" is the euphemistic phrase that for decades justified perceptions of the country as unfit for democracy. Its roots run deep in the scholarship on Spanish history and politics. In the late nineteenth century, historians routinely depicted Spain as a "semi-African" nation, owing to the country's proximity to North Africa and nearly eight centuries of Arab occupation.[10] One can presume that this accounts for the origins of the phrase "Africa begins at the Pyrenees." In more recent times, historians have been prone to descriptions of the Spanish people as violent and fanatical. James Michener's best-selling *Iberia* (1968), which introduced millions of Americans and Europeans to Spanish history, drew upon the Inquisition, the expulsion of the Moors and Jews from the Iberian Peninsula in 1492, and the horrors of the conquest of the Americas – to portray the Spaniards as austere and cruel, fiercely individualistic, fanatically religious, and generally contemptuous of modernity.

Political scientists wanting to explain the persistent absence of democracy in Spain, decades after it had become the norm in most of western Europe and several Latin American countries, promoted their own version of the argument about Spanish difference. In their thinking, Spain was "different, unique and distinctive," a contention that in turn gave rise to the notion of "Spanish exceptionalism" (Wiarda 2000: 30). The basis for this diagnosis was not the national character of the Spanish people but rather the country's political culture as expressed by the behavior of its political leaders and the composition of its political institutions. For advocates of Spanish exceptionalism, Spain was home to a unique "Iberian-Catholic" political culture and sociopolitical order that at its core was "essentially two-class, authoritarian, traditional, elitist, patrimonial, Catholic, stratified, hierarchical, and corporate," and thus at odds with the values and practices of liberal democracy (Wiarda 1973: 209). The root of this anti-democratic "heritage" was a historical trajectory that set Spain (and by extension its colonial possessions in the Americas) apart from European civilization (see Morse 1964). Spain, it was noted, was bypassed by the great intellectual and social transformations thought to have engendered stable democratic governance elsewhere in Europe, such as the Protestant Reformation, the Enlightenment, and the Industrial Revolution.

Curiously, the idea of Spanish difference is also deeply rooted in the rhetoric and mythology of the Franco regime. At the end of the civil war in 1939, Franco skillfully used the slogan "Spain is Different" to legitimize his authoritarian regime and make the case that Spaniards were unfit for democracy.[11] In Franco's words, "every people is haunted by familiar demons, and Spain's are an anarchistic spirit, negative criticism, lack of solidarity, extremism and mutual hostility" (Trythall 1970: 265). These inherent traits of Spain, in Franco's mind, set the nation apart from others and rendered its people incapable of handling democracy. Predictably, Franco also reasoned that Spain's peculiarities made a strong authoritarian hand a necessity to prevent the country from falling back into the kind of human and material destruction occasioned by the civil war. Democracy, he argued, made Spain weak by encouraging the country's inherent propensity toward anarchism, individualism, and extremism.

Considering the pervasiveness of the notion of Spain as "different," and therefore unsuitable for democracy, it is probably safe to assume that the most pleasing thing that anyone can say about Spain today is that the country (politically speaking, at least) is rather ordinary. Howard Wiarda (2000: 61), who popularized the view of Spanish exceptionalism during the early 1970s, said it best when he declared that Spain "has made it to the ranks of being a normal country." Of course, nothing has done more to support the view of political normalcy in Spain than the civility with which Spanish politicians undertook to build the institutions of the country's new democracy. Thus, something as unpretentious as making Spain normal may well be the most meaningful and lasting accomplishment of the post-transition settlement.

Side-effects and unintended consequences

To be sure, the post-transition settlement has not been a political panacea. Oddly enough, some of the central conflicts in contemporary Spanish politics flow from either the settlement's limitations or the very nature of its compromises. The post-transition settlement did not solve Spain's most vexing problem: national identity, which ensues from the historic challenge to the legitimacy of the Spanish state posed by culturally distinct minority communities. It is obvious that the decentralization of the state, intended to create a pluralist nation, did not erase separatist tendencies in the Basque Country or prevent a bloodbath between radical Basque nationalists and the Spanish army. Ironically, the advent of democracy gave a tremendous boost to anti-democratic groups such as Euskadi Ta Askatasuna (ETA), the terrorist branch of the Basque separatist movement. Since ETA embraced armed struggle on behalf of Basque independence in 1968, it has committed 3,391 acts of terrorism, which have killed 836 people, and injured 2,367, of whom 1,294 were rendered physically incapacitated.[12] This terrorist campaign is intended to provoke a wave of indiscriminate violence against the public by the government, in the hope that this would cause the population to respond with increased protest and support for the resistance.

Seeking to solve some old problems, the post-transition settlement ended up creating new ones. The most widespread complaint about the political agreements of the Spanish transition is that, alongside having assisted in the creation of a successful democracy, they sapped the life out of politics by depressing political participation. One version of the argument contends that the secrecy of pact-making during the democratic transition fueled widespread cynicism about politics (see Encarnación 2005: 190). A more familiar contention is that the tactical demobilization of mass actors, such as the labor movement, imposed by the culture of compromise and consensus prevalent among the political elite during the democratic transition, had the unintended consequence of severely retarding (if not crippling) the development of civil society. Summarizing the effects of Spain's "pacted" transition upon the development of civil society in the post-Franco era, McDonough et al. (1998: 1) have observed that: "The good news, the efflorescence of tolerance – is partly responsible for the bad news, the extraordinarily low levels of mass involvement in politics." Either argument points to the same ironic point. What Spain lacked for much of its history as it struggled to get democracy off the ground – the capacity of its political leaders to summon any degree of compromise to allow democratic practices and institutions to rise and flourish – is what the country appears to have enjoyed too much of as it created its new democracy.

Underscoring the validity of the claim that the elite-driven nature of the political transition in Spain accounts for what has been termed a "deficit in political participation and civic engagement" (McDonough et al. 1998: ix) is the empirical data on the evolution of the Spanish political culture in the post-Franco era. It suggests two unmistakable trends. The first is a disinterest (bordering on apathy) in politics (see Morlino and Montero 1995; Martín-Cortes 2007). Despite the very high level of legitimacy that democracy enjoys in Spain, two-thirds of all Spaniards express negative feelings towards or non-involvement with politics, amongst the highest in Europe. The second is exceptionally low levels of membership in secondary associations, such as political parties, trade unions, and religious organizations (see McDonough et al. 1998; Encarnación 2003; Gunther 2007). Only about a third of the Spanish public claims to belong to such groups, a strikingly low percentage compared to that found in younger democracies, like Brazil, to say nothing of older democracies, such as the United States, where more than two-thirds of the public profess to be active in a wide range of "associational" endeavors.

A more obvious by-product of the post-transition settlement is the issue of political memory, which today stands alongside national identity as a major fault line in Spanish politics. It is fair to conclude that the deliberate attempt to bury the memory of painful episodes in Spanish history, a linchpin of the democratic transition, has been a mixed blessing. On the one hand, it did wonders for speeding the institutionalization of democracy. Much of the acrimony in civil–military relations caused by the decision to put the military on trial on charges of human rights abuses in countries like Chile and Argentina (where military trials proved so destabilizing to the new democratic regime that the government was forced to put an end to them) was averted in Spain. Relations among civilian leaders were also aided by the decision to forget the past. Spain was spared the negative consequences of bureaucratic purges that can be seen throughout the post-communist world, such as creating an embittered political opposition to democracy led by those forced out of the government positions they enjoyed under the old regime.

On the other hand, the official silence over the past imposed by the Pact of Forgetting had many unintended negative consequences that go well beyond the survival of Franco's material legacy. Sparing the old regime any accountability for its political crimes meant leaving many myths of the Francoist era relatively undisturbed, and none more prominent and problematic than the claim that Franco's 1936 military uprising was warranted; that it was an act of national salvation from the chaos of the Second Republic. This claim became the chief rationale for the establishment of the Franco dictatorship in 1939. Addressing this troublesome legacy, which was conveniently swept under the rug during the transition to democracy, is the purpose of the Law of Historical Memory, approved by the Spanish parliament on October 31, 2007. It aims to help Spaniards reconcile the past by establishing a commission to investigate the fate of those who perished during the civil war, by offering compensation to those victimized by the Franco regime (including those who lost their jobs, were forced into exile, and served time in labor camps), and by vanishing from public view the remaining monuments and memorials from the Francoist era.

THE PLAN FOR THE BOOK

The dynamics of Spain's post-transition settlement frame the central questions animating this book. Foremost among them, what made this settlement possible in the first place? This is a compelling question given that prior to Franco's death there was no tradition of cooperation across class and ideological lines in Spanish history. Moreover, the level of cooperation and consensus underpinning Spanish democratization is virtually unmatched by any other nation which entered the democratic age late in the twentieth century. Just as compelling are the questions about the settlement's consequences; key among them, what has been the long-term impact on the quality of Spanish democracy? As seen previously, widespread cynicism permeates Spanish political culture, something conventionally associated with the origins of Spanish democracy in secret political pacts. Yet, Spain shows few signs of a "democratic freezing," or a monopoly on power by political oligarchs, the most common side-effect attributed to democratic transitions assisted by political pacts. Why was Spain spared this problematic outcome?

A final concern about Spain's post-transition settlement regards its future. Recent developments in Spanish politics suggest that it has deteriorated significantly; indeed, it may be broken altogether. At least since 2004, when the government declared the "recovery" of political memory official state policy, the silence over the past imposed by the democratic transition has effectively been shattered. Policy making no longer depends upon reaching consensus between the parties of the left and the right. The right took Spain into war in Iraq in 2003 against vehement opposition from the left and the public. For its part, the left legalized homosexual marriage in 2005 over strong opposition from the Catholic Church and conservatives. Spain's future as a unitary state has never been more uncertain than at the present time. The recent expansion of regional autonomy to Catalonia authorized by the parliament in 2006 has triggered a rush by other regions to demand similar autonomy deals from the central state. This appears to suggest that the country is on an irreversible course toward full-fledged federalism. So, as the post-transition settlement recedes into history, what are the consequences for the future of Spanish democracy?

Chapter 2 locates the historical roots of Spain's post-transition settlement in the "pro-democratic political learning" derived from past political misfortunes, especially the sense that extreme political polarization had doomed previous forays into democ-ratization. This political learning crystallized as a consequence of the sheer trauma of the Republican era, which saw the attempt to democratize degenerate into a gruesome civil war, and the political socialization of the public under the Franco dictatorship. A key mission of Francoism was to instill into the Spaniards the high price the nation had paid for its past political excesses. Chapter 3 illustrates how political learning interacted with the crafting of a new democracy in Spain. It showcases the determina-tion of political actors to craft compromises that consciously addressed obstacles that for centuries had made democracy an uphill struggle in Spain. This explains not only the "pacted" nature of the Spanish transition but also many of the institutional innova-tions incorporated in the new political regime, such as the monarchy, a bicameral par-liament, an asymmetrical type of federalism, and a proportional electoral law. Finally, this chapter suggests how the consensus-driven approach to democratization that pre-vailed in Spain averted the emergence of a "frozen" democracy by creating an inclusive process of political bargaining that incorporated actors from across the political spectrum.

Chapter 4 explores the evolution of Spanish political parties, the architects of the post-transition settlement, from symbols of revolution and radicalism during the inter-war years to pillars of moderation and pragmatism in the post-Franco era. In explaining this transformation, the chapter considers the political learning from the past together with the role of external influences coming from European parties, especially those on the left, and the repudiation by the general public of radical ideologies and "maximal-ist" political projects. Chapter 5 investigates the effects of Spain's "pacted" transition on the development of civil society, especially a much-discussed "civil society deficit." It finds that political pact-making did have a devastating effect on a variety of social movements, but that the overall weakness of civil society in Spain is a complex phe-nomenon owed to a unique cocktail of cultural and historical factors in place well before the democratic transition. Special attention is paid to the "corporatization" of society that took place under Francoism and the manner in which it robbed civil society of its autonomy and undermined its capacity for organization. On the other hand, this legacy is also responsible for one of the brightest spots in Spanish civic life: a vigorous culture of popular protest and mass demonstrations.

Chapter 6 examines the most complex and consequential institutional outcome of the post-transition settlement: the "state of the autonomies," a federal-like structure within the confines of a unitary state. This compromise explains why, unlike on two previous occasions in Spanish history, the decentralization of the state did not derail the process of democratization, but also why there still is so much tension between Madrid and the regions. Chapter 7 reviews the political economy of the post-Franco era. It showcases the "social-democratic" approach that ruled over the modernization of the Spanish economy during the 1980s and 1990s. Rooted in the political comprom-ises of the democratic transition and the economic philosophies of those managing the economy, it emphasizes the gradual introduction of painful economic policies, the expansion of the welfare state to compensate those most directly affected by economic change, and social pacts with national trade unions and employers' associations to solidify societal support for the restructuring of the economy. This approach explains much about Spain's success in modernizing outmoded economic structures without eroding the citizenry's faith in democracy, as has been the case in other new democracies.

Chapter 8 explains the breakdown of the agreement to suppress the memory of the past, the most controversial component of the post-transition settlement. Front and center are the unintended consequences of Spain's indictment of Chilean strongman Augusto Pinochet on charges of crimes against humanity. An event rich in irony (and hypocrisy), it ended society's complicity with the effort to repress the past by launching a vigorous movement to "recover" Spain's historical memory. The chapter also examines the ongoing attempt to reconcile Spain's difficult past signaled by the passage of the 2007 Law of Historical Memory, exactly three decades after the country became a paradigmatic example of democratic consolidation. Among the many provocative lessons this experience reveals is that, contrary to the received conventional wisdom, confronting the past is not a prerequisite for democratization.

Chapter 9 closes the study with a review of the policies of the socialist administration of José Luis Rodríguez Zapatero and what they might portend for the future of Spanish politics. Gay marriage, amnesty for illegal immigrants, and negotiations with ETA account for Zapatero's reputation as a "radical democrat." The chapter concludes that Zapatero's political gamble reveals the surprising capacity of Spanish democracy to adapt to change, a paradoxical legacy of the post-transition settlement. His radical reforms are being facilitated by the political maturity made possible by the conservative strategies of the democratic transition.

2

POLITICS AND THE LESSONS OF HISTORY

As Spain began to take infant steps toward democracy following Franco's death on November 20, 1975, at the ripe age of 82, the country's historic reputation as a setting for entrenched ethnic conflicts, bloody military coups, and epic civil wars, to say nothing of a marked propensity toward authoritarian government, provided little in the way of hope for the rise of a stable democratic society. The Spaniards' experience with democracy was scant. Absolutist rule was, for the most part, the political norm, sustained by the unholy trinity of the army, the Church, and the monarchy; military coups, rather than elections, were the most common vehicle for orchestrating a change in political regimes. More importantly, what little experience Spain had with democracy did not provide much confidence or inspiration about the prospect for a democratic future. Prior to 1975, Spain's democratic experience was limited to a series of brief, chaotic and often tragic episodes with democracy that left very little doubt about the incapacity of the Spanish people to govern itself under democratic rule. The last foray into democratization, the short and traumatic Second Republic (1931–6), had descended into political chaos and a bloody civil war.

Not surprisingly, the political forecasts issued by the experts for Spain as the end of the Franco era was approaching were uniformly bleak and did not preclude the possibility of the advent of another civil war or another dictatorship. J. W. D. Trythall (1970: 274) concluded his biography of General Franco by observing that: "If Franco's departure may be followed closely by a liberalization, it is only too likely to be followed at a distance by a profound disillusionment. So many have nourished dreams over so many years, and when their aspirations cannot be satisfied overnight, those of them whose politics are at present moderate may all too easily take up more impatiently radical attitudes." The historian Richard Herr (1971: 27), writing in the twilight of the Franco era, concluded: "Like every country that has been ruled recently by a strong man, it is subject to the question; after he goes, what? Should the ban on politics end, many persons, both friends and enemies of Franco, anticipate that the Spaniards will return to their former habits." More certain and pessimistic was the Spanish scholar José Amodia (1976: 233), who concluded a volume on Franco's political legacy (a year after Franco's death) with an ominous warning: "It is naive to expect Franco's death to work a miracle. In the political future of Spain I see a great deal of darkness and hardly any light, my forecast must be pessimistic."

Conspicuous by its absence from the experts' forecasts was any indication that Spanish political leaders would enter democracy determined to put the past behind them and radically change their political behavior by trading old political habits of confrontation and intransigence for consensus and compromise, as was in fact the case. As seen in this chapter, coincident with the coming of democracy, Spanish politicians experienced a dramatic case of what has been termed "pro-democratic political learning," understood to mean "the process through which people modify their political beliefs and tactics as a result of severe crises, frustrations, and dramatic changes in environment" (Bermeo 1992: 273). Ironically, the facilitating roots of this political learning rested deep within the same history that raised fears among scholars and political observers of the possibility of another democratic failure in Spain in the wake of the demise of Franco's authoritarian rule. The lessons from past political misfortunes actually showed the way forward in Spain.

This chapter explores two sources of pro-democratic political learning in Spain. Foremost is the country's traumatic struggle to get democracy off the ground, especially under the Second Republic. This brief and ultimately tragic experiment with democracy provided a powerful example of how not to undertake democratization. It furnished the core lesson that over-polarization was the main cause behind the fall of the Second Republic and that depoliticization was the most effective antidote to over-polarization. A second and less apparent source of political learning was the collective memory of the pathos and savagery of the Spanish Civil War manufactured under Franco. Through both its structures and its policies, the Franco regime instilled in the Spanish citizenry the high price the nation had paid for the political excesses of the interwar years together with a determination to not repeat them ever again. This socialization ensured a broadly based desire to avoid conflict during the transition to democracy within society at large, for fear of recreating the cycle of political chaos, civil war, and dictatorship of the interwar years. The process of social and economic modernization experienced by Spain during the late Franco era reinforced the desire to avoid conflict by creating a widespread desire for democracy.

PROMISING STARTS AND FRUSTRATED ENDS

There is much irony in Spain's delayed transition to a stable and well-functioning democracy.[1] Spain is one of the oldest states in Europe, having existed in its present political configuration since 1492, when the "Catholic Monarchs" (Queen Isabella of Castile and King Ferdinand of Aragon) expelled the Jews and the Muslims from the Iberian Peninsula. Also notable is that for centuries after its "creation," Spain enjoyed remarkable political stability, at least when compared to other European nations. The country was spared the revolutions that rocked the continent during the seventeenth and eighteenth centuries. This internal political stability helps explain why Spain was able to hold on to its vast colonial empire from 1492 until the 1830s. It was not until Napoleon's invasion of Spain in 1807 that the Spanish empire began to fall apart.

Finally, few European states undertook to democratize as early and with as much vigor as Spain. Indeed, the country's first brush with democracy was one of the most robust in all of Europe.

Taking advantage of the political upheaval created by the French occupation of the Iberian Peninsula (1807–14), liberal politicians boldly enacted in 1812 the Cádiz constitution, an extraordinary document that sought to "turn Spain and its former colonies into a vast democratic nation that bridged the ocean" (Herr 1971: 73). By far the most liberal constitution of its time written by a European nation, the Cádiz constitution declared Spain to be sovereign and its subjects free, stripped the monarchy of its absolutist powers, and provided for a one-house legislature to be elected by universal male suffrage. This document greatly influenced the spread of independence and democracy throughout the Spanish-speaking world, but in Spain, where it originated, it failed to engender a liberal, democratic regime.

With the restoration of the monarchy that followed the expulsion of the French army from Spain in 1814, after years of intense popular resistance memorable for having originated the term "guerilla warfare," the dream of the Spanish liberals who drafted the Cádiz constitution was crushed with the triumphant return of absolutism. Political stability remained elusive, however. Between 1814 and 1874, there were 37 attempted coups in Spain, of which 12 were successful (Beevor 1982: 15). The last one (1874) put an end to the country's first constitutional democracy. Declared in 1873, Spain's first republic lasted a mere 11 months. Ensuring its quick demise was the introduction of a controversial plan to federalize the country by creating self-governing cantons, 13 peninsular and four overseas, each with its own constitution, legislature, and control over a host of issues like taxes and education. The plan struck fears of national disintegration into the very heart of an ultra-nationalistic military, which promptly moved to put an end to this first experiment in republican government.

Having derailed democracy, military officers turned to an enlightened and very able conservative politician, Antonio Cánovas del Castillo, whom they tasked with the responsibility of creating a new political regime that would wed Spain's monarchical structures to those of a democratic system, such as an elected parliament. The Cánovas constitution of 1876 established the "Restoration monarchy" of Alfonso XII and later Alfonso XIII (1875–1923). This political regime was supported by a virtual "who's who" of Spain's privileged classes: rural oligarchs from Andalusia, Extremadura, and La Mancha – where *Latifundismo* (Iberian-style feudalism) was the principal mode of economic activity and a major source of political power – bankers from the Basque Country, and manufacturers from Catalonia.

A limited democracy

Under the Restoration period inaugurated in 1876, Spain enjoyed remarkable political stability together with significant economic progress ensuing from the country's position of neutrality during World War I. Democratic development, however, stagnated and came to a screeching halt in 1923 with the establishment of the dictatorship of General Miguel Primo de Rivera. A key factor contributing to the demise of the Restoration regime was its political limitations. Scholars have correctly characterized this regime as a "limited democracy" because the political franchise was severely constrained (Gunther et al. 2004: 2). For much of this period, the right to vote was restricted to males and the system of *turno pacífico* (peaceful turn) permitted the nation's two major parties, the Conservative and Liberal parties, to trade places at the helm of the government, making a mockery of the electoral process. These exclusionary practices reflected dominant elite attitudes about democracy during this era, and more specifically, a suspicion of the capacity of the masses to behave as democratic citizens. "Universal suffrage means the dissolution of society. It is the negation of the national will and the parliamentary regime," remarked Cánovas during the deliberations leading to the creation of the Restoration regime in 1876 (Herr 1971: 114).

Political life in the Restoration period was also famously corrupt. It saw the birth of the powerful *caciques* (a term borrowed from the Americas, originally intended to mean Indian chiefs), bigwigs and political bosses who functioned as transmission belts between the national parties and the peasants. In typical patron–client fashion, the *caciques* channeled favors and services to the masses in exchange for political support. This way of doing politics was undoubtedly aided by the vast numbers of poor and illiterate peasants who populated Spain in the late nineteenth century, especially in remote areas of the country such as small villages in Galicia, where vestiges of *Caciquismo* are thought to persist to this day (Gunther et al. 2004: 141). Those most disadvantaged in society saw in the *caciques* the principal means for escaping their often-desperate economic situation.

Challenges from below

The limitations of the Restoration regime made it all but impossible for it to absorb the pressures from groups excluded from politics. Indeed, it was the mobilization of these groups that led the King to give his blessing to the establishment of the Primo de Rivera dictatorship. Although Primo de Rivera is often depicted as a "benign despot," and his regime as a "gentle dictatorship," he was not a friend of democracy (Herr 1971: 114).[2] He shut down the parliament, suspended the 1876 constitution, repressed the press, and outlawed many political organizations, all in the name of securing social peace. A principal target of Primo de Rivera's repression was a thriving anarchist movement. Spanish anarchists espoused a libertarian form of socialism that advocated a society free of such institutional trappings as political parties, a centralized state, and a capitalist economy.[3] To achieve their revolutionary ends some anarchists advocated violence, leading to the rise of a veritable reign of terror in Spain during the twilight of the nineteenth century and the dawn of the twentieth century. Among the spectacular acts of terrorism carried out by anarchist groups was the bombing of the Liceo Opera House in Barcelona in 1893, which killed 20 people. Also notable were the murder of Cánovas, the architect of the Restoration regime, in 1897, and the bombing of the wedding of Alfonso XIII in 1906. The bomb missed the royal couple but killed 24 people.

A more consequential development of the anarchists' rise was the infiltration of the nascent labor movement. This tactic succeeded in giving them control of the Confederación Nacional del Trabajo (CNT), the largest workers' movement in Spain during the interwar period and one of the most revolutionary organizations ever created in the country. Founded in 1911, and outlawed until 1914, the CNT grew by leaps and bounds after 1914, reaching a membership of 1.58 million by 1934 (Beevor 1982: 21). Owing to its anarchist origins and inherent suspicion of Marxism, the CNT rejected overtures from socialists and communists to join their movements. The CNT also shunned the strategy of collaboration with the state and the employers that characterized the behavior of other unions of the era. Instead, the organization adopted a strategy of "systematization of the doctrine of collective violence" to achieve its revolutionary goals (Payne 2004: 14). This strategy, as seen shortly, is greatly responsible for the political chaos and violence for which Spain became infamous during the Republican era.

Another popular force clamoring for political change during the 1920s was the socialist movement, organized around the Partido Socialista Obrero Español (PSOE), and its sister institution, the Unión General de Trabajadores (UGT). Founded in 1879, the PSOE, together with the UGT, played an important role in organizing a growing and increasingly politicized urban working class. This mission received a huge boost with the success of the 1917 Russian revolution, which brought a sense of exhilaration to the Spanish working class and fears among Spanish conservatives that the country was turning into "the Russia of the West." Indeed, in Spanish history, the years 1919–21 are known as the "Bolshevik Triennium" in consideration of the unprecedented number of strikes that rocked the nation, a reflection of a rapidly expanding labor movement.

Calls for political change were also coming from the influential "Generation of '98," a group of intellectuals who contemplated Spain's fate in the wake of the "Disaster of '98," the nation's humiliating defeat to the upstart United States during the 1898 Spanish-American War. It entailed the loss of the last remnants of the country's once vast colonial assets in the Americas (Cuba and Puerto Rico) and the Pacific (Guam and the Philippines) and with it the end of any serious claims of Spain to empire.[4] For the members of the Generation of '98, only a complete program of "political regeneration," entailing not only a new political regime but also the expansion of education and economic opportunities, could save Spain from outright ruin.

Regional nationalists, driven by the desire to have their distinct cultural-linguistic heritage recognized by the central state, also adopted the cause of political change, hoping that a new regime would be more sympathetic to their plight. This was notably the case in Catalonia, where nationalism and republicanism were successfully wedded. For Catalan nationalists, only a republic could guarantee the advance of greater autonomy for the region. Even some conservatives joined in the effort to uproot the monarchy. Fearful of a revolution by the disenfranchised masses and the establishment of a Russian-style dictatorship of the proletariat, many conservatives became convinced that a republic would be a safer alternative than a discredited monarchy vulnerable to a popular uprising.

THE SECOND REPUBLIC: SPAIN'S FIRST DEMOCRACY

Facing mounting social unrest, public hostility, and loss of support from his conservative allies, King Alfonso XIII dismissed Primo de Rivera as head of the government in

January 1930 and shortly thereafter abdicated his throne and fled the country. This opened the way for the declaration of Spain's Second Republic on April 14, 1931, Spain's first real attempt to live under democratic rule. Notwithstanding the popular clamoring for a republican type of government, the Second Republic proved unstable from the start and ultimately incapable of implementing its ambitious social and political agenda.[5] It included land reform, divorce, the separation of church and state, and the expansion of education, labor rights, and regional autonomy. These policies reflected the leading forces behind the Second Republic – the representatives of "Modern" Spain (republicans, socialists, organized labor, and regionalists) – and incorporated all the things that the conservative political system of the Restoration regime had either overlooked or neglected. The dream of modernizing Spain from top to bottom was not to be, however, and eventually succumbed to a right-wing, nationalist uprising begun in 1936, just five years after the creation of the Second Republic. What went wrong?

The international climate into which the Second Republic was born was certainly not auspicious to the consolidation of democracy. The interwar years were especially hard on democracy in Europe. No fewer than 13 democratic governments perished in Europe between the years of 1920 and 1938, in places as varied as Germany, Austria, Estonia, Greece, and Portugal (see Bermeo 2003: 21). Most of these regime collapses are attributed to the economic dislocations created by the economic crash of 1929 and the growing popularity of fascism across Europe. To a significant extent, this was the case in Spain, which saw its share of economic travails during the interwar years (unemployment and inflation) as well as the rise of very influential fascist or fascist-leaning organizations. But the most serious problems faced by the Second Republic were all homegrown, either manufactured by the Republican leaders themselves or born out of the resistance from conservative elites to the republican liberal project.

Chief among the contributing factors leading to the collapse of the Second Republic was the erratic political behavior of its leaders. In pursuit of a wholesale modernization of Spanish society, many Republican leaders adopted an impolite, moralistic, and uncompromising attitude that ended up hurting the Republican cause by hardening the opposition and creating a host of unnecessary enemies. "Intransigence will be symptomatic of integrity" is a famous quote attributed to Manuel Azaña of the Republican Action party, the Second Republic's first prime minister (Payne 1970: 91). Republican intransigence was most famously displayed when it came to dealing with the Catholic Church, which many Republicans regarded as their principal nemesis. A Republican assault on the Church was needlessly aggressive and confrontational, and did little to advance the popularity of Republican policies with the masses. As church historians have pointed out (Martínez-Torrón 2006: 777), "there was something anomalous in the anti-religious policy of the Second Republic for the clergy was not fascist, although it was largely conservative, and peasants were not anti-clerical, notwithstanding the gradual de-Christianization of the working class."

The Republican attack on the Catholic Church began at the opening of the constitutional debate of 1931 with Azaña declaring: "Spain is no longer a Catholic country, even though there are many millions of Spanish Catholics" (Amodia 1976: 17). The new constitution itself, inspired by other radical democratic constitutions of the era, including those of Mexico (1917) and Weimar Germany (1919), emphasized the absence of an official religion in Spain. Articles 26 and 27 recognized freedom of religion, ended financial support for the clergy, and nationalized the Church's vast property holdings. The anti-religion obsession of the Second Republic reached its lowest point with the decision to deny the right to vote to women in the 1931 constitution; some leftist members of the congress feared that this would create "a reactionary and anti-republican force," since women could be more easily influenced by the clergy (Martínez-Torrón 2006: 782). Adding insult to injury, the Republican leadership failed to condemn the wave of church burnings and other forms of anti-clerical violence that spread throughout Spain in the early 1930s. These actions upset the Catholic sensibilities of ordinary Spaniards (even many who had supported the creation of the Republic) and triggered the resignation of several of the Catholic members of the Azaña government, outraged by the government's virulent anti-clericalism.

A flawed institutional design also contributed to the problems of the Second Republic. In direct response to the exclusionary nature of the Restoration regime, the architects of the Second Republic sought to create as inclusive a political regime as possible (notwithstanding the initial exclusion of women from the political franchise). This led to the unwise passage of an electoral law that allowed for representation in parliament of a plethora of political parties, and, by extension, the creation of a very fragmented party system. In turn, political diversity largely prevented the creation of a stable government capable of unifying an increasingly polarized public and generating broad support for its contentious policies. Unsurprisingly, almost from the onset the Republic became an emblematic symbol for governmental instability. More than 20 parties were present in each of the three legislatures elected during the Republic (1931, 1933, and 1936), the largest party in each of the legislatures never had more than 24 percent of seats, and in each at least 11 parties had ten or more seats.[6] Between April 1931 and July 1936, there were 19 different governments under eight different prime ministers, a feat that accorded the Second Republic the dubious honor of "the most unstable parliamentary regime in interwar Europe" (Gunther et al. 2004: 30).

A third problem afflicting the Second Republic was deep (perhaps even insurmountable) ideological divisions within the ruling left–republican leadership. The Republican alliance incorporated an assortment of left-wing and republican organizations, ranging from the Socialist party on the left to the conservative Radical party and the Catholic republicans on the right. This heterogeneous coalition in time proved to be a huge political liability for both the stability of the Republic and the survival of democracy. On the one hand, leftists and republicans had little in common beyond their distaste for the old regime. In fact, they shared a mutual distrust of one another and this became the source of multiple intra-regime squabbles about the scope and speed of the government's reform agenda. Consequently, a consensus about the kind of democratic society that Spain was to become under the Second Republic remained elusive, with some regarding the establishment of a republic as a goal in itself, while others viewed it as a stepping stone toward a more radical transformation of politics and society, such as socialism or communism. These ideological divisions made it all but impossible for the government to gain popular support for its policies. For instance, while sections of the Spanish lower-middle class were sympathetic toward the policies of the Republic, especially in industrialized Catalonia and Madrid, much of it remained "highly traditional in outlook, devoutly Catholic, exaggeratedly status-conscious towards the working class, and bitterly hostile towards anything that smacked even vaguely of socialism" (Blinkhorn 1988: 9). On the other hand, the lack of internal cohesion within the Republican government hardly helped the left–republican coalition confront its opposition from either the left or the right and prevent the nation from falling into outright political chaos.

The consolidation of political polarization

On the left, the anarchists posed the biggest threat to the Republic. Led by the secretive and uncompromising Federación Anarquista Ibérica (FAI), Spanish anarchists were not on the whole supporters of the Second Republic. They opposed all political activity and therefore shunned parties, elections and parliaments, ensuing from their view that the Republic was just as repugnant as the monarchy. Indeed, some anarchists saw the advent of democracy as an opportunity to advance the goal of creating a self-regulating society by means of revolutionary action. This was certainly the intention of the anarchist CNT, which greeted the Republic with open contempt, if not outright hostility. At its 1931 Congress, the CNT leadership declared that the organization should remain in "open war against the state," arguing that "the greatest danger facing Spain was democracy because the workers might accept its false promises and be led away from their hatred of capitalism and the state" (Malefakis 1970: 294).

In Barcelona, where the CNT dominated the labor movement, the organization's tactics of labor terrorism, such as the killing of high-profile industrialists, left Spanish employers in a state of a "panic and shock" and placed traditional structures of industrial control and authority "under mortal threat" (Martin 1990: 215). More moderate groups, such as the socialist UGT, were often forced to adopt similar tactics in the hope of keeping up with the CNT. According to one analyst: "Socialist workers in Madrid often acted as radically as anarcho-syndicalist workers in Barcelona. They established their own militias, formed street patrols, and expropriated a number of strategic factories, placing them under the control of workers' committees" (Bookchin 1977: xiv). In the countryside, the CNT mobilized the peasantry into a war against the landed oligarchy whose impact on property relations is hard to overstate. By 1933, one-third of all land and between half and two-thirds of all cultivated land had been seized by anarchist groups in Republican Spain (Malefakis 1970: 372).

Ironically, the leaders of the Republic had a direct hand in assisting in the rise of the right, since their policies had the unintended outcome of mobilizing the political forces behind "Traditional" Spain: the Catholic Church, big business and the military. These groups found their political voice in the Confederación Española de Derechas Autónomas (CEDA), the most important Catholic, right-wing party in Spain during the interwar era. The fascist-leaning CEDA rose to political prominence during the 1933 elections, as a consequence of the convergence of several factors favoring a conservative, Catholic victory, including the Socialists' decision to seek electoral success on their own (thereby breaking the left–republican coalition) and the move by the CNT to boycott the elections in protest for what they perceived to be the shortcomings of Republican policies.

By September 1935, five CEDA ministers were serving in the government and in control of some of the most politically sensitive ministries (labor, justice, and agriculture) giving the Second Republic a distinct right-wing orientation and marking a period known among left-wing circles as the *bienio negro* (two black years). This period is noted by the CEDA's assault on the early policies of the Republic, which meant an effective reversal of the religious, social and economic reforms undertaken by the Republic between 1931 and 1933. The *bienio negro* is best known, however, for the repression of the left. The most famous act of left-wing repression took place in 1934 in the mining region of Asturias, where government forces (led by none other than General Francisco Franco) employed extraordinary violence to put down a rebellion by miners. Over 1,000 dead, more than 30,000 prisoners, and numerous executions of workers without trial was the outcome of the Asturias massacre.

Convinced that the Second Republic was quickly becoming a fascist state, in 1936 the left–republican coalition regrouped for the last election of the Republican period under the banner of the Popular Front, backed by a "Workers' Alliance" embracing socialist, communist, and anarchist trade unions. This was a remarkable collaborative effort if only because of the "unconscionably venomous" relations among the leading unions of the Republican period (Bookchin 1977: 230). The Popular Front managed a thin electoral victory in 1936, bringing the Second Republic back to its liberal roots. By then, however, the fate of the Second Republic was cast with the country set on an irreversible course toward civil war. Spain was gripped with an acute case of political polarization with the political center having effectively disappeared and extremism and violent tactics taking hold of both ends of the political spectrum. War seemed to be the only option for both the left and the right to achieve their political goals.

Spain against itself

General Franco, backed by a nationalist coalition comprising big business, the Catholic Church, and the military staged a coup d'état on July 18, 1936, generally considered the opening act of the Spanish Civil War.[7] This conflict divided the country into two bands: the "Republicans," on one side, and the "Nationalists," on the other. The Nationalist forces would emerge victorious from the end of hostilities on March 28, 1939, when Madrid fell to Franco's forces. A few days later, on April 1, Franco declared the war over. More than half a million casualties (the vast majority of them from the Republican side) was the human toll of the war, making the Spanish Civil War the bloodiest of the many that arose in interwar Europe.[8] By contrast, Ireland's civil war resulted in 3,000 casualties, Finland's in 30,000, Greece's in 60,000, and Hungary's in 6,000 (Kissane and Sitter 2005: 186–8).

Why did Franco and his rebel army win the war? Several factors aided in the Nationalist victory. Although the Republican government controlled the nation's economic resources, especially the gold reserves of the Bank of Spain and the nation's leading industrial zones, it was unable to hold on to the national army, much of which defected for the Nationalist side. While the majority of colonels stayed loyal to the Republican government, the lower-echelon and particularly younger officers sided with the Francoist rebellion. More important, perhaps, the most experienced troops in the Spanish army were those stationed overseas, in Spanish Morocco, and they were under the command of General Franco. Their arrival on the Spanish mainland would greatly tip the military advantage in favor of the Nationalist side.

The Republican side also made many tactical errors and none more evident than choosing to concentrate on a socioeconomic revolution rather than on developing a military strategy to defeat the right-wing insurgency. As argued by Stanley Payne (1985: 15), at the inception of the civil war the CNT and the UGT devoted much of their energies to collectivizing industry and farmland while ignoring the military conflict. This "revolution" was staged most dramatically and effectively in Catalonia, where the CNT and other workers' organizations seized hundreds of factories, but it also spread to other parts of the country, such as Asturias, Valencia, and New Castile. The consequences of this strategy for the Republican side were significant. According to Payne (1985: 16), "What was left of the Spanish army in the Republican zone was largely disbanded in favor of leftist militia battalions that were full of revolutionary zeal and reasonably well-equipped but lacked discipline, leadership, or military skill." He adds that the early battles of 1936 were "uniform disasters" for the leftist forces, who were driven back to Madrid by the small but experienced veterans from the Moroccan garrisons.

Geographic considerations also favored the Nationalist uprising. Republican strongholds included all the major cities in the nation, including Barcelona, Madrid, and Valencia, where the economic disruptions of the war were felt most dramatically. Across urban centers the war created vast unemployment and food shortages that in time would lead to widespread hunger, malnutrition, and low morale. The Nationalist zone, by contrast, included the principal agricultural regions of central and northern Spain where work and food were plentiful. Also important were the international dynamics generated by the war, which greatly favored Franco. The Nationalists enjoyed the active support of sympathetic regimes in Germany and Italy. It was these countries' assistance that allowed Franco to airlift his army from Morocco to Seville across the Straits of Gibraltar in July 1936. The bombing of the Basque town of Guernica, arguably the most emblematic event of the war (if only because of the eponymous painting by Picasso) was executed by planes of Germany's Condor Legion.

The Republicans, by contrast, could only dream of external help. Saving Spain's young republic did, of course, become a cause célèbre among western liberal intellectuals, who vigorously helped to publicize the plight of the Republicans. The poetry of W. H. Auden, George Orwell's war memoir *Homage to Catalonia*, Ernest Hemingway's wartime novel *For Whom the Bell Tolls*, and the gripping photography of Robert Cappa are among the most important artistic works inspired by war. But in its most trying hours not a single democratic government came to the rescue of Spain's Republican government against the Nationalist assault. The British, French, and American governments agreed on a policy of non-intervention, based on the assumption that intervention would only serve to escalate the conflict and lead to a wider European war. Abandoned by its fellow democracies, most pointedly France, which like Spain was ruled by a Popular Front government, the Republican government turned to the Soviets for help. Soviet aid in the form of aircraft, tanks, and political and military advisors helped the Republic resist the Nationalist rebellion but proved, in the end, incapable of stopping it. The same can be said of the assistance provided by the 40,000 volunteers from 53 countries that comprised the International Brigades (including the 3,000-member American Lincoln Battalion) that fought Franco's forces alongside the Republican army. For them, participation in the Spanish Civil War became an epic struggle between the forces of good and evil with Franco representing fascism, the greatest evil of the day.

THE FRANCO REGIME

Upon assuming control of the nation in 1939, Franco's most immediate and urgent task was to clean house by eradicating any remnant of Republican opposition. This made the immediate post-civil war years seem just as violent, if not more so, than the civil war itself. A strong believer that Spain was suffering from an infectious, malignant "red cancer" which had to be cured, Franco proved to be a brutal, vindictive ruler (Trythall 1970: 140). The 1939 Law of Political Responsibilities provided legal justification for the arrest and sentencing of virtually anyone opposed to the dictatorship. Punishment for conviction under the law included fines, confiscation of property, imprisonment for no less than six months and no more than 15 years, exile to a remote part of the country, and disqualification from holding any form of public office. By 1941, the prison population in Spain had soared to 233,037 (Trythall 1970: 142), and over the life of the regime it is estimated that some 400,000 people were imprisoned as a consequence of the 1939 law (Preston 1995: 230).

Those convicted of high crimes against the state paid with their lives. The number of postwar executions remains in dispute and estimates range from a low of 40,000 (Trythall 1970: 136) to a high of 200,000 (Jackson 1965: 539). The bulk of those executed were members or supporters of the guerilla movement, comprised of communists and anarchists, that formed after Franco's military victory in 1939 with the hope of sparking a mass movement against Franco. Its swift and violent defeat ensured that no serious challenge to the Franco regime would emerge within Spain for at least two decades. It would not be until the 1960s, with the rebirth of the labor movement and the rise of the terrorist organization ETA, that opposition groups would begin to have any meaningful influence over Spain's political direction.

Institutional and philosophical foundations

The political regime that Franco consolidated in Spain after 1939 was purposely designed as the very antithesis of the Second Republic.[9] This was no accident, for it was the very institutions of the Second Republic – its secular constitution, ideologically charged parties, revolutionary social movements, and quasi-federal structure – that Franco blamed for driving the nation into civil war. In Franco's eyes, these institutions made Spain weak by encouraging the country's inherent propensity toward individualism, anarchism, and extremism. Accordingly, Franco's nationalist "crusade" endeavored to strengthen Spain by undoing much of the political work of the Republican era. All political parties and independent trade unions were banned, on grounds that politics was a poisonous and divisive activity. Spain was declared a "Catholic confessional state," a pendulum reaction to the radical anti-clericalism of the Second Republic. It granted the Catholic Church state protection in all forms, including at the cost of the freedom of other religions. The hard-won statutes of autonomy granted by the Republic to the Basques and the Catalans were declared void and replaced by a policy of cultural homogeneity.

Franco's plans to strengthen Spain also demanded the development of governing institutions that stood as an alternative to democracy. In Franco's view, this was key to avoiding *el error de Primo de Rivera*: that is, "the failure to develop a fully o. and institutionalized political system" (Payne 1985: 19). Franco designed for himself the position of Chief of State and "Caudillo" (Leader), his official title, around which all political power rested. This gave him the authority to name the President of the government (the Prime Minister), who, in consultation with Franco, appointed the other members of the Council of Ministers. Franco also possessed the authority to name the President of the national parliament (the Cortes) who in turn selected the members and heads of each parliamentary committee. These leaders were recruited from a small coterie of Catholic, right-wing and monarchist organizations that comprised the so-called Francoist family. Key members of this political family included the fascist organization Falange, the Asociación Católica Nacional de Propagandistas (ACNP), an elite Catholic organization that provided many of the regime's ministers, the Carlists, representatives of Spain's monarchical tradition, the Movimiento Nacional, the closest institution resembling a political party under Franco, and Opus Dei (Work of God), a fundamentalist Catholic organization active in business, law, and higher education.

Notwithstanding the obvious influence of fascist groups within the Franco regime, Franco disavowed any official affiliation to any guiding ideology or philosophy. Indeed, he professed an overt apathy toward ideology, leading some to refer to him as "the least ideological of the modern dictators" (Gunther 1980: 23). In contrast to Italy under Mussolini or Germany under Hitler, no elaborate ideology to mobilize the masses was ever formulated by Franco in Spain, and no central party structure was ever developed to organize societal support for the authoritarian regime. Instead, Franco adopted what Juan Linz (1970) has famously referred to as "mentalities," a mix of values such as conservatism, nationalism, and religiosity that gave the Franco regime its core political identity. "We believe in God, Franco and Spain" was the motto of the Movimiento Nacional.

Franco's pragmatism permeated most aspects of governance and state–society relations. Instead of a constitution, the Franco regime was guided by a set of "Fundamental Laws," a total of seven decrees enacted on an ad hoc basis during the life of the regime. In keeping with the predominantly pragmatic nature of Franco's rule, on the whole, the Fundamental Laws dispensed with conceptual or philosophical matters of governance and instead covered such practical matters as labor relations, the composition of the Cortes, and Franco's succession. State–society relations were organized in classic corporatist fashion. The antithesis of pluralism with its emphasis on individual freedoms and rights and unrestricted competition among interest groups for access to the state, "corporatism" emphasizes class harmony, national solidarity, and social order as dictated by the state. Franco's reliance upon the ideals of corporatism served multiple, interrelated purposes, all aimed at organizing and maintaining political control.

Foremost was the organization of political representation. In keeping with the corporatist desire for an orderly and non-competitive society, the national parliament incorporated representation from the most important institutions in the country, including the regime's syndicate institutions, professional associations, local government and cultural and governmental bodies. Rules governing election to the parliament varied over time but they largely depended upon the discretion of Franco himself. After 1967, election procedures were amended to allow for "family representation" in the parliament, which permitted two representatives by province. An even stronger sense of corporatism was injected into the organizations that regulated labor and industrial relations. In an attempt to replace the independent trade union movement and employers' associations that flourished during the Second Republic, the Franco regime created a universal "vertical syndicate" (Organización Sindical Española, OSE) that incorporated compulsory participation by both workers and employers into a single, state-controlled institution. This was in keeping with the corporatist notion that there is no inherent conflict in the relations between workers and employers.

The politics of socialization

To legitimize its rule, and help assure its long-term survival, Franco's authoritarian regime relied upon the extensive socialization of the citizenry, a process that entailed manipulating the history of the regime's origins. This effort centered on politicizing the history of the Spanish Civil War. It began almost as soon as the war itself ended. As the victor, Franco and his Nationalist crusade had the upper hand in shaping what was to be remembered about the war. The Franco regime took full advantage of this opportunity and moved rapidly to make the chaos and violence of the civil war the main justification for its existence. Indeed, saving Spain from war and destruction became the principal way for Franco to legitimize his illegitimate rise to power, at least through the late 1950s when that justification was replaced by the promotion of peace and economic prosperity. Harnessing the theme of "national salvation" often entailed an elaborate rhetorical handiwork designed to link the Franco regime and its actions to Spain's mythical past as a great conqueror and savior. As expressed by Franco himself (Herzberger 1991: 35), "Our victory was the triumph of Spain against the anti-Spain. The heroic re-conquest of the Fatherland that was moving headlong down the path of destruction. Therefore, our victory was for all men and for all classes in Spain."

To drive home the point about having saved the country from ruin, Franco was in the habit of actually exaggerating the number of people who died in the civil war, a conflict that he himself provoked. *Un millón de muertos* (one million deaths) was the phrase commonly used by Francoist authorities when accounting for the number of Spaniards who perished in the war, a figure that historians have put into serious question. Gabriel Jackson's excruciatingly detailed account (1965: 539) puts the number of deaths related to the civil war at 580,000. The point of exaggerating the number of casualties, according to Jackson, was a very calculated one: "to impress upon the people the high cost of the war." This mission proved very successful. The phrase "one million deaths" became engraved in the minds of the Spaniards, having become the title of one of the better-known fictionalized accounts of the civil war by the novelist José María Gironella. Oddly enough, Franco's enemies (the communists and the socialists) became willing participants in Franco's ploy to exaggerate the human cost of the civil war by accepting the 1 million mark, since it served their purpose of underlining the violent nature of the Franco regime.

A vast propaganda machine organized around a national news and documentary service, Noticiarios y Documentales Cinematográficos (NODO), facilitated the Franco regime's manipulation of Spanish history. These vehicles of official state culture distilled for the nation both domestic and international news. Franco himself was a frequent subject of NODO documentaries, invariably with the purpose of emphasizing some social or economic achievement of the dictatorship. Between 1943 and 1975, he appeared in over 900 NODO reports (Ellwood 1995: 202). NODO's most important role, however, was the promotion of the Franco regime's myths, especially those linked to the civil war. The agency's most famous statement on the civil war was the 1959 documentary *El camino de la paz* (The Path to Peace), a highlight of the "20 years of peace" campaign, which conveyed the message that Franco's nationalist uprising was necessary to restore order to the Spanish nation as a consequence of the Second Republic's attacks on Spanish institutions and culture.

The state's educational system also paid service to the Franco regime by promoting a new narrative of Spanish history. Post-civil war textbooks retell the events of the interwar years from a unique Francoist perspective. References to the Second Republic are made usually in connection to "convent burnings, disorder, social conflict, separatism and communism" (Boyd 1997: 249). The point was to tie republicanism to partisan squabbling and endemic anti-clericalism. Even more distorted was the telling of the civil war: the Nationalist victors are portrayed as "saviors" while the losing Republicans are depicted as "traitors." What is referred to as "The Spanish War" is characterized not only as a struggle between good and evil but also as a conflict fought by Spaniards against hostile foreigners, communists and anarchists in particular. These textbooks are also remarkable for the extent to which they sought to whitewash some of the most troublesome aspects of Spanish history. A key purpose was to deny any truth to the *Leyenda Negra* (Black Legend) promoted by Spain's enemies during the fifteenth century, which depicted the country as brutal and bloodthirsty, and was based largely on the violence and repression of the Spanish Inquisition. The violent expulsion of the Moors and the Jews from the Iberian Peninsula and the colonization of the Americas begun in 1492 are glorified as pivotal events in the history of the Spanish nation and as a testament to its devotion to spreading Christianity.

Memorializing the 1936 nationalist uprising was another strategy employed by the Franco regime to shape public perceptions about the civil war. Undoubtedly, the ultimate (and most controversial) act of consecration of the memory of "the Spirit of 1936" and its protagonists was the construction of *El Valle de los Caídos*, a monument intended to serve two seemingly contradictory goals: to honor Franco's victory and to function as a symbol of national reconciliation. Commenced in the early 1940s and completed in 1959, *El Valle de los Caídos* was built by Republican prisoners, many of whom died while working on the monument. They were forced to quarry the huge cavern (250 meters deep) into the rocks of the Sierra de Guadarrama that today houses the body of Franco and that of José Antonio Primo de Rivera, the founder of the Falange. In a direct affront to the Republican victims of the civil war, alongside the bodies of some 50,000 Francoist supporters are those of a few Republicans, a gesture intended to underscore a spirit of national reconciliation.

Ironically, by the time *El Valle de los Caídos* was finished and unveiled in 1959, the Franco regime had begun to de-emphasize the civil war as the central justification for its existence. Instead, after 1959 the Franco regime embraced the exaltation of "peace and prosperity" as the new rationalization for the continuation of dictatorship in Spain (Aguilar 2002: 29). This could be seen as a strategy of desperation on the part of the Franco regime, as it was clear by then that the argument of national salvation no longer possessed much resonance with the general public. But it also reflected the extraordinary social and economic advances attained by Spain during the late Franco period. By the mid-1960s, the Franco regime could make a credible argument that in Spain authoritarianism and social and economic modernization were mutually supportive.

Modernization and the twilight of Francoism

During the Franco regime, Spain took gigantic leaps out of poverty and economic backwardness, albeit not overnight. With the exception of pockets of industrialization in Catalonia and the Basque Country, Spain remained an agrarian society well into the twentieth century. In 1950, for example, 47.6 percent of the Spanish population was still employed in agriculture; by contrast, by the 1930s, only 10 percent of Britain's economically active population was still engaged in agriculture, 22 percent in Germany, and 22 percent in France (Gunther et al. 2004: 27). Overall levels of wealth were also markedly lower in Spain than in the rest of Europe. By 1950, per capita GDP for western Europe stood at $4,594, versus $2,397 for Spain (Chislett 2002: 17). Even some of Spain's former colonies were better off. Argentina's per capita GDP in 1950 was $4,987, higher than the European average and almost twice that of Spain (Chislett 2002: 16).

Two factors conspired to undermine economic performance and living standards in the early years of the Franco regime.[10] Hoping to accelerate its downfall, after the end of the civil war in 1939, the West imposed an economic boycott upon the Franco dictatorship. This isolation effectively prevented the country from benefiting from postwar economic recovery programs such as the Marshall Plan, which channeled billions of American dollars into the major European economies after the end of World War II. On the other hand was the economic ideology adopted by the Franco regime. Between 1939 and the late 1940s the Spanish economy strived for autarky, a utopian form of economic self-sufficiency. It reflected the Franco regime's belief in the political virtues of shutting off the country to all external influence. Autarky imposed "a form of quarantine" during which the state could cure society of its ills, particularly the contamination of the Spanish proletariat by Bolshevism during the Second Republic (Richards 1995: 181). The consequences of this ill-conceived economic strategy were nothing short of catastrophic.

By the 1950s, the mythical pursuit of economic autarky had combined with a disregard for market realities and rampant economic mismanagement had conspired to create an economic environment dominated by "favoritism, corruption, the emergence of a black market, galloping inflation and crucial shortages of basic foodstuffs, raw materials and capital goods" (Harrison 1993: 19). This bleak economic picture forced millions of Spaniards into abject poverty and made the postwar years seem more devastating than the civil war itself. *Los años del hambre* (the years of hunger) is the phrase used by the Spaniards to describe the first decade of Francoist rule. According to a journalistic account of the era, "In the cities, cats and dogs disappeared from the streets having either starved to death or been eaten. In the countryside, the poorer peasants lived off boiled grass and weeds" (Hopper 1986: 24). Merciful intervention from the sympathetic Peronist regime in Argentina between 1942 and 1947, which sent massive amounts of grain and beef to Spain, kept the nation from mass starvation. Argentina also became the preferred destination for Spaniards trying to escape the misery of the era. During the early 1950s, more than 300,000 Spaniards left for Latin America, with the majority of them going to Argentina (Foweraker 1989: 64).

An abrupt sea change in Spain's economic climate arrived with the introduction of a plan of economic stabilization and liberalization, as stipulated in the July 1959 Decree-Law of the New Economic Order. It marked the second phase of the Franco regime, 1959–77. This era, remembered in Spain as *los años de desarrollo* (the years of development), is characterized by a transition to international market capitalism, the liberalization of labor relations, and unprecedented economic expansion and social progress. Economic technocrats affiliated with Opus Dei, who by the mid-1950s had penetrated the upper echelons of the Franco regime and managed to wrest control of the economy from the Falange and the military, were responsible for the design and implementation of the 1959 plan. Highlights of the 1959 plan included the liberalization of domestic and foreign trade (including opening the country to tourism), a 50 percent devaluation of the peseta, which aimed to make Spanish exports more attractive, and price increases on a wide range of goods and services (see Anderson 1970).

In revamping the Spanish economy, Opus technocrats were aided by economic experts from the International Monetary Fund (IMF), the World Bank, and the Organization for Economic Cooperation and Development (OECD). Spain was given membership in these organizations in 1958, signaling a break with tradition by the West towards the Franco regime. By the late 1950s the world's geopolitical map had changed dramatically and the Franco regime, however repugnant to the West, had emerged as a useful ally in its fight against the spread of communism in Europe and elsewhere. As observed by Herr (1971: 233), "Spain with its anti-Communist government and its strategic location controlling the entrance to the Mediterranean Sea while entrenched behind the wall of the Pyrenees became more and more attractive to American military planners." The fact that Franco frequently boasted of being the only western leader to have successfully put down communism only added to his appeal to the Americans. Spanish–American cooperation was formalized with the 1953 Pact of Madrid, a ten-year economic and military agreement that called for the joint operation of naval and air bases in Spain and the supply of American economic and military assistance to the Franco regime. With the United States as an ally and friend, Franco effectively ceased to be an international pariah and any remaining hope that the West would play any role to accelerate the demise of the Franco regime all but vanished. In 1955, Spain was welcomed into the United Nations and dozens of ambassadors returned to Madrid.

After 1959, the Spanish economy grew at a miraculous pace. Growth in industrial output between 1960 and 1967 was the fastest in the world at 10.5 percent per annum and real industrial wages increased by 40 percent in this period, propelling the Spanish economy to the rank of the world's tenth largest by the time of the transition to democracy in the mid-1970s.[11] The engine behind this economic expansion was tourism; between 1960 and 1975, the number of visitors to Spain soared from 6 million to 35 million, contributing $3 billion to the national economy. Alongside the economic boom came a dramatic expansion of social services and consumer spending. By 1975, the percentage of those of school age covered by compulsory education reached 90 percent, and the number of university students had quintupled since 1960. Although Spanish television began broadcasting only in 1959, when the state created a state-run television service, by 1974 the proportion of all households in Spain with a television set had reached 74 percent. That same year saw 85 percent of households in possession of a washing machine and a refrigerator. Automobile ownership rose from 500,000 (one car per 55 inhabitants) in 1960 to over 3,300,000 (one for every nine) by 1974. A surge in the purchasing power of Spanish workers propelled this revolution in consumer spending. Between 1960 and 1974 per capita income rose in Spain from $400 to $1,300. At long last the level of affluence in Spanish society was catching up with the western European average. While in 1959 per capita GDP in Spain stood at 51 percent of the western European average, by 1975 it had reached a "respectable" 77 percent (Harrison 2006: 6).

The dramatic expansion of the economy had profound social consequences, such as the integration of women into the labor force. Between 1961 and 1981, women rose from around 14 percent to 25 percent of Spain's working population, with much of this expansion concentrated in the service industries, most notably tourism (Brooksbank Jones 1995: 386). Relentless urbanization was another dramatic manifestation of an expanding economy. The number of Spanish cities with a population of over 100,000 went from 20 in 1960 to 40 in 1975, propelling the move of 6 million Spaniards from one province to another one. This period also saw the rise of the mega-metropolis in Spain. Between 1955 and 1975, 2 million people migrated to Madrid and 1.8 million to Barcelona seeking better economic opportunities. By 1981, the percentage of Spaniards living in cities larger than 100,000 had reached 42 percent, making Spain as urbanized as the average European country.

As modernization theory would predict (Lipset 1959; Rostow 1960), the social and economic transformations of the late Franco era engendered a strong desire for democracy among the Spanish public. Survey data from the Instituto de Opinión Pública show that between 1966 and 1976 approval for the "democratic principle of government" increased within the adult population from 35 to 78 percent (Wert Ortega 1985: 74–5). Sentiments in favor of democracy were especially notable within the working class, which experienced a marked decline in revolutionary ideologies, as millions of workers were able to join the ranks of the middle class. Edward Malefakis (1995: 73–4) writes that "having escaped poverty for the first time, and thus being able to participate in the consumerism which was sweeping the entire Western world, a kind of *embourgeoisement* transformed the Spanish working classes." He adds that the effects of this moderating process were reinforced by the greater political sophistication being bred among the workers by massive urbanization, the partial erosion of class barriers, higher educational levels, and the increasing influence of the media.

Modernization, however, did not make the advent of democracy a foregone conclusion in Spain. It is telling that although Spain was pushed out of the category of a "developing" society, as determined by the United Nations, by 1963, when its per capita GDP reached the $500 mark, the Franco regime remained firmly in place during the peak years of economic expansion. Ironically, the economic expansion of the late Franco period may have actually worked to delay the advent of democracy. Rising incomes and standards of living had a moderating effect on the masses that made it easier for the government to justify the continuity of the authoritarian state. A significant pro-democratic opposition in authoritarian Spain did not appear until the early 1970s, when the labor movement began to stage politically motivated strikes, and no serious steps to liberalize the Franco regime were taken until after the dictator's death in 1975.

Nor did modernization ensure that the consolidation of the transition to democracy begun after Franco's death would prove successful. As seen in the next chapter, the consolidation of a new democratic regime depended largely upon the expert political craftsmanship of national leaders, especially their capacity to reach pivotal compromises on historical obstacles to democratization, such as the accommodation into the new democratic framework of the monarchy and the Catholic Church, and demands for autonomy from culturally distinct regions. Despite the modernization of the country, some of these problems had become more complex and dangerous to democracy than ever before, such as the rise of a radical Basque separatist movement in the late 1960s. The agency that the political class brought to the task of restoring democracy in Spain did not develop in a vacuum. It was closely informed by the lessons that political actors took from the misfortunes of the past, and none more prominent than the recognition that a dearth of political consensus had doomed previous forays into democratization.

Telling signs that pro-democratic political learning would be playing a major role in the restoration of democracy in Spain were apparent well before Franco's death. At the 1962 Congress of Munich, the leaders of the republican–socialist exiled community signed a document that called for "political prudence" in the reintroduction of democracy, with an eye toward encouraging renunciation of "all active and passive forms of violence, before, during and after" the process of democratization (Aguilar 2002: 103). This document reflected years of introspection by the leaders of the exiled community about what had gone wrong in Spain during the interwar years and what responsibility they shared for having contributed to the series of tragic events that the country experienced during the interwar period. A sentiment strongly felt among the participants of the Munich gathering was that a monarchical democracy was the most appropriate form of government for Spain in a post-Franco future. Republican government, contended one influential participant, "was at the very heart of a tragic conflict. How could we go beyond it?" (Aguilar 2002: 104). Within Spain, an analogous process of political learning was also afoot, led by the Spanish Communist Party (PCE), Franco's principal domestic opposition. The words of Communist leader Santiago Álvarez (Gunther 2007: 24), who had been tortured and sentenced to death by Franco, eloquently express the sentiment of many within the party about the unique opportunity that the democratic transition provided for extraordinary political gestures that could effectively reverse the course of Spanish history:

This memory of the past obliges us to take these circumstances into account, that is, to follow a policy of moderation. We feel responsibility for this process of democratization and the need to make a superhuman effort so that this process is not truncated. This is a unique moment in Spanish history. After more than a century of civil wars and a vicious cycle of massacres among Spaniards, which began after the War of Independence and that ended in June 1977 with the first elections based on universal suffrage, this is the moment when it is possible to end this cycle and to open a period of civilized life, politically speaking. In this sense we cannot allow ourselves the luxury of expressing opinions which might be misunderstood, which could be, or appear to be extremist.

Virtually guaranteeing that a process of pro-democratic political learning would prove viable and successful in Spain were the sentiments of ordinary Spaniards. Survey data of the mid-1970s show that the public placed "peace, order and stability" as their "top priorities" for the post-Franco era (Aguilar 2001: 94). This is hardly surprising considering the process of political socialization to which the public had been subjected under Franco, especially the fear of another civil war. During the late Franco period, ordinary Spaniards had also been deeply affected by new discourses about the causes and consequences of the civil war developed by the anti-Franco intelligentsia. Rather than taking sides and placing blame, the narrative of the civil war constructed by the most influential journalists, novelists and film-makers of the era saw the civil war event as an act of collective madness with devastating consequences for future generations irrespective of their social status and ideological differences (see chapter 8). Their message to the nation with respect to the civil war was essentially the same one that Franco had stressed for decades: "never again."

CONCLUSION

History did not augur well for a successful experience with democratization in Spain. Prior to 1977, the country had no significant tradition of stable democratic governance. This meant that in Spain democratic institutions and practices would have to be invented from scratch. What little democratic experience Spain did have, however, served as a powerful, memorable example of how not to undertake a process of democratization. Fears of falling back into the cycle of political chaos, civil war, and dictatorship (as was the case during the interwar years) induced a process of political learning during the restoration of democracy begun in 1975 that encouraged political actors and society at large to avoid what were perceived to be the main political mistakes of the past: lack of consensus and excessive polarization. This demanded an approach to politics that placed political pragmatism ahead of ideological purity.

Of course, traumatic historical episodes, like a democratic breakdown or a civil war, are never a reliable source of political learning. Nations are very good at repeating their mistakes, and political actors can derive dramatically different lessons from the same political experience. Not surprisingly, across the world, the attempt to use the past to re-imagine nations and forge new political paths is not always successful and in fact often results in fights over history and memory (see Friedman and Kenney 2005). So a key question about political learning raised by the case of Spain is why were the Spaniards so successful at mining their painful history for positive political lessons as democracy approached? As seen in this chapter, this question cannot be fully understood without unpacking how the Franco regime handled the memory of the collapse of the interwar Second Republic and the violence of the Spanish Civil War. Without the old regime's historical myths, manipulations, and distortions, it is unlikely that history would have emerged as a useful foundation for democratization in Spain.

3

THE PRIMACY OF DEMOCRATIC CRAFTING

On June 15, 1977, some 20 million Spaniards went to the polls for the first time since February 15, 1936, just months before the outbreak of the civil war, to elect a new government to replace the Franco dictatorship. Befitting the nation's first free elections in over four decades, the public's enthusiasm for democracy was high, bordering on delirious. As chronicled by the American journalist Stanley Meisler (1977: 190) in the pages of *Foreign Affairs*, the first freely contested parliamentary election in Spain following decades of fear and repression "produced scenes that Franco would have abhorred: Communists brazenly waving red banners, chanting slogans, and singing the *Internationale*; the young dynamic leader of the Socialist Workers' Party entering rallies with his left hand in a clenched fist salute, his right signaling V for *victoria*; politicians exhorting Basques in Euskera, Catalans in Catalan and Galicians in Gallego, all forbidden languages a few years before; and newspapers belittling their government and its leader."

Virtually all indicators suggest that the hopes for a democratic future expressed by the Spaniards on June 15, 1977, have been fulfilled. Although political scientists have yet to agree on what it means for democracy to become consolidated, there is a broadly based consensus that Spanish democracy is fully consolidated. By some estimates (Linz and Stepan 1996: 108), Spain met all the requirements for "democratic consolidation" with the 1982 elections (and perhaps even earlier), just a few years after enacting a new democratic constitution in 1978.[1] Underscoring the characterization of democracy in Spain as consolidated is the prevailing sense among leading scholars of Spanish politics of the improbability that the country will ever again live under a nondemocratic regime. Stanley Payne (1986b: 279) has observed that the destabilization of Spain's democracy "will only result from major national failure in political leadership or massive overloading of problems." "Democracy has become business as usual, an expected and accepted part of the everyday life of all Spaniards," writes Victor Pérez-Díaz (1990: 17). "No serious observer of Spanish politics today acknowledges even a remote possibility of a military coup or return to authoritarianism by some other means," observes Richard Gunther (1992: 40).

What explains the apparent ease with which democracy consolidated in Spain? Surely, the country benefited tremendously from undertaking to democratize in the aftermath of the social and economic progress of the late Franco period. This created a cross-class constituency for democracy before the actual dismantling of the dictatorial regime (Malefakis 1995). Spain also enjoyed the advantage of entering democracy with a civilianized state bureaucracy, which explains the surprising speed at which the Spanish military accepted the transition to democracy (see Agüero 1995). Another positive factor in the democratization of Spain was the prospect of entry into the European Economic Community (EEC), the precursor to the European Union (EU), which served as a powerful incentive for the Spaniards to modernize their political institutions (Huntington 1991; Pridham 1995; Whitehead 1996). Spaniards have long believed that their history, culture, and religious values belong squarely within the European tradition. Many of them have also sustained the view that closer ties to Europe were the answer to the country's many problems, from its economic poverty to its political backwardness to its struggles with peripheral nationalisms. José Ortega y Gasset (1963: 521), Spain's foremost twentieth-century philosopher, best expressed this point of view when he declared, "Spain is the problem and Europe the solution."

None of the factors highlighted above, however, provides a satisfactory explanation for the success of democracy in Spain. In fact, as some have argued, they can fool us into thinking that the process of democratization in Spain was an "over-determined success" (Linz and Stepan 1996: 89). A stable democracy was a far from certain outcome in Spain, given the multiple obstacles to democracy that arose following Franco's death. Thus, it is imperative that any analysis of Spanish democratization be mindful of the primacy of "political crafting": in other words, how democracy was engineered.[2] This approach recognizes the agency that individual actors bring to the task of getting democracy off the ground. It also emphasizes the particular "institutional arrangements" put in place to facilitate regime efficacy and stability (Linz and Stepan 1989: 42). As demonstrated in this chapter, building a political regime that could ensure the long-term viability of democratic institutions and practices was first and foremost in the minds of the architects of Spain's new democracy. A central goal was to virtually eradicate the possibility for political polarization and radicalization, which everyone agreed rested at the heart of the collapse of democracy during the interwar years. Thus, revisiting the past with an eye toward applying its lessons to the present was critical to the making of every major decision concerning the institutions of the new democratic regime, from the configuration of the state, to the design of electoral laws, to the adoption of national symbols like the flag.

This analysis of Spanish democratization politics opens with an account of the transition to democracy that emphasizes the role of two unlikely political reformers: King Juan Carlos, who assumed absolute control of Spain after Franco's death, and Adolfo Suárez, a former Francoist insider hand-picked by the King to orchestrate the transition to democracy. It continues with an examination of the construction of democratic institutions in Spain as incorporated into the 1978 constitution, which suggests the deliberate and dispassionate manner in which political actors in Spain went about creating flexible constitutional compromises intended to ensure the sustainability of democracy. The conclusion uses evidence from the Spanish experience to challenge the widespread claim that transitions to democracy anchored on political pacts create "frozen" democracies.

TWO UNLIKELY DEMOCRATIC REFORMERS

Remarkably, the political infrastructure of the Franco regime remained virtually unchanged until its final days; and it was the dictator's wish that things would remain that way even after his death. As a way of ensuring its longevity, during its twilight years the Franco regime developed an elaborate strategy of *continuismo* aimed at creating "Francoism without Franco." It was anchored upon the restoration of the Spanish monarchy, the subject of the last "fundamental" law passed by the Franco regime. Banking on political allegiance and longevity, Franco passed over the exiled King (Don Juan, Count of Barcelona, Alfonso XIII's third son) and instead named the King's son, the young prince Juan Carlos, as his successor. To make sure that the young King would not veer off from Franco's well-laid-out plans, the last Prime Minister named by Franco was Admiral Luis Carrero Blanco, an able and trusted advisor. All this was designed to leave things, as Franco once said, *atado y bien atado* (safely tied up).

However, even before Franco's death on November 20, 1975, his carefully arranged plans for the transition from one authoritarian regime to another began to unravel. Barely six months into his premiership, Carrero Blanco was assassinated by ETA, an ominous sign of the kind of terror that the organization would impose throughout the democratic transition. His successor, Carlos Arias Navarro, presided over three very chaotic years (1973–6) when no one knew for sure in which direction Spain was heading. As observed by Gunther (2007: 8), Arias Navarro promised *apertura* but instead delivered "institutional stagnation, confusion and agitation in the streets and periodic repression." Just before Franco's passing, Arias Navarro proposed a new set of political reforms in response to growing demands for political liberalization, including the legalization of political "associations" rather than the much-dreaded "parties." These reforms, however, never made it out of the parliament. More ominous, around this time the Arias Navarro government ratcheted up its repressive policies in direct response to the assassination of Carrero Blanco. Much to the horror of international observers and against threats of a boycott from its democratic neighbors, the Arias Navarro government executed five people suspected of terrorism in a clear sign that the old political order remained very much in place. Thirteen countries withdrew their ambassadors from Madrid in protest.

The indecision that gripped the Arias Navarro government reflected deep divisions within the state concerning the future of the authoritarian regime. Advocating political reform (albeit gradually) were the *aperturistas* (the progressive wing of the Franco regime), to which Arias purportedly belonged. On the other side stood the *inmovilistas*, the conservative wing of Francoism, which preferred the maintenance of the authoritarian regime without any significant modification. The impasse between the *aperturistas* and *inmovilistas* created the opportunity for the first critical and unexpected step of the Spanish transition to democracy. In July 1976 King Juan Carlos dismissed the Arias Navarro government and appointed his own man, Adolfo Suárez, a young Francoist insider, with the mandate to execute a speedy and complete process of political liberalization leading to democratic elections. Perhaps more than any other, this decision earned the King the title of *El piloto del cambio* (the pilot of the change), to say nothing of the affection of the general public for the monarchy.[3]

Of course, the King's actions did not take place in a vacuum. As will be seen in chapter 5, even before Franco's death, civil society had begun to mobilize and demand the country's return to democracy. Strikes in particular were successfully employed by the workers to convince the ruling elite of the unfeasibility of *continuismo*. External events in Portugal also played an important role in the King's decision to order a speedy process of democratization, by suggesting the potential for chaos and violence in the aftermath of prolonged dictatorship. The Portuguese transition to democracy, which had begun a few months earlier, featured revolutionary activity, such as land seizures, not seen in western Europe since the Spanish Civil War, and it served for Spain as an alarming negative example of how not to do a democratic transition.

The King's pro-democracy actions stunned the nation. Juan Carlos had been personally groomed to assume the reigns of the authoritarian regime. He arrived in Spain at the age of ten (from his exile home in Portugal) to attend military school and be socialized in the ways of the Franco dictatorship by the dictator himself. On July 12, 1969, he was anointed Franco's successor in a ceremony in which the young Prince swore his oath of loyalty to Franco. A more convincing reason for the people's surprise at the actions of the young King was that few believed that he had it within him to boldly effect political change in Spain, whether for good or bad. For much of the late Franco period, Juan Carlos was barely seen and much less heard. This had occasioned widespread mockery about his future in the post-Franco era. Many Spaniards nicknamed him "Juan Carlos the Brief," for it was assumed that his tenure at the helm of the nation would be a short and insignificant one.

Notwithstanding most Spaniards' enormous satisfaction with the King's act of political betrayal, his appointment of Suárez to lead the nation into democracy was not universally praised. "A grave, grave error" declared *El País*, a liberal leading daily born around the transition to democracy, which quickly became the newspaper of record. The most serious reservations about Suárez had to do with his intimate association with the Franco regime. Under Franco, he had been director of propaganda services and head of the Movimiento Nacional, the closest thing to a party under Franco's rule. Ironically, what made the opposition hesitant about Suárez was exactly what made him the ideal man for the job of transforming Franco's authoritarian institutions. His familiarity with the Franco regime was critical to convincing the old guard to relinquish power through peaceful means. Suárez was also something of a transitional figure within the Franco regime. "He was young enough to have a political future beyond Franco and yet not burdened by a particularly strong ideology of political preferences" (Mujal-León 1985: 279). This made Suárez the ultimate pragmatist; someone willing to enter into a dialogue with any group in society for the sake of creating broadly based societal compromises.

Pacting regime change

Suárez orchestrated the first ever process of regime change to democracy anchored upon the transformation of an authoritarian regime from the inside out. The very institutions of the authoritarian state were employed in the construction of the new democratic order. This was no ordinary political operation. As noted by Linz and Stepan (1996: 92): "The equivalent in the USSR would have involved Gorbachev convincing the Communist Party and the legislative organs of the complex constitutional structure of the Soviet Union to allow multiparty, freely contested elections for a parliament of the union which then would have the duty and power to form the government." Of course, this never happened in the USSR, or in any other hyper-institutionalized authoritarian state, so why was it possible in Spain? The self-transformation of the Franco regime depended largely upon Suárez's negotiating capacities, as he simultaneously engaged in negotiations with representatives of the old regime and its democratic opposition.

Suárez's first major accomplishment was persuading the Francoist parliament to pass a law that essentially put the Franco regime out of business. The 1976 Law of Political Reform legalized parties and independent unions, guaranteed freedom of the press, granted amnesty for political prisoners, ordered the dissolution of the vertical syndicate, and called for the country's first democratic vote in nearly four decades. Key to understanding why the Francoist parliament would go along with Suárez's plan was that the law was passed in accord with the Francoist legal framework. Accordingly, political reform was legislated as a "fundamental" law. This gave political reform in Spain "backward legitimacy" or legitimacy under the laws and procedures of the existing political system (Di Palma 1990). To ensure "forward legitimacy," the law of political reform was approved in a national referendum by an overwhelming majority of the Spanish public: 94.2 in favor and 2.9 opposed (Gunther 2007: 8).

Emboldened with his success in organizing the self-liquidation of Francoism, Suárez began to engage in negotiations with the democratic opposition led by the Communist and Socialist parties. In doing so, he capitalized on an ongoing process of political moderation percolating within the left that was initiated years before the democratic transition and which was rooted in the reawakening of the memories of historical misfortunes, especially the collapse of the interwar Second Republic. The 1970 *Pacto por la Libertad* (Pact of Freedom) affirmed the willingness of the Spanish Communist Party (the PCE), the main opposition to the Franco regime, to "reach agreements with virtually all political parties, including those on the right" (Gunther et al. 2004: 93). This pact also committed the Communists to reconciliation with the army and the Church, and to the construction of socialism through the democratic process. These decisions by the Communist leadership were pivotal in shaping Spain's "pacted" transition. Until the early 1970s, the Communists held on to the view that the Franco regime "could not be reformed but had to be brought down" by means of a revolutionary overthrow (Mujal-León 1985: 165). Following Franco's death, the Junta Democrática, an inter-party coalition, brought Socialist and Communist leaders together with the purpose of bringing a peaceful end to the Franco regime. "It is time to pact with the system," Santiago Carrillo, the Secretary General of the Spanish Communist Party, is quoted as saying on March 26, 1976, on the occasion of the formation of the Junta Democrática (Elordi 1996: 126).

The Communists' acceptance of negotiations opened the door for a series of secret deals between state insiders committed to liberalizing the Franco regime and the democratic opposition. At meetings that often took place late into the evening, at locations like José Luis, a Madrid restaurant, the architecture of Spain's new democracy began to emerge even before the first free vote was cast. Among the major compromises of the "restaurant agreements" was the left's decision to give up on creating a "Third Republic," by agreeing to the restoration of the monarchy, in exchange for the legalization of political parties and the trade unions and free elections. The left also joined Suárez in recommending that King Juan Carlos grant pardons to all political prisoners, a prelude to the 1977 amnesty law that prevented prosecution of anyone associated with past political crimes, which in turn became the foundation for the *Pacto del Olvido*, the agreement to relegate memory of the past to the dustbin of history. This deliberate attempt to bury the past, the first pillar of Spain's post-transition settlement, sought to avoid recriminations about who had done what to whom and when, so that the nation could move forward with the business of institutionalizing the emerging democratic system. Like so many other political compromises of the transition, this one was inspired by the past. Guided by the desire "to live harmoniously with the enemy" (Aguilar 2001: 98), the political regime created in 1977 is the first in twentieth-century Spain not to have called the previous regime to account for its political excesses.[4]

Future political compromises were purposely designed to minimize the prospect of political fragmentation and excessive polarization, in a deliberate effort to avoid the fate of the Second Republic. The new electoral law passed by the Francoist parliament called for universal suffrage, the secret ballot, and the establishment of a bicameral system of representation: a Senate elected by a plurality system and a Chamber of Deputies elected through proportional representation. The law also made the Spanish provinces the official electoral district. These were all conscious political choices. The framers of the new electoral law believed that a bicameral system would make it more difficult for radical parties to exert influence in national politics, since they would have to gain control of two representative bodies. Undoubtedly, the memory of the Second Republic's radicalized unicameral system helped create this impression. The decision to base electoral representation around provinces rather than regions should also be read as an obstacle to any potential evolution of the country into a federation.

A royal decree of March 18, 1977 passed by the Francoist parliament defined how political competition was to be organized in the new democracy. The legislators sought to strike a delicate balance between being inclusive enough to guarantee broad political diversity and restrictive enough to weed out small groups wielding disproportionate influence. With these goals in mind, the 1977 decree adopted the d'Hondt system of translating votes into seats. Named after its inventor (a Belgian mathematician), this system of political representation explicitly favors large parties to the detriment of smaller ones. The law also required that representation in the 350-member Congress of Deputies was limited to parties that obtained a minimum of 3 percent of the votes in at least one district. It also provided financial subsidies to the parties to remedy their desperate economic situation, according to a system by which the state promised to reimburse the parties by a fixed amount for each parliamentary seat gained in the parliament. Clearly, the central purpose of the new electoral law was to streamline the slate of political organizations allowed to field candidates for public office.

In April 1977, the final adjustment to the electoral process was made with the legalization of the PCE, which the political reform of 1976 had purposely excluded. This had been a concession to the military, which viewed the party as a threat to national security, almost in the same way in which it regarded ETA. Suárez boldly reversed this decision during the Easter week vacation, while military officers were away from their offices, in time for the PCE's participation in the June 1977 elections. He wisely recognized that the emerging democratic system had more to gain from legalizing the PCE than from keeping it in its illegal and clandestine status. As he argued on the floor of the Cortes, "I do not think that our people want to find itself fatally obliged to see our jails full of people for ideological reasons. I think that in a democracy we must all be vigilant of ourselves, we must all be witnesses and judges of our public actions" (Linz and Stepan 1996: 97). Suárez also recognized that the exclusion from the 1977 elections of the PCE, at the time the largest and best-organized party in Spain, would have certainly posed a serious problem of legitimacy for the new democracy.

Ensuing largely from his successful negotiation of the end of the Franco regime, Suárez emerged the undisputed winner of national elections held on June 15, 1977, Spain's first since February 16, 1936. His centrist coalition, the Unión de Centro Democrático (UCD), scored a decisive victory with 34 percent of the popular vote and 118 parliamentary seats (48 percent of all seats). With this victory, Suárez was entrusted with the responsibility of governing the nation through the "Constituent" period, 1977–9. His main responsibility was drafting a new democratic constitution that could settle issues that in the past had hindered democratic development, and that would be acceptable to a majority of the Spanish public, a tall order to be sure.

CONSOLIDATING DEMOCRACY WITH CONSENSUS

To inaugurate democracy and accelerate the process of democratic consolidation, Prime Minister Suárez negotiated with the leading opposition parties the epoch-making Pacts of Moncloa. These agreements, which contained specific steps for dealing with the economic crisis that accompanied the democratic transition, especially runaway inflation, institutionalized the second pillar of the post-transition settlement: the commitment by the country's leading political forces to a collaborative approach to policy making.[5] Signed to great fanfare on October 27, 1977, the Moncloa pacts are rightly characterized as "extra-parliamentary" because the bargaining took place behind closed doors, at the residence of the Spanish Prime Minister (the Moncloa Palace). In keeping with Suárez's intention to be inclusive, the Moncloa pacts incorporated political representation from virtually the entire ideological spectrum, including Christian Democrats, Social Democrats, Communists, Socialists, conservatives, and regional-nationalists.[6] Only groups on the far fringes of Spanish politics, such as the neo-Francoist Fuerza Nueva (FN) and Herri Batasuna (HB), ETA's political wing, remained outside of the sphere of consensus created by the accord. Subsequent to its signing, Moncloa was debated in the national parliament, where it was rapidly turned into law.

Why the need for so much consensus in the aftermath of the inauguration of a new democratic government? The principal reason was the desire by the Suárez administration to create an aura of political consensus around the drafting of a new constitution. This explains the accord's impeccable political timing: right after the first democratic elections of 1977 and immediately before the parliamentarians began to debate the various articles that would go on to become the foundation of the 1978 constitution.

The need to integrate the political class in anticipation of a process sure to revive all the contentious issues in Spanish history was highlighted to this author in an interview with the main architect of the Moncloa pacts, Enrique Fuentes Quintana, Vice President for the Economy. He acknowledged that the pacts' chief purpose "was to neutralize the political arena as a way to facilitate the acceptance of a democratic constitution by all the relevant political forces" (Encarnación 1997: 407). Fuentes Quintana's insistence that democracy be inaugurated in Spain with a broad political accord flowed directly from his reading of Spanish history, especially the collapse of the Second Republic, his central historical reference for his design of the Moncloa pacts. In his view, the principal lesson from the Republican era was that over-polarization occasioned the erosion of the legal and social order and the eventual collapse of democracy. This lesson was of relevance to Spain in 1977 because, in Fuentes Quintana's own words, "while history does not repeat itself, historical conditions do" (Encarnación 1997: 407).

Political violence, that old familiar demon of Spanish politics, was another motivating factor behind the rise of the Moncloa pacts. Because Spain's democratic transition was dominated by consensus, contemporary observers tend to forget the very violent context in which it unfolded. In fact, political violence was more "pervasive" in Spain than in "revolutionary" Portugal (Bermeo 1997: 39). The assassination of Admiral Carrero Blanco, Franco's alter ego and apparent political heir, by ETA in 1973 was eerily reminiscent of the rash of political assassinations that started the civil war in 1936. ETA killings intensified as the transition progressed, rising from 43 in 1975, the year Franco died, to 78 in 1978, the year the new democratic constitution was enacted, to 118 in 1980 (a record for a single year to date), the year of the first regional elections (Maravall and Santamaría 1986: 105). This killing campaign was intended to unleash an "action–repression–action spiral," a classic strategy of insurgencies intended to provoke a wave of indiscriminate violence against the public by the government, in the hope that this would cause the population to respond with increased protest and support for the resistance.

Political violence from other parts of Spanish society, such as the state and extreme right-wing and left-wing movements, served to further stoke fears of another civil war and/or the possibility of a military intervention to derail the process of democratization. In December 1976, shortly after Franco's death, the extreme left-wing organization GRAPO kidnapped two important figures of the Franco regime, the President of the Council of the State and the President of the Superior Council of Military Justice. In March 1976, just before the trade unions and the political parties were legalized, the police opened fired on a demonstration in the Basque city of Vitoria killing five workers. In January 1977, in what came to be known as the "Atocha Massacre," neo-fascist groups murdered six members of the Spanish Communist Party, including five labor lawyers, a handful of the more than 70 assassinations carried out by extreme right-wing movements between 1977 and 1980.

Finally, there was the desire from virtually the entire political class to demonstrate to the general public and sectors of Spanish society still ambivalent or opposed to democracy (ETA and the military, most notably) that it could comport itself politically and that it had the capacity and the means to address the nation's most pressing problems in a responsible and orderly manner. Getting this message across was especially important for the left-wing parties (PSOE and the PCE), which used the Moncloa pacts to underscore to the electorate that they no longer stood on the margins of politics and that they belonged squarely within the political mainstream. Both parties (but especially the PCE) saw their performance in the 1977 elections as evidence that the public still harbored some suspicion of their democratic credentials.

The Moncloa pacts had immediate, positive results, especially in the economic realm. The annual rate of inflation fell from almost 25 percent in 1977 to 16.5 percent by 1978, barely missing the target rate of 15 percent predicted by the pacts (Harrison 2006: 20). This success was due in no small measure to the support the pacts received from the public. Aside from complaints from the media that the pacts created the impression that the nation had a "shadow government," and from employers that the pacts granted too much influence to the left-wing parties, most Spaniards simply accepted them, including the workers (Encarnación 2005: 190). One survey found that 55.6 percent of technicians and 38.2 of clerks found the economic mandates of the Moncloa pacts "reasonable" (Wert Ortega 1985: 79). A 1978 survey by the Centro de Investigaciones Sociológicas (CIS) found that an overwhelming majority of Spaniards had a positive impression of the Moncloa pacts. Interestingly, many citizens saw a link between "pacting" and the successful democratization of the nation. The CIS survey found that 23 percent of the public thought that the Moncloa accord was "very necessary" to the nation's democratic well-being while 43 percent deemed it "sufficiently necessary."

Notwithstanding their economic importance, it is in the political realm that we find the most important legacies of the Moncloa pacts. This is hardly surprising since, as noted already, it was the political situation rather than the state of the economy that truly drove both the government and the opposition to the bargaining table. The most important contribution of the Moncloa pacts to the consolidation of democracy was integrating the political class around the project of democratic consolidation, while isolating, simultaneously, the forces most likely to disrupt or derail Spain's new democracy: the military, ETA, and extreme right-wing groups. To no small degree, the Moncloa pacts introduced a radical way of doing politics in Spain. They allowed politicians to think of their opponents as "adversaries" rather than "enemies" (Capo Giol 1981: 159). Prime Minister Leopoldo Calvo Sotelo, who replaced Suárez as prime minister in 1981, observes that "After the drafting and implementation of the Moncloa accord there was a consolidation within the political class of the sentiment that the democratic project was best served by a process of negotiation; and as a result, any actor opposed to it was seen as outside of the political mainstream."[7]

Framing the 1978 constitution

Neither the negotiated manner in which the constitution was drafted, nor the spirit of political accommodation incorporated into its various articles, can be imagined without the Moncloa pacts serving as a template for intra-elite collaboration. Unlike previous Spanish constitutions, most notably that of the Second Republic, a ruling government did not impose the 1978 constitution. Instead, it was a negotiated settlement involving all the major political parties, much like the drafting of the Moncloa pacts. Indeed, the constitution is the ultimate political pact in the democratization of Spain. The framework of the constitution was laid out by a group of seven notables representing all the major political groups, who worked in private to craft a document that represented a broad political compromise and that incorporated specific mechanisms to ensure the stability of the new regime. The committee's deliberations were kept strictly confidential from their inception in late August 1977 through to completion in November 1977, when a draft copy of the agreement was leaked to the press. The aim was, as recalled by the Socialist representative, to work "without interference or pressure" (Peces-Barba 1988: 33).

The secrecy that surrounded the writing of the constitution, as argued by Gunther (2007: 13), "shielded the politicians from criticisms that they were selling out their interests in the interest of establishing a broad inter-party consensus." These criticisms were also muted by the political inclusiveness of the membership of the constitutional drafting committee. It was made up of three members from the centrist UCD (the governing party), two from the left (one from the PSOE and one from the PCE); one from the right (a representative of AP, a right-wing party), and one from the "Grupo Mixto," representing "regional-nationalist" parties from Catalonia and the Basque Country.[8] The committee's business was haunted by the traumatic memory of the failure of the Second Republic. Its president, Emilio Attard Alonso, opened the committee's deliberations by remarking, "We are fully conscious that the dialectical undertakings of 1931 began in a quarrel and ended in civil war" (Gunther 1992: 77).

The negotiated approach to constitution making adopted by the Spaniards had clear benefits, since it took into consideration the views of all the relevant political forces, thereby virtually assuring its acceptance by the general public. It had some drawbacks as well, most notably that some of the historic problems of the country would not be settled once and for all by the constitution. Therefore, reaching a broad consensus on many of the issues that had divided Spain for centuries often boiled down to proposing a framework for their future resolution. Consequently, the resulting document was notable above all for many exquisite ambiguities which democratic governments established after 1977 have endeavored to disentangle. Yet ambiguity was, arguably, what was in the best interest of Spain in 1977 as it commenced its new democratic future. As contended by Miguel Roca, the Catalan representative in the constitutional drafting committee, "Consensus means accepting ambiguity . . . the kind of ambiguity that opens the way for any democratic party to rule without creating a dangerous constitutional crisis" (López Pina 1985: 32).

The many ambiguities contained in the new constitution begin with the definition of the Spanish state. Article 1 states that the political form of the Spanish state is that of a "parliamentary monarchy," a political arrangement that ensured the survival of the Spanish monarchy in the new democratic regime. This was a radical constitutional innovation for Spain, given the country's strong republican traditions, and a major concession on the part of the left. Since the declaration of Spain's first republic in 1873, democracy and republicanism had become part and parcel of the same thing for the left. Carrillo (1965: 111), the PCE's Secretary General, best expressed this point prior to Franco's death when he declared: "democracy is synonymous with republican government."

Carrillo was hardly alone in holding this view. Many of the parliamentarians who participated in the constitutional debate were of the belief that "in Spain, freedom and democracy came to have one name only: republic" (López Pina 1985: 36). Popular sentiments among left-wing voters leaned heavily toward another republic. A 1979 poll showed that Communist voters preferred a republican government to a parliamentary monarchy by 65 percent to 14 percent (Gunther 1992: 45). The left, however, had the good sense not to push for the republican option during the constitutional debate. Republicanism did not have a good reputation in Spain, given its association by the general public with the democratic breakdown of the interwar era. Surveys from the early 1980s show that only 5 percent or less of the population had favorable impressions of the Second Republic and it consistently scored lower than the Franco regime (Aguilar and Humlebaek 2002: 145).

In any case, before the inception of the parliamentary debate on the constitution, King Juan Carlos had already secured a role for the monarchy in the new democracy by his brave betrayal of Francoism. A 1977 survey indicated how high the popularity of the monarchy was among ordinary Spaniards: 59 percent professed to be pro-monarchical, 19 percent were indifferent, and only 18 percent chose a republic (Conversi 2002: 230). Just as important in guaranteeing a role for the monarchy in the new regime was the tremendous respect that the King enjoyed within the political class, including many on the left. The politicians saw the King as a man who could not only help solidify democracy in Spain but also keep the nation together at a time when flaring ethnic tensions were threatening national unity. The King played this role of national unifier to brilliant effect. In 1976, during his first official trip to Catalonia, he addressed the locals in Catalan (a first for a Spanish monarch) proclaiming, "Long live Catalonia, long live Spain." The effect of this attempt at multiculturalism was "highly favorable throughout Catalonia and the Monarchy's popularity soared, despite the rather cold reception the Monarch had received on his arrival" (Conversi 2002: 230).

Ambiguity also prevailed in the making of the constitutional compromise on church–state relations. In this respect, as in other aspects of political development in Spain in the post-Franco era, the eventual church–state compromise inserted into the new constitution bears no connection to models from the past, especially the Republican era, although it was directly inspired by the past. It contrasts radically with the shrill anti-clericalism found in the 1931 Republican constitution, which bluntly stated, "The Spanish State has no official religion," as well as with the "Confessional Catholic State," of the Francoist era, which made Catholicism the state's official religion. Instead, as aptly characterized by one American newspaper, in conceiving church–state relations in the post-Franco era "the authors of the Spanish constitution opted for a handshake between the two institutions" (*Christian Science Monitor*, October 1, 2004). The 1978 constitution guarantees freedom of religion and worship, the absence of an official state religion, and state neutrality on religious issues, but nonetheless manages to recognize the historic importance of the Catholic Church in the public life of the Spanish people.

Article 16 states that "public authorities shall maintain the consequent relations of cooperation with the Catholic Church and other confessions." This stipulation has allowed the Catholic Church to retain extensive public financing from the state, to finance the wide range of educational, cultural, and ecclesiastical activities conducted by the Church, the chief reason why the left initially opposed it.[9] The Socialist party argued that the mention of the Catholic Church in the constitution violated the spirit of equality among religious faiths. The Communists, however, arguing for the need for avoiding the social polarization of the 1930s, joined Suárez's center-right government in endorsing the constitutional compromise on the Church. In the end, the most persuasive argument was that set forth by the Church itself. Especially influential in shaping the role of the Church in the new constitution was Cardinal Vicente Enrique Tarancón of Madrid. During the constitutional debate, he warned the parliamentarians that "The Church is a social reality . . . and politics has to bear in mind and respect the real life of the people; it cannot ignore the fact that the majority of the Spanish people belong to the Catholic Church" (Brasslof 1998: 95).

Equally ambiguous was the economic order suggested by the constitution, which sought to marry the right's desire for constructing a free economy with the left's plans for a strong role for the state in regulating the activities of the market and in protecting workers' rights. At the demand of the employers, article 38 of the constitution notes that "the free enterprise system is recognized within the framework of a market economy." This statement appears to be contradicted by article 128 of the constitution, which states that "essential resources or services may be restricted by law to the public sector and that intervention in companies may be decided upon when the public interest so demands." To help minimize class conflict, which everyone agreed had contributed mightily to the collapse of the Second Republic, the constitution provides institutional mechanisms for the formulation of national economic policy. It stipulates that the government "shall make economic policy with the collaboration of the trade unions and other professional employer and economic organizations." To that end, the constitution authorizes the creation of an extra-parliamentary Social and Economic Council designed to facilitate social negotiation of national economic policy and labor and industrial relations matters among the state, the employers, and the trade unions. This makes the Spanish constitution unique among modern constitutions for the extent to which it stipulates specific roles for economic actors such as unions.

The most ambiguous and complex constitutional compromise of them all concerns the decentralization of the state in response to demands for regional autonomy from ethnic minority communities. But this would be no ordinary process of devolution of powers from the central state to the regions. On the one hand, the framers of the constitution had to reconcile seemingly contradictory demands: the right's insistence that the unitary nature of the state be protected, and the call from the regions that the state be decentralized, which was supported by the left. On the other hand, any reconsideration of the configuration of the state in Spain had to confront such politically charged subjects as "the Spanish nation" and "the Spanish state," both of which had been appropriated and heavily abused by the Franco regime, thereby turning them into highly polarizing concepts. As noted by Aguilar and Humlebaek (2002: 133), "For any Spaniard who had lived under the dictatorship, expressions such as 'Spain' and 'the Spanish Nation' or cheers of 'Viva España' immediately evoked Francoist discourse."

The difficulties of reconceiving the Spanish state forced the parliamentary debate on the constitution to last for 16 months. In the end, the resulting compromise aimed to satisfy everybody, which of course means that in the long run it has pleased nobody. Article 2 of the constitution notes the "indissoluble unity of the Spanish nation." This formally rules out the nation becoming a federal state. Indeed, the term "federalism" is studiously avoided in the text of the constitution. But the constitution also recognizes the existence of a variety of "nationalities" within the Spanish territory and the right of the regions to seek self-governance from the central state. This reference to "nationalities" was a hard-won victory for the nationalists of Catalonia and the Basque Country, who have traditionally questioned the existence of a Spanish nation.

A task related to the decentralization of the state was the reconstruction of national symbols as a means to "refound" the state and provide the country with a shared sense of nationhood. Here again the lessons from the past ruled the day. In striking contrast to the refounding of the state after the declaration of the Second Republic in 1931, which saw the nation adopt a new flag and national anthem, the framers of the constitution sought a more conciliatory approach by incorporating elements from the recent past. The Francoist national anthem and flag were retained, although in the new constitution the description of the flag was changed from "red, gold and red" to "red, yellow and red" on the assumption that "yellow sounded more democratic and, to some extent, liberated the flag from its controversial recent past" (Gimeno Martínez 2006: 56).[10] To prevent any discussion in the parliament or heated debates within society at large, the decision on the anthem and the flag was introduced as a royal decree.

The framers of the constitution and subsequent democratic governments took no decision with respect to Franco's material legacy (statues, monuments, and street names) and it was basically left to individual localities to determine how to proceed. It would not be until 2007 that the government would attempt to legislate this explosive issue at the national level. In the nationalistic regions, like Catalonia and the Basque Country, symbols with regional significance quickly replaced those of the dictatorship. In bastions of republicanism, like Madrid, Francoist symbols were substituted with old Republican ones. In much of the rest of the country, however, especially towns and villages, the material legacy of the old regime endures. The framers of the constitution also skirted the decision of choosing a national holiday. When the idea of a national holiday was revisited in 1987, the government settled on Columbus Day (October 12), now renamed "Spain's National Day," with an eye toward erasing any reference to "conquest and colonization, to Christopher Columbus, and even to Latin America" (Aguilar and Humlebaek 2002: 139).

A FROZEN DEMOCRACY?

An obvious concern that ensues from the heavy reliance on secret intra-elite negotiations and political pacts employed to introduce democratic governance in Spain is whether any of this had a negative impact on the quality of Spanish democracy. This concern is prompted by a very well-known contention in the democratization literature that democracies assisted in their birth by political pacts are destined to evolve into "frozen" democracies. Terry Karl (1987: 88) has made this point most forcefully when observing that "pacts hinder the prospects for the future democratic self-transformation of society, economy or polity thereby producing a frozen democracy." This "freezing" outcome, it is argued, is an almost inevitable consequence of the long-term negative side-effects created by the inherently elitist, corporatist, and exclusionary nature of political pact-making. Consequently, political pacts negotiated at the time of the

Table 3.1   Governments in democratic Spain, 1977–2004

Government	Time in office	Duration (months)	Party	Percentage of parliamentary seats	Majority/minority
Suárez I	1/77–4/79	22	UCD	47	Minority
Suárez II	4/79–1/81	22	UCD	48	Minority
Calvo Sotelo	2/81–10/82	21	UCD	48	Minority
González I	12/82–6/86	43	PSOE	58	Majority
González II	7/86–10/89	40	PSOE	53	Majority
González III	12/89–6/93	43	PSOE	50	Majority
González IV	7/93–3/96	33	PSOE	45	Minority
Aznar I	5/96–1/00	45	PP	45	Minority
Aznar II	4/00–1/04	46	PP	52	Majority
Zapatero	4/04–present	–	PSOE	43	Minority

Source: Adapted from Gunther et al. (2004: 167). The data are updated to 2004

transition to democracy are generally viewed as a double-edged sword. They can do wonders for introducing democracy by minimizing conflict among politicians (see O'Donnell and Schmitter 1986), but at the high price of compromising the quality of the emerging democracy (see Karl 1987; Przeworski 1991; Hagopian 1992; Diamond 1998). Among the many negative side-effects attributed to political pacts, three stand out: (1) stifling political competition by concentrating power in the hands of a few elite actors; (2) hindering democratization by retarding the development of civil rights and political liberties; and (3) undermining popular support for democracy by fueling cynicism among the citizenry.

Little, if anything, about the development of democracy in Spain supports the "freezing" hypothesis. The numerous transfers of government experienced by the country since the "foundational" elections of 1977 suggest the overall vitality of Spanish democracy. As can be observed in table 3.1, since 1977 Spain has undergone six general elections and four of them have brought about a change in the ruling party of the government (1982, 1996, and 2004). Moreover, despite the "consensual" nature of post-transition politics, Spain has consistently behaved as a majoritarian political system with one single party in control of the government, which some have credited with enhancing the quality of democratic governance by promoting "decisiveness" and "consistency in policy-making and implementation," and "democratic accountability" (Gunther 2007: 29).

As it happens, the many changes in government experienced by Spain also suggest that the country is already a mature democracy, since it meets one of the methods most commonly employed by political scientists for determining which democracies are consolidated and which are not: the "two-turnover test." According to Samuel Huntington (1991: 266–7), who devised this test of democratic consolidation, democratic regimes achieve consolidation if "the party or group that takes power in the initial election at the time of the transition loses a subsequent election and turns over power to those election winners, and if those election winners then peacefully turn over power to the winners of the later election." Spain met this test in 1996 with the defeat of the Socialist party to the conservative Popular Party.

Of course, routine elections, even clean and competitive ones, do not a democracy make. This is the principal reason why many democratization scholars insist that for any democracy to become fully rooted in any society it must be capable of delivering more than regular and fair elections (Linz and Stepan 1996; Diamond 1999; Encarnación 2000a). Three things, in particular, are generally seen as suggesting a high level of overall quality of democracy: (1) civilian control over the military; (2) adherence to a broad menu of civil rights and political liberties; and (3) widespread acceptance of democracy by the citizenry as the best form of government: in other words, "democratic legitimacy." On all three fronts, the Spanish case excels.

Comparative studies of civilian–military relations (Agüero 1995; Zaverucha 1993) hold Spain as the paradigmatic case of "civilian supremacy" over the military, no small accomplishment considering the military origins of the Franco regime. Attaining this status requires that the military be socialized into "accepting the superiority of democratic institutions and procedures" (Agüero 1995: 153). Rather ironically, the fact that Spain had achieved civilian supremacy over the military was revealed with the coup attempt of February 21, 1981. The "Tejerazo," an attempt to derail democracy led by Lieutenant Colonel Antonio Tejero and triggered by the extension of self-governance to Catalonia and the Basque Country, failed in no small measure because the majority of military officers did not support it, to say nothing of the resolute defense of democracy by all the principal political forces and the general public.

The best snapshot of what has been accomplished in Spain in the post-Franco era with respect to civil rights and political liberties can be found in the comparative data from Freedom House, frequently cited as the standard for judging the quality of democracy worldwide.[11] With the death of Franco in 1975 and the initiation of democratic reforms, Spain moved from the category of "not free" to "partly free." After the democratic elections of 1977, Spain became "free," a classification the country has retained ever since. More suggestive is that, as demonstrated in table 3.2, Spain's record for protecting civil rights and political liberties has remained consistently high since the advent of democracy and today is virtually indistinguishable from those of older and presumably more mature democracies. Freedom House's data for 2006 give Spain the perfect score of 1, the same as for Canada, the United States, and Britain. More meaningful, perhaps, is how favorably the quality of democracy in Spain fares when compared to that of other new democracies.

The very high regard on the part of the general public for the democratic political process in Spain is suggested by the fact that, since the democratic transition, Spanish public opinion has been strongly pro-democratic and has overwhelmingly rejected the major possible alternative to democracy, a military government. By 1978, just one year into the new democracy, 77 percent of Spaniards were deeming democracy preferable to any other kind of government with only 15 percent preferring authoritarianism (Linz and Stepan 1996: 108–9). As noted in figure 3.1, this favorable impression of democracy has held steady over the years and despite the travails faced by the nation's new democracy, including widespread terrorism courtesy of Basque separatist groups and western Europe's highest unemployment rate.

Table 3.2 Civil and political freedoms in selected countries[a]

Country	Political rights	Civil rights	Freedom rating
Argentina	2	2	Free
Brazil	2	2	Free
Chile	1	1	Free
China	7	6	Not free
Cuba	7	7	Not free
France	1	1	Free
Iraq	6	5	Not free
Japan	1	2	Free
Malaysia	4	4	Partly free
Nigeria	4	4	Partly free
Russia	6	5	Not free
Spain	1	1	Free
United Kingdom	1	1	Free
United States	1	1	Free
Venezuela	4	4	Partly free

[a] 1 represents the highest level of respect for civil and political rights; 7 represents the lowest.
Source: Freedom House, "Freedom in the World, 2006"

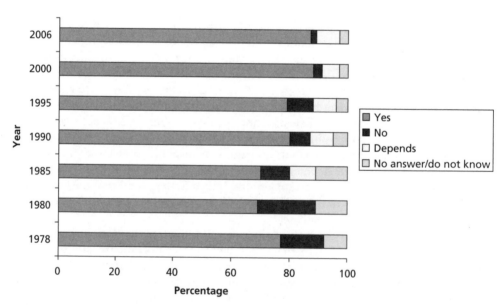

[a] For the years 1978 and 1980, people were asked to agree or disagree with the following statement: "Democracy is the best political system for a country like ours." After 1981, the statement posed was "Democracy is preferable to any other form of government."
Source: CIS

Figure 3.1 Support for democracy in Spain, 1978–2006 (%)[a]

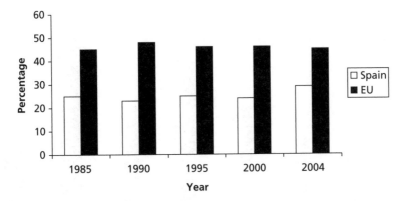

Source: Adapted from Martín-Cortés (2007)

Figure 3.2   Interest in politics in Spain and the European Union, 1985–2004 (%)

Public support for democracy in Spain is more impressive still when compared to that of other countries. According to the survey data from *Eurobarometer*, the 78 percent of Spaniards who prefer democracy to any other type of government is the average for the European Union, and is actually higher than the average for older democracies such as Britain (73 percent), Italy (73), and Ireland (63). More revealing still is the contrast that can be drawn with other new democracies, especially major Latin American nations. According to survey data from Latinobarometer, national averages for the statement "Democracy is preferable to any other kind of government" range from 77 percent in Uruguay to 73 percent in Argentina, 59 percent in Chile and Mexico, and 37 percent in Brazil.

One aspect of political life in Spain that does appear to support the "freezing" hypothesis is an utter disengagement from politics by the general public. Across the board, studies of contemporary Spanish political culture show a clear disinterest in politics bordering on apathy and cynicism. Summarizing the views of numerous scholars, Morlino and Montero (1995: 252) describe Spanish political culture as "characterized by lack of popular interest in politics, perceptions of inefficacy, a critical skepticism, and a lack of confidence in the political elites." This characterization is supported by cross-national data from the Eurobarometer that trace the issue of "interest in politics" across European publics, generally defined as how frequently people discuss political matters with their friends. These data consistently rank Spain well below the EU average. As seen in figure 3.2, since the early 1980s the percentage of Spaniards professing an interest in politics has rarely exceeded 25 percent versus the EU average of above 40 percent (Martín-Cortés 2007). During the early 1990s the percentage of the population professing an interest in politics actually fell to the mid-teens.

Some studies have suggested that the apathy and cynicism prevalent in Spanish political culture is an enduring legacy of the demobilization of the public that took place during the democratic transition, the result of intense intra-elite political bargaining (see especially McDonough et al. 1998: 145–64). This impression, however compelling, is broadly contradicted by cross-national research on levels of interest in politics in the

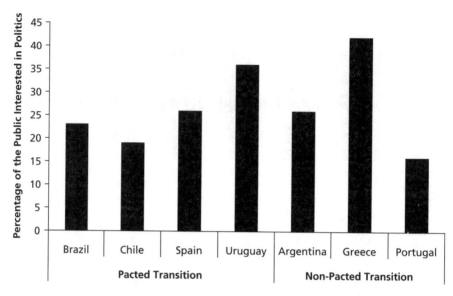

[a] These categories have been questioned for representing simplistic typologies (see Encarnación 2005; Gunther 2007). Although they capture something about the dynamics of regime change, they clearly tell us little about the long-term qualitative characteristics of the democratic regime that consolidates.

Note: The percentage data represent annual averages for 1996.

Source: Adapted from Martín-Cortés (2004, 2007)

Figure 3.3   Interest in politics and mode of democratic transition[a]

new democracies of Iberia and South America by Martín-Cortés (2003, 2007). Figure 3.3 shows no obvious connection between the level of interest in politics and whether the transition to democracy featured pacts or not. Uruguay, a case whose democratic transition was anchored on pacts between civilian and military leaders, is noted as having the highest level of interest in politics in South America (36 percent), well ahead of Argentina (25 percent), which experienced the region's best-known "non-pacted" transition. Portugal, a country that entered democracy via a revolution, lags behind Spain, whose democratic transition was anchored on political negotiations. Such findings lead the author to the conclusion that "it may not be pacts by themselves that keep citizens away from politics but something else" (Martín-Cortés 2007: 13). That something else may be rooted in the historical experience. Maravall and others have argued that "a cynical view of politics has long been a central trait of Southern European political culture and that this trait could even be a rational judgment based on a long experience of politics as the abuse of power" (Morlino and Montero 1995: 252). In other words, decades of dictatorial rule have instilled into Spanish citizens a deep-seated suspicion of governmental authority and politics in general, but this does not preclude them from offering a very positive evaluation of the current democratic regime.

CONCLUSION

Two broad lessons about democratization are provided by the success of Spanish democracy. Arguably the most compelling is the need to take into consideration the agency of real-life political actors and their skills at engineering political conditions that can help in overcoming obstacles to democratic living. This lesson is often overlooked by the popularity of the view of democracy as the outcome of structural preconditions such as a relatively advanced level of social and economic development. The more recent trend to privilege the behavior of collectivities in determining the fate of political events has further obscured attention to individual political actions. Surely, individual agency does not develop in a vacuum. In the case of Spain, it was conditioned by the painful memory of past political misfortunes. Every major institutional feature of Spain's new democracy – a bicameral parliament, an electoral law premised on proportional representation, a labor and industrial relations regime based on explicit collaboration among key economic actors, and an asymmetrical type of federalism, to name the most notable – reflects a studied approach to what would work best for the country based on past political experience.

A second lesson is that how nations enter democracy does not determine the long-term qualitative aspects of the political regime. Spain pointedly challenges the popular impression that a "pacted" transition is destined to produce a "frozen" democracy. Why a democratic freezing was successfully averted in Spain is clearly tied to the broadly based commitment to democracy on the part of the Spanish political class. A less evident but arguably more decisive factor was the inclusiveness of the bargaining process, which incorporated actors from across the ideological spectrum. This political inclusiveness, a reflection of the desire to avoid the political polarization of the past, served to legitimize the political compromises, to ensure that they served the national interest of democratic consolidation, and to facilitate their acceptance by society at large. Indeed, the extraordinary inclusion represented in the Spanish pacts is what separates them from analogous agreements found in other democratizing environments. The political pacts that aided in the introduction of democracy in Venezuela and Colombia in the late 1950s, and Brazil in the 1980s, readily come to mind. In all of these cases, often held as examples of frozen or flawed democracies, political pact-making was the product of a small coterie of elites brought together for the explicit purpose of excluding the left from politics. Only in Spain did the regime of political pacts incorporate representation from the left.[12] In sum, the Spanish experience suggests that whether the transition to democracy is pacted or not is not sufficient for determining the long-term quality of any democratic regime. Many other factors come into play, including what actors are involved in the construction of democracy.

FROM CONTENTION TO MODERATION: PARTY POLITICS

Historically a symbol of political extremism and polarization, Spanish political parties in the post-Franco era have served as a model of political restraint and moderation. Extensive inter-party collaboration made for a very efficient and orderly transition out of the Franco regime. The same can be said about the role of the political parties in the institutionalization of democratic governance. Less evident is the moderation prevalent within the party system itself and its individual components. Two large parties have dominated post-Franco politics: the left-wing Partido Socialista Obrero Español (PSOE) and the right-wing Partido Popular (PP). Each party draws political support from across society and appeals to the political center to win elections. Moreover, for the most part, both parties have remained committed to pragmatic rather than ideologically driven policies, which reflect a common understanding of Spain as a modern democratic society within the larger community of European nations.

The pragmatism and ideological moderation that permeate the politics of both the PSOE and the PP are also evident across the entire political party system. It is telling that the traditional dominant feature of Spanish political parties, ideological extremism from either the left or the right, appears extinct today. On the left, the Partido Comunista de España (PCE), following its failure to sustain the vibrancy and control over civil society that it gained during the late Franco period and the collapse of communism in the early 1990s, has folded itself into Izquierda Unida (IU). This new left-wing coalition is to the left of the PSOE, but hardly a revolutionary or anti-system force. It is best described as the Spanish version of the "New Left," given its concerns with post-material issues such as the environment, gender parity, and gay rights.

Things on the right are even more revealing, especially when seen through broad comparative lenses. In recent years, the radical right has surged across western Europe, fueled by a radical, populist agenda that at its core is often xenophobic and blatantly racist (Betz 1995). The paradigmatic case is France, where Jean-Marie Le Pen's National Front, an extreme nationalist party whose motto is "France for the French," has become a major player in the country's politics. In the 2002 elections, Le Pen rocked the French political establishment by gaining nearly 20 percent of the vote in the second round of the presidential elections. But the phenomenon of the extreme right hardly stops at France's borders. In Italy, Switzerland, and even the Netherlands, a country notorious for its liberal politics, extreme right-wing parties have enjoyed stunning electoral successes. In all of these cases, curbing the flow of immigrants and/or curtailing or eliminating access to social services is at the heart of their political platforms.

Spain, however, appears to have successfully averted the distressing trend of the rising extreme right. Despite their popularity across Europe, no militant anti-immigrant or populist party has taken root in the country to channel citizens' increasing anxiety about immigration. To be sure, extreme right-wing groups do exist in Spain. In fact, due to the country's long and rich experience of ultra-right government, the Spanish universe of such organizations is one of the most diverse in all of Europe, encompassing "fascist, neo-Nazi, anti-regional, ultra-Catholic, anti-Semitic and xenophobic organizations" (Encarnación 2004: 182). But their influence over national politics is basically non-existent. This is most tellingly suggested in the complete absence of representation of the extreme right in the Spanish parliament, a body that encompasses significant political pluralism, including conservative, social democratic, communist, and regionalist parties. The collective vote for extreme right parties in the 2004 general elections was statistically insignificant.

As seen in this chapter, a complex process of institutional modernization accounts for the robust prominence of moderation in Spain's party system in the post-Franco era. It was conditioned by at least three major factors. The first is the desire of party leaders from both the left and the right to move away from the ideological rigidity of the past. From the onset of democracy, party leaders were bent on keeping political polarization at bay. This meant, in essence, a moratorium on familiar demons of party politics in Spain: excessive partisanship and ideological extremism. A second factor is the moderating influence of European political trends, especially on the left. During their long absence from Spain, the left-wing intelligentsia underwent a process of "renovation" as a consequence of their exposure to moderate left-wing philosophies such as "Euro-Communism" and "Social Democracy," which emphasize the wedding of capitalist structures to Marxist economic models. The third factor is the preferences of the Spanish electorate. From the very onset of democracy, the Spanish public has favored pragmatic policies and has rejected political platforms calling for radical change.

The chapter is arranged chronologically, following three pivotal phases in the development of the party system in Spain in the post-Franco era. The first phase (1977–82), a period dominated by the transition to democracy, covers the return of party politics in Spain after a four-decade absence and the rise and fall of the political center, the dominant political force in the early years of democratic development. Its main legacy was to formally establish consensus as the new ethos of Spanish political culture. The second (1982–96) examines the resurgence of the left with an emphasis on the long reign in power of the PSOE beginning with the landmark 1982 elections, which marked the return of the left to power in Spain for the first time since the volatile Republican era. During this period Spain attained democratic consolidation and ended its isolation from Europe with the country's entry into the EEC in 1986. The third phase (1996–2004) looks at the rebirth of the right and the emergence of the PP as the face of modern Spanish conservatism.

A discussion of the 2004 elections, Spain's most controversial in the post-Franco era, concludes the chapter. Coming on the heels of the March 11, 2004 attack on Madrid's Atocha train station, the 2004 elections brought worldwide attention to Spanish politics and a bitter political fallout has left many wondering if the culture of political consensus that has defined party politics in Spain in the post-Franco era has come to an end. This is underscored by the rise of unprecedented acrimony and rancor in the relations between the nation's two major parties.

THE RETURN OF PARTIES

Ensuing largely from Franco's longstanding ban on political parties, an abundance of parties (well over 200) registered with the central electoral committee as soon as parties became legal in 1976 and in anticipation of the 1977 elections. They covered the entire political spectrum and then some. On the left were the historic parties of the Second Republic, the PSOE and the PCE, which had miraculously survived a 40-year-old ban on parties. The strongest of the two was the PCE, which emerged from the dictatorship as the country's most resourceful political party and the one with "the most visible presence in many influential sectors of society" (Gunther 1986b: 57).[1] Its membership around the time of Franco's death in 1975 stood at an estimated 35,000, an impressive number considering that the party remained illegal until 1977 (Foweraker 1989: 133).

The PCE's success in organizing itself prior to the demise of the Franco regime is a testament to the party's endeavors to maintain a presence in Spain following the end of the civil war. After giving up on an early strategy of guerilla struggle, the PCE began to form clandestine organizations that incorporated workers, students, women, and neighbors in an all-out societal effort to fight the authoritarian regime from within its very structures. In doing so, the PCE's organizing capacity presented the most effective societal opposition to the Franco regime. Paradoxically, what made the party so effective under Franco made it politically unpalatable for most Spaniards in the new democracy. Since its creation in 1921, the PCE has battled a reputation for intransigence, revolutionary postures, and Stalinism, which did not dissipate after its leader, Santiago Carrillo, embraced Euro-Communism and "a parliamentary path" (Maxwell 1986: 264). These negative impressions ensued largely from the party's historic connections to Moscow, which provided the party with much-needed financial support to underwrite its clandestine opposition to Franco (Mujal-León 1985: 165). The PCE was also notorious for the iron hand that its leaders wielded in imposing party discipline. One scholar writes that while the PCE "did provide a structure for organization and coordination which proved effective in fighting the dictatorship, the party itself was not a very democratic institution" and "was often as nasty and as authoritarian as the regime it was committed to combating" (Foweraker 1989: 133).

The post-civil war trajectory of the PSOE, Spain's oldest party (founded in 1879), differs markedly from that of the PCE. After the end of the civil war in 1939, its leadership went into exile in France, hoping to promote regime change in Spain from the outside.[2] This meant that during the Franco dictatorship the PSOE lost significant ground to the PCE in organizing many of the grassroots movements advocating democratic change. Consequently, unlike the PCE, the PSOE had little if any significant presence in Spain as democracy commenced. In the early 1970s the PSOE's membership within Spain did not exceed 2,000 (Gunther 1986a: 11). Fortunately for the PSOE, upon the return of its leadership from exile, the party could tap into a long history as the standard-bearer of working-class interests in Spain.

Assisting in the resuscitation of the PSOE was the survival of left-wing loyalties across generations in communities and families across Spain, especially in traditional enclaves of working-class militancy such as mining communities in Asturias, metal- and steel-workers in the Basque Country, and urban industrial workers in Barcelona and Madrid. It is estimated that as many as 37.3 percent of the delegates to the twenty-eighth congress of the PSOE in 1979 were children of parents who had been affiliated either to the PSOE or to the historic socialist trade union, the UGT (Maravall 1985: 147). Also important to the PSOE's rehabilitation were its European connections. The PSOE has always been "unabashedly pro-European" and continental leaders like Willy Brandt, François Mitterrand, Pietro Nenni, and Olaf Palme "lent their prestige to a campaign that offered the PSOE as the best vehicle for European integration" (Mujal-León 1985: 166). Private socialist organizations like Germany's Friedrich Ebert Foundation were also useful in helping revive the UGT by providing "advice, money and organizational expertise" (Maxwell 1991: 39).

In the new regime, the Alianza Popular (AP) claimed to represent the right. Headed by Manuel Fraga, Franco's former Minister of Information and Tourism, the AP stood for the traditional concerns of Spanish conservatives and had strong ties to the Catholic Church, Catholic groups such as Opus Dei, and the military. This profile often put the party squarely outside of the political mainstream and limited its ability to reach out to a broader electorate. Indeed, during its earliest days, the AP was regarded as a reactionary, right-wing force, which made the party unpalatable even to natural constituencies like the Catholic Church and the business community (González Cuevas 2000; Baón 2001). Fraga openly criticized the new democratic constitution because of its recognition of the right to regional self-governance, and sought to mobilize the AP against it. The extent of opposition of the right to the constitution is best suggested in the fact that, although the text of the new constitution was overwhelmingly approved by the Spanish electorate, half of AP deputies (4) voted against it during its deliberation in the national parliament.

Actions such as opposition to the constitution put the AP in the company of some unsavory anti-democratic organizations, such as the extremist Fuerza Nueva (FN), which entered parliament in 1979 as a self-declared fascist organization. This party was formed in 1966 by former combatants of the Franco regime as a reaction to the new forces emerging in opposition to the dictatorship. FN also attacked reformist politicians within the Franco regime, accusing them of betraying Francoist ideology and failing to contain the opposition to the authoritarian order. During the very brief time it had representation in the national parliament (1979–82), the party focused its energies on attacking the country's new democratic constitution for nurturing multiculturalism and the "mutilation" of Spain with the creation of regional self-governments in regions like Catalonia and the Basque Country (Encarnación 2004: 182).

The most significant development during the re-emergence of the party system was in the center, with the emergence of the Unión de Centro Democrático (UCD), which

Table 4.1   Representation in the Spanish Congress of Deputies, 1977–2004

Party	% of votes	No. of seats	% of seats	% of votes	No. of seats	% of seats	% of votes	No. of seats	% of seats
	1977			**1979**			**1982**		
PCE/IU	9.3	20	5.7	10.8	23	6.6	4.0	4	1.1
PSOE	29.4	118	33.7	30.5	121	34.6	48.4	202	57.7
UCD	34.6	166	47.4	35.9	168	48.0	6.5	12	3.4
AP/PP	8.8	16	4.6	6.1	9	2.6	26.5	106	30.3
CiU	2.8	11	3.1	2.7	1	0.3	3.7	12	3.4
PNV	1.7	8	2.3	1.5	7	2.0	1.9	8	2.3
	1986			**1989**			**1993**		
IU	4.5	7	2.0	9.1	17	4.9	9.6	18	5.1
PSOE	44.6	184	52.6	39.9	175	50.0	38.3	159	45.4
AP/PP	26.3	105	3.0	25.9	107	30.6	34.8	141	40.3
CiU	5.1	18	5.1	5.1	18	5.1	4.9	17	4.9
PNV	1.6	6	1.7	1.2	5	1.4	1.2	5	1.4
	1996			**2000**			**2004**		
IU	10.6	21	6.0	5.5	8	2.3	5.3	5	1.42
PSOE	37.5	141	40.3	34.1	125	35.7	43.3	164	46.85
AP/PP	38.8	156	44.6	44.5	183	52.3	38.3	148	42.28
CiU	4.6	16	4.6	4.2	15	4.3	3.3	10	2.85
PNV	1.3	5	1.4	1.5	7	2.0	1.6	7	2.0
ERC	0.7	1	0.3	0.8	1	0.3	2.5	8	2.28

Source: Spanish Interior Ministry

as seen in table 4.1 managed impressive electoral victories in 1977 and 1979. This party was headed by Adolfo Suárez, the former Francoist insider whom the King hand-picked to bring the Franco regime to a peaceful conclusion (see chapter 3). Both elections gave the party a near absolute majority in the national parliament and control of about 60 percent of all Spanish cities and towns. These early UCD successes reflected in no small measure the obstacles to victory that the parties of the opposition had to overcome. The electoral system crafted by the Francoist parliament just prior to its disablement has an obvious anti-urban bias that penalizes industrial, leftist areas. Representation in the Congress of Deputies allows all provinces, however small, a minimum of three deputies. Thus, in the 1977 elections the 15 smallest provinces, with a total population of 3.4 million, had a total of 53 seats in the Congress, while the largest province, Barcelona, with a population of 4.5 million, had only 33 seats (Meisler 1977: 194). The opposition was also disadvantaged by the control that Suárez, as a former Francoist official, had over the state and its resources. Notable among them was the state-controlled media. Suárez's every move was dutifully covered by the government-controlled television channels, while those of his rivals from the left were by and large ignored (Roldán Ros 1985: 265).

Built-in advantages alone, however, do not explain the UCD's electoral success. More important was Suárez's enormous popularity. As a result of his successful management of the democratic transition, he was perceived by the public "as the most capable politician for solving a whole series of problems – prices, public order, unemployment, and strikes and the inauguration of democracy" (Tusell Gómez 1985: 95). Suárez also perfectly captured the zeitgeist of the political moment in Spain. He "incarnated the modern Spaniard, who was ready to turn his back on the old-fashioned dictatorial Franco state and make Spain acceptable to Western Europe. In short, he was an articulate, charming, energetic heir of Franco smart enough to know that Franco belonged to the past" (Meisler 1977: 192–3). His youth (42 years) and very photogenic good looks served to underscore this point.

A second source of success for the UCD was its moderate political platform, which emphasized a desire to cool off political passions for the sake of securing a new democratic order. "To vote for the Center is to vote for Suárez" was a slogan of the UCD's 1977 campaign (Meisler 1977: 195). This message stood in contrast to those coming from the parties of the left, whose platforms called for the nationalization of the economy and the purging of all remaining elements from the old regime.[3] The UCD also cultivated an "inter-class" image, which stood in striking contrast to the rigid working-class identity promoted by the Socialist and Communist parties. The party's platform stated that the UCD was "at the service of the diverse peoples of Spain and of all social, generational and human sectors" (Gunther et al. 1980: 174). By contrast, through the late 1970s, the PSOE saw itself exclusively as a working-class party, although the term "working class" was defined broadly enough to incorporate "from the dean of the university faculty to the student, from the liberal professional and the executive to the carpenter, fisherman, laborer or bricklayer" (Gunther et al. 1980: 176).

In aiming squarely for the political center and a multi-class constituency, the UCD successfully tapped into the electorate's mood for political moderation and national unity. Survey data from the Instituto de Opinión Pública show that in the immediate aftermath of Franco's death in 1975 the majority of Spaniards favored a "democratic evolution" of the Franco regime through the reformation of its fundamental laws (Wert Ortega 1985: 74–5). This sentiment clearly favored Suárez going into the 1977 elections and gave his politics of consensus considerable legitimacy among the general public. Also indicative of the moderation of the electorate were the patterns of political self-identification. As seen in figure 4.1, in the post-Franco era, the bulk of the Spanish electorate has remained comfortably lodged in the political center with a slight leftward orientation. The table describes self-placement on a left–right dimension scale, with 1 being furthest to the left, and 10 the furthest to the right. Clearly, among national political parties, the political preferences of the Spanish electorate favored the UCD, which occupied the center-right of the political spectrum, and to a lesser extent the PSOE, which occupied the center-left. Their combined vote in the 1977 elections amounted to over 60 percent of the total vote (34 percent for the UCD and 29.9 percent for the PSOE).

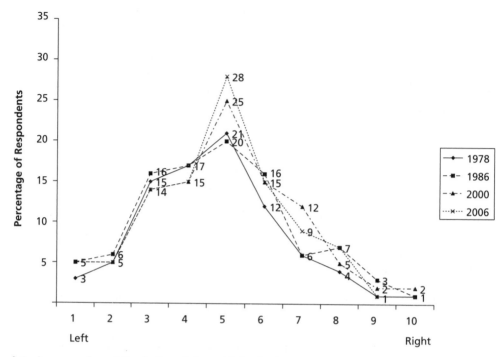

[a] Scale ranges from 1 for furthest left, to 10 for furthest right. The numbers for 1978 and 1986 do not add to a full 100 percent due to non-respondents.
Source: Data for 1978 from Wert Ortega (1985: 87); data for 1986–2006 from CIS.

Figure 4.1 Voters' self-placement on the left–right dimension, 1978–2006 (%)[a]

The center at the helm

While in power (1977–82), the UCD accomplished a great deal. The party is mainly responsible for institutionalizing democracy in Spain and it did so by adopting a consensus-driven approach to governance. The UCD oversaw the negotiation of the 1977 Pacts of Moncloa with the opposition parties from the left, which stabilized the economy and labor relations in the wake of the dismantling of the Franco regime. More importantly, these accords set a tone of consensus in anticipation of the drafting of a new democratic constitution, which the UCD successfully managed to get approved by the Spanish people in a national referendum. The party was also successful in negotiating the autonomy charters of Catalonia, the Basque Country and Galicia, which opened the way for the decentralization of the state. It also enhanced civilian control over the military by merging three military ministries under a civilian-led Ministry of Defense. Under the UCD, Spain was incorporated into NATO and negotiations for Spanish entry into the EEC were started, milestones in ending Spain's international isolation.

The UCD's brief but remarkable career ended with its defeat in the 1982 general elections, widely regarded as a watershed event in the life of Spain's new democracy. These elections simultaneously brought about the near total collapse of the UCD and the stunning rise to power of the PSOE. In 1982, the UCD saw its share of the popular vote plunge from 35 percent in the 1979 elections to 6 percent in 1982, bringing a decrease in parliamentary representation from 168 seats to a mere 12 seats. The UCD never recovered from what has been characterized as "an electoral defeat without precedent in contemporary European politics" (López-Pintor 1985: 305) and soon vanished from the electoral map, leaving the country's political landscape without a political center. For its part, the PSOE saw its share of the popular vote increase to 48 percent in the 1982 elections, which translated into a significant gain in its representation in the parliament from 121 seats to 202 seats. The biggest beneficiary of the UCD's collapse, however, was the right, represented by the neo-Francoist AP. Its share of the popular vote soared, from 6 percent to 27 percent, and its representation rose from 9 seats in the parliament to 106 seats. This extraordinary reconfiguration of the electoral landscape in 1982 gave Spain the highest level of electoral volatility recorded by a European nation in the twentieth century (Gunther et al. 2004: 199).

An inability to overcome its diverse ideological clientele is the conventional wisdom to explain the UCD's spectacular meltdown (Huneeus 1985; Hopkin 1999). The party embraced a heterogeneous coalition of 14 small parties and political groups that incorporated conservatives, liberals, Social Democrats and Christian Democrats. This ideological heterogeneity served the UCD well going into the 1977 elections, since it enabled the party to successfully tap into the prevailing sentiment of national integration. Once in office, however, the UCD proved incapable of overcoming its internal squabbles. As explained by López-Pintor (1985: 302), "The difficulties in agreeing to common ideological and political goals led to sterile pseudo-ideological debates within the party elite and among cadres: they argued about topics of no serious interest to their voters: whether the UCD should be a party of the center left, center right, or just pure center."

Another reason for the UCD's inability to grow as a center-right party was the re-emergence of powerful regional parties in Catalonia and the Basque Country that combined centrist economic policies with demands for autonomy from Madrid. In Catalonia, for instance, at the inception of democracy the centrist vote was clearly split between the UCD and the Convergència i Unió (CiU), the leading nationalist party. Both parties competed for voters who did not identify with the parties from either the left or the right. In the end, the CiU proved more viable than the UCD in Catalonia due to its success in depicting the government in Madrid as an obstacle to the development of Catalan autonomy. A similar situation developed in the Basque Country, where the Partido Nacionalista Vasco (PNV) competed directly with the UCD for the political center. And, as in Catalonia, the regional party prevailed over the national one.

The most immediate cause of the UCD's demise, however, was the severe blow to the organization dealt by Suárez's sudden resignation from the government in January 1981. This event remains shrouded in mystery, although it is rumored to have been caused by pressure from the military, which was unhappy with many of Suárez's decisions, including legalizing the Communist party and granting self-rule to the Basques and the Catalans. Another theory is that Suárez was too weak to lead the party to victory in 1982. In 1980, he survived a vote of no confidence by UCD leaders following the party's defeat in the regional elections in Catalonia, the Basque Country and Andalusia (a harbinger of things to come in 1982), though he was able to gain a vote of confidence shortly thereafter. In any case, Suárez's resignation threw a fragmented organization into outright chaos and left a vacuum in the party that his replacement, Vice President Leopoldo Calvo Sotelo, was unable to fill. Although a competent politician, Calvo Sotelo had neither the prestige nor the charisma to compensate for the UCD's many institutional shortcomings. As he himself would acknowledge, "The UCD was a government desperately trying to become a party."[4]

THE REBIRTH OF THE LEFT

By the time of its historic electoral victory in 1982, the PSOE had successfully reinvented itself as a political organization by shedding almost all traces of political radicalism. In a bitter struggle for the very soul of the party, Felipe González, a young and charismatic Andalusian politician who, as head of the *renovadores* (renovators) battled both the Franco regime and the exiled Socialist leadership, succeeded in forcing the PSOE to drop the Marxist label from the party's definition. This opened the way for the rise of the multi-class, social democratic party that the PSOE has become today. Whereas the party's platform in 1976 described the PSOE as "a class party, Marxist and democratic," by 1979 this definition had been altered to "a class party, of the masses, democratic and federal" (Gunther 1986a: 21). The party also ceased to use street demonstrations as a tactic to pressure the government into changing its policies. These decisions, which were by no means universally accepted by the party's faithful, reflected González's calculus that the party's losses in 1977 and 1979 were rooted in its radical image and that becoming a "catch-all" party was the way for it to reach a larger electorate. As explained by Gunther (1986a: 15), "An abandonment of mass mobilization rhetoric and radical ideological commitments was dictated by the very moderation of the Spanish populace."

The PSOE's reinvention paid off handsomely in the 1982 election. Not only did the PSOE bury the UCD in the elections; it became the first party in the new democracy to enjoy an overall parliamentary majority. As seen in table 4.1, under González's leadership, the PSOE governed the nation for 14 years (until 1996), often with large electoral pluralities, and well past the point when most political observers deemed Spain to have become a fully consolidated democracy. During this period, the PSOE accelerated its own transformation from a class-based party to a catch-all party while pushing the country toward a relentless modernization drive that was reflected in both domestic and foreign policy.

On the domestic side, the most important (and controversial) changes introduced by the PSOE concerned the economy. Rather than advancing the Marxist-inspired economic agenda that had brought the party into power in 1982, and which had characterized the party since its founding in the nineteenth century, once in office the Socialists embraced a vigorous neoliberal economic program that called for the dismantling of much of Franco's public sector economy (see chapter 7). Another about-face took place in foreign policy. As head of the opposition, the PSOE had opposed Suárez's decision in 1981 to incorporate Spain into NATO, on grounds that it violated Spain's long history of neutrality in major international conflicts such as World Wars I and II and ran contrary to the country's traditional image as a bridge between Europe and the

Third World – Latin America and North Africa, in particular. These positions, histori-cally cherished by the Spanish left, led the party during the 1982 electoral campaign to promise to put the issue of NATO membership to a referendum in the hope that the public would choose to pull Spain from the organization. Once in office, however, González made NATO membership a key component of his plan for the Europeaniza-tion of Spain. In campaigning for Spain's continued presence in NATO, he argued that membership could serve to facilitate foreign policy goals such as obtaining membership in the EEC and enticing France to cooperate with the Spanish government in the fight against ETA.

In the end, González succeeded in getting 52 percent of the vote on the referendum on NATO, aided greatly by the inclusion of a clause calling for the reduction of Ameri-can military personnel in Spain. With the NATO headache behind him, González suc-cessfully completed incorporation of the Spanish economy into the EEC, his greatest accomplishment on the international front, after years of protracted negotiations that started in 1979. The fact that by the mid-1980s both Paris and Madrid were under a Socialist administration was certainly a contributing factor in France's decision to moderate its longstanding hesitation about Spain's entry into the EEC, which ensued principally from stiff opposition by French farmers to having to contend with cheaper agricultural imports from Spain.

A disgraceful exit

The string of Socialist victories (1982, 1989, and 1993) ended with the 1996 general elections, won by the upstart PP, a reinvented AP. Numerous factors account for this reversal of fortunes for the once unbeatable PSOE. The first was the defection of labor from the party, a consequence of the government's economic policies. In 1988, the UGT, in collaboration with its rival union, the Communist-affiliated Comisiones Obreras (CCOO), pulled off the first successful general strike in the post-Franco period. This was the first obvious expression of labor disillusion with the Socialist government. At the PSOE's thirty-second party congress of 1990, the divorce between the UGT and the PSOE became official. Ironically, the conflict between the PSOE and the UGT was not rooted in the party's betrayal of its historic commitment to socialism. Much to the dismay of many of its members, the UGT leadership supported the party's decision to pursue market-friendly policies. Instead, the real friction was over how to distribute the benefits of a rapidly growing economy. The 1988 general strike was provoked by the government's decision to recommend to employers that wage increases be capped at 5 percent. This proposal was rejected by union leaders, who argued that their sacri-fices under the first Socialist government (1982–6) entitled them to a more generous piece of the pie in light of the recovery of the economy.

Of course, by the time of its split with the UGT, the PSOE could well afford to lose its formal affiliation with the labor movement, given the party's new image as a multi-class party. But the UGT's defection took a heavy toll on the party at a time when it could least afford it. In particular, the general strike of 1988 brought tremendous humili-ation and embarrassment to a party that historically had seen itself as the standard-bearer of working-class interests in Spain. The UGT's defection from the PSOE also had a demoralizing effect upon the most activist wing of the party, which began to openly criticize the party leadership (including González) as arrogant, authoritarian, and out of touch with reality (Burgess 2000: 26). The effects of these internal attacks were tellingly reflected in the electoral results of the 1993 elections.

Although the PSOE won the elections, for the first time since 1982 the party failed to gain an absolute majority of seats in the parliament, forcing the party to seek other parties to form a coalition government. González rejected the option to govern with legislative support from IU, which had been harshly critical of the PSOE's economic program, and instead chose to bring into government the Catalan party CiU, a strategy that ultimately backfired. While the alliance with CiU allowed the PSOE to continue to govern, it seriously compromised its future electoral prospects. The rise to national prominence of a regional party mobilized the right, which feared that CiU would exploit its newly gained political clout to further advance the cause of Catalan independence. At the same time, the entry of the right-leaning CiU into the socialist government left PSOE voters depressed and demoralized, since this was seen as an unambiguous rightward turn for the party.

A stunning string of corruption scandals that seriously tarnished the image of the PSOE sealed the fate of the PSOE in the 1996 elections.[5] The opposition parties successfully exploited these scandals by portraying the PSOE, and the González government in particular, as a sleaze machine. The PSOE and the González administration gave the opposition more than enough to work with in constructing these attacks. In 1991, it was revealed that PSOE officials had been running a scam to finance party activities that involved running front corporations that paid the party's bills with money obtained from charging companies for fictitious work. In 1992, Julián García Valderde, the President of RENFE, the national railroad company, was embroiled in a scandal involving the award of contracts to build the high-speed rail link between Madrid and Seville and to construct and operate Expo '92 in Seville. In 1993, Aida Álvarez, the Director of the *Boletín del Estado* (BOE), the state's official journal of record, was arrested for overcharging companies for the purchase of paper and keeping the earnings for herself. In 1994, Mario Rubio, the former governor of the Bank of Spain, was accused of fraud and insider trading, and Luis Roldán, the first civilian leader of the Guardia Civil, was arrested for bribery and misappropriation of funds. These scandals featured prominently in the fall of the once mighty Carlos Solchaga, one of the architects of the PSOE's neoliberal economic program.

Most damaging to the PSOE, however, was the scandal involving the secret financing of death squads as part of the state's effort to stamp out Basque terrorism (see chapter 6). These activities included not only the torture of individuals suspected of terrorism, but also the killing of innocent civilians (see Woodworth 2003; Encarnación 2007). Although the scandal did not touch González personally, it consumed the last two years of his administration and reached the highest levels of his cabinet. As discussed in chapter 6, the only silver lining of this depressing episode, certainly a stain on Spain's otherwise sterling reputation as a democracy, was the capacity of the Spanish state to investigate itself and to punish those responsible for breaking the law. By the time the investigations were over in 1998, both the former Minister of the Interior and the Director of State Security had been sent to jail for illegal detention and misappropriation of state funds.

THE REFOUNDING OF THE RIGHT

It is a testament to the general weakness of the right in Spain in the democratic period that it took nearly 20 years to elect a right-wing government, which came about in 1996 with the election of the PP.[6] This is made more compelling still by the fact that, for much of the last three decades (especially during the 1980s), the right was on the ascent in many democratic societies, including the United States, the United Kingdom, Germany, and other European countries. Of course, in Spain things were quite different because of the country's distinct political history in the twentieth century. The right had ruled the nation from 1939 through 1977 with a heavy authoritarian hand. Thus, having denied the country basic political and civil rights for nearly four decades, it is hardly surprising that in the democratic era right-wing parties have faced an uphill struggle in refashioning themselves into democratic entities.

During the long run of the PSOE during the 1980s and early 1990s, the AP underwent a political metamorphosis by shedding its "neo-Francoist" reputation and eventually emerging as a mainstream conservative organization, now renamed the Partido Popular. By the time of its electoral victory in 1996, the PP had dropped all serious opposition to abortion, divorce, and regional autonomy in a clear effort to increase its electoral appeal. This transformation of the right is perhaps just as important to the consolidation of democracy in Spain as that of the left that took place around the time of the democratic transition, when the PSOE dropped its Marxist identity and mobilizational model. As contended by Kenneth Maxwell (1991: 46), the emergence of a conservative alternative in Spain filled a vacuum in the opposition that had encouraged "hegemonic tendencies within the PSOE."

The mastermind behind the AP's transformation was José María Aznar, a former tax inspector from the interior of the country (La Rioja), who has come to embody the face of modern-day Spanish conservatism. After sidelining AP founder Fraga, Aznar re-defined the party as a European Christian Democratic organization, and in 1989 changed its name to the Partido Popular. Aznar's own political trajectory mirrors the transformation of the right in Spain. As a teenager in Franco's Spain, Aznar was active in far-right organizations. It has been widely reported that at the age of 16 he wrote a letter to his local newspaper "attacking the official Francoist movement and declaring his membership in the independent Falangists, the authentic incarnation, in his own words, of José Antonio Primo de Rivera, the founder of the fascist Falange" (Balfour 2005: 150). The not so subtle point of Aznar's letter was to criticize Francoist officials for having abandoned the true principles of Spanish fascism. As an AP regional leader during the late 1970s, Aznar attacked the new constitution for its support of regional rights, which he regarded as a threat to the nation. By the early 1980s, however, Aznar was leading those seeking to modernize the right.

As illustrated in table 4.1, the PP dominated Spanish politics from 1966 to 2004. During its first years in control of the government, the party stuck to a moderate and pragmatic political agenda. Indeed, to a significant extent, the party's early policies can be seen as a continuation of those of the outgoing Socialist administration. Despite pressures from the Catholic Church, an important political ally, the party did not seek to overturn many of the PSOE policies that had so angered devout Catholics, such as the legalization of abortion. In a bow to social progressivism, and in an effort to close the gender gap with the left, the PP began to encourage participation of women in the party, which had lagged significantly compared to the PSOE. By 2000, the percentage of PP members in the national parliament had risen to 25 percent, a striking contrast to the 6 percent registered by its predecessor (the AP) during the 1977–9 parliament (Balfour 2005: 157). The PP adopted an accommodating stance toward the unions, engaging them in "concertation" accords with greater success than the preceding Socialist government (Hamann 2005). On the economic front, the PP accelerated the policies of economic liberalization, especially privatizations, and European integration championed by the PSOE, with generally positive results. Sound macroeconomic indicators allowed the Aznar government in 1998 to fulfill the criteria for joining the circle of founding nations of the European Monetary Union (EMU) established by the Maastricht Treaty.

Several factors conditioned the PP's moderation. Lacking a majority in the national parliament, the party was forced into political alliances with the nationalist parties of Catalonia and the Basque Country. One of the great ironies of this development is that the PP, which bitterly complained during the Socialist era about the central state's dealings with the regions, expanded the autonomy of the Catalans and the Basques in an unprecedented way. For instance, it agreed to transfer 30 percent of tax revenue to each region. Aznar was also keenly aware that the PSOE's defeat in 1996 was caused mainly by the corruption that surrounded the party rather than by a rejection of its policies. Finally, Aznar did not want to spoil all the work that had gone into making the PP a mainstream conservative party. In his mind, the PP was no different in ideological orientation from other modern conservative parties like the Christian Democratic party in Germany, the Conservative party in Britain, and the Republican party in the United States. As if Aznar needed any reminder of the need to burnish his credentials as a mainstream conservative politician, during the 1996 campaign many on the left sought to scare voters by suggesting that a PP victory would entail a vote for a return to Francoism.

Largely due to its moderation and pragmatism, to say nothing of the disarray that gripped the PSOE following its defeat in 1996, the PP was easily re-elected into office in 2000. This time around the party was rewarded with a clear parliamentary majority, which meant that it could now advance its political and economic program without the complications of having to negotiate or compromise with other parties. The elections of 2000 also revealed the extent to which the PP had succeeded in converting itself into a catch-all party by branching out beyond its core conservative base comprised principally of former Franco supporters, devout Catholics, the business community, and ardent Spanish nationalists. Large sections of the young, the middle class, and urban professionals were now voting for the PP. Most impressive and surprising of all, however, was the PP's success with working-class voters, historically a bastion of left-wing sympathizers. In 1982 only 9 percent of the working-class vote went to the PP, but by 2000 that support had soared to 27 percent (Balfour 2005: 175).

A right-wing turn

Emboldened by its 2000 victory, and armed with an unassailable parliamentary majority, the PP began to pursue a more conservative political program that in some respects can be seen as the first significant departure from the politics of consensus of the post-Franco era. One of the most radical policies implemented by the PP came in 2003, just before leaving office, when the government unveiled a new educational curriculum intended to "shape the values of new generations of Spaniards along traditionalist lines" (Balfour 2005: 158). It made religious instruction taught by Vatican-approved teachers and texts a compulsory subject in primary and secondary schools. In effect, this new curriculum attempted to return education policy in Spain to its Francoist days and blurred the very delicate church–state division established by the architects of the 1978 constitution, which sought to reconcile the historic influence of the Catholic Church in Spain with the institutionalization of a democratic system.

The new curriculum was part and parcel of a project of "Constitutional Patriotism" approved by the PP at its fourteenth congress in 2002, an attempt to cast traditional ideas of Spanish nationalism and dogma in a new light. It advanced a new Spanish historicism that eerily echoed the thinking of Spanish conservatives in the late nineteenth century and that emphasized the idea of Spain as an ancient, diverse but indivisible land. Before it was modified in response to opposition from nationalist regions like Catalonia and the Basque Country, the new curriculum required the teaching of Spanish history to allow students to understand that "Spain is a country with an identity that is not ethnically based, but politically, historically and culturally based, which developed through its contribution to universal History and Culture" (Núñez Siexas 2005: 134). The new curriculum also sought to portray Spain as a modern, civilizing state, a view that replaces the more common and pessimistic view of Spain as a decadent and inefficient empire. Contemporary episodes of Spanish history such as the Spanish Civil War and Francoism were treated as aberrations (and in the case of the civil war as an externally induced conflict) and secondary to the great forces that shaped the nation, such as the genius behind the conquest of the Americas.

The government's new cultural program was pushed through initiatives such as the rewriting of textbooks, grants to private foundations and research think tanks intended to reconsider Spanish history, and attempts to influence the work of public institutions (museums and universities) devoted to the study of Spanish humanities and social studies. Undoubtedly, the most controversial grant was the one awarded to the National Francisco Franco Foundation, which is dedicated to the memory of Franco and is administered by his daughter. It organizes events to mark Franco's death every year and maintains fresh flowers on his tomb at *El Valle de los Caídos*. Rethinking Spanish history was undertaken by the PP hand in hand with an effort to revive national symbols, most notably the Spanish flag, which under Franco had become intimately tied to a culturally and politically repressive state.

Aznar raised a few eyebrows and the ire of many on the left when his government planted an enormous Spanish flag in the very center of Madrid's Plaza Colón. His government also began to require that the national anthem be played during the King's travels throughout the country. The not so hidden purpose behind such policies was to promote national unity and to undermine the growing perception of Spain as a multicultural society. In the post-transition period, this view of the country is being promoted not only by the creation of the autonomous regions but also by the recent influx of immigrants into Spain. Aznar left very little doubt about how he felt about multiculturalism when pushing his agenda for a democratic nationalism. "Multiculturalism divides society; it is not living together, it is not integration," he was quoted as saying by *El País* (June 10, 2002).

The PP also created a big splash in the foreign policy arena. Under the UCD and the PSOE, Spanish foreign policy had remained firmly set in the directions suggested by the European Union and its continental leaders, France and Germany. But after 2000, Spanish foreign policy became unabashedly pro-American with Aznar's decision to back George W. Bush's decision to go to war in Iraq in March 2003 and to send Spanish troops to Iraq to back up the American invasion. Indeed, Aznar became the most visible supporter of American policy in Europe after British Prime Minister Tony Blair. The Spanish involvement in Iraq brought foreign policy into the realm of domestic politics in a manner rarely seen before in Spain. It did not help matters that Aznar sidelined the Spanish parliament completely. He argued that a parliamentary debate and vote on Spain's involvement in Iraq was not needed because the decision to send 1,300 Spanish troops to Iraq did not amount to a declaration of war against another state, but rather was a diplomatic mission. Moreover, he contended that the intended purpose of Spanish troops in Iraq was not combat but rather peacekeeping and postwar reconstruction. Neither argument sat well with the opposition parties or with the general public. As in the rest of Europe, public opinion in Spain was overwhelmingly against the war in Iraq, exceeding 90 percent in some polls.

What possessed Aznar to undertake such a bold step in foreign affairs is somewhat puzzling. As a leader of the opposition in 1990, he had criticized the PSOE's very limited support for the first Gulf War, arguing that all diplomatic channels had not yet been exhausted. Moreover, in siding with the Americans on the war in Iraq, Aznar was not only antagonizing Spain's continental EU partners, but also embracing the foreign policy of a country intensely disliked and even resented by many Spaniards. Spanish anti-Americanism is especially virulent, and is rooted in Spain's humiliating defeat at the hands of the Americans in the 1898 Spanish-American War, the decision of the Americans not to intervene in the Spanish Civil War, the exclusion of Spain from American postwar economic recovery programs (the Marshall Plan), and the explicit support given by American administrations to the Franco regime since the signing of the 1953 Pact of Madrid, which authorized the establishment of American military bases in Spain in exchange for economic and military aid. In the post-Franco period, Spanish–American relations have often been tense, the result of clashes over American policy toward Latin America but also of notable gaffes about Spanish politics by American presidents, and none more notorious than Ronald Reagan's 1985 comments about the Americans who volunteered to fight alongside the Spanish Republican army against Franco during the 1930s. On the eve of his arrival in Madrid he remarked that "the individuals that went over there were, in the opinion of most Americans, fighting on the wrong side" (Maxwell 1991: 39).[7]

Among the reasons often cited for Aznar's support for the war in Iraq was his friendship with Bush, a fellow conservative, and Aznar's desire to escape the realm of influence of the Paris–Berlin axis by seeking closer relations with the Americans. Aznar came into office thinking that Spain's relations with Washington should be at least as important as those with France and Germany, a view that stood in striking contrast to the strong pro-European policy of Spanish governments in the post-Franco era. Finally, there was the hope that Spanish support for Bush on Iraq would translate into greater

American help in the fight against ETA, or at the very least help in bringing international attention to his government's struggles with ETA. Thus, Aznar must have been very pleased when the American government, following the attacks of September 11, 2001, included ETA in its list of terrorist organizations and began to refer to the organization as a "terrorist" rather than as a "separatist" organization. These positions strengthened Aznar's controversial contention that "ETA and Osama bin Laden are the same thing" (Woodworth 2004: 13).

Support for the war in Iraq was an audacious policy for the PP to adopt, but it eventually came to haunt the party at election time. The March 2004 elections turned out to be a referendum on the PP's support for the Bush administration's policy in Iraq. Sensing an opportunity to capitalize upon the unpopularity of the war in Iraq among the Spanish people, the Socialist challenger, José Luis Rodríguez Zapatero, ran a vigorous anti-war campaign. His PP opponent, Mariano Rajoy, who succeeded Aznar at the helm of the PP in 2003, hoped that the positive economic record of the Aznar years would trump people's unease with the war. But this was not to be. On March 11, 2004, just three days before the general elections of March 14, the bombing of Madrid's Atocha train station significantly altered the dynamics of the political campaign.

2004: BALLOTS AND BOMBS

Attributed to Moroccan terrorists affiliated with the al Qaeda organization (the mastermind behind the terrorist attacks of September 11, 2001), the attack on Atocha train station was designed to create the maximum amount of carnage and suffering. No fewer than nine bombs went off between 7.00 a.m. and 7.15 a.m. as trains packed with morning commuters were entering Atocha station. The explosives managed to kill 190 people and left over 1,500 wounded. This was the deadliest terrorist attack in Spanish history, far surpassing the bombing of a Barcelona supermarket by ETA in 1987 that killed 21 people, and the worst event of its kind on European soil since World War II.

What had been widely predicted to be a tight race turned out to be a resounding victory for the PSOE. Zapatero emerged as the undisputed victor, winning almost 1.3 million votes more than the PP. The Popular vote plunged from the 44.5 percent it had received in 2000 to 38.3 percent. The PSOE saw its share of the vote soar from 34.1 percent to 43.3 percent. The impact of the vote on the number of legislative seats assigned to each party was very significant. The PP lost 35 of the 183 seats that it had attained in 2000. The PSOE saw its number of seats in parliament increase to a total of 164, sufficient to see the party easily form a strong minority government in coalition with IU, which retained five of its previous eight seats. This election also made electoral history in Spain by representing the first time that a majority party had lost complete control of the government.

The convergence of terror and ballots made the March 2004 elections the most debated in Spain since 1977, with endless speculation about the extent to which the terrorist bombs influenced the outcome of the vote. The prevailing explanation of the 2004 vote (especially outside of Spain) is that the terrorist attacks altered the dynamics of the race in favor of the PSOE. According to the conventional wisdom, coming just days before the elections, the attack served as a painful reminder to the Spanish electorate of the price Spain was paying for its participation in the war in Iraq. In sum, the PP paid dearly at the polls for its support of American policy. An even more cynical and offensive view, especially popular in the United States, saw the Spanish electorate bowing to the fear of Islamist terrorism. The pro-Bush editorial page of the *Wall Street Journal* (March 16, 2004) noted that "By murdering innocents they [the terrorists] were able to topple one of the pillars of the Western anti-terror alliance."

Giving credence to the conventional wisdom about the outcome of the 2004 elections are the national surveys taken in the weeks prior to the elections by the pollsters at the Center for Sociological Investigations (CIS 2004), which consistently showed the PP enjoying a 2- to 5-point lead over the PSOE. This had led PP party leaders to confidently predict a safe but narrow victory. The CIS data (2004) show that voters appeared content with the PP's economic performance. The party had given Spain eight years of solid economic growth (averaging 3.2 percent per year) and had cut the unemployment rate from 22 to 11 percent (*Economist*, June 24, 2004). Prospective voters also gave the PP high scores for handling the all-important issue of terrorism, especially for the tough stance Aznar had taken toward ETA. They were also impressed with Aznar's willingness to keep his word that he would step down after eight years in office and approved of his successor at the helm of the party, Interior Minister Mariano Rajoy. By contrast, prospective voters viewed Zapatero as inexperienced.

An examination of the political factors that influenced the 2004 vote, however, reveals that the simplistic interpretation that the PP lost the election due to the terrorist attack does not stand up to rigorous scrutiny. This is not to say that the bombings did not themselves play a pivotal role in determining the outcome of the elections; they did, but not in the way suggested by the American media. Even before the terrorist attack it was clear that the PSOE was closing in on the PP in public opinion surveys. Indeed, political analysts generally accept the view that during the final stretch of the campaign the PSOE and PP were virtually in a tie (Chari 2004: 956). This was not apparent to outside observers because Spanish electoral law prohibits the publication of polling information during the final week of the political campaign. But the parties' own internal polls (taken not for public consumption but rather to gauge the direction of the elections) were predicting a very close contest.

Numerous factors independent of the attack of March 11 helped the PSOE close the gap with the PP and eventually win the race. Zapatero promoted himself as the leader of a new generation of Socialists by distancing himself from the party's old guard and all the baggage of corruption inherited from the party's reign during the 1980s and early 1990s. He also promised not to tinker with the economic policies pursued by Aznar. This meant, above all, continuing liberalization of the economy (including further relaxation of the labor market), a path that, oddly enough, was first introduced in Spain by the Socialists in the mid-1980s. Most noticeable of all, however, was Zapatero's decision to go full force against the PP on the issue of Iraq. During the last weeks of the campaign, Zapatero renewed the controversial debate over Aznar's decision to participate in the US-led invasion of Iraq without consulting the parliament, which in Zapatero's view made the presence of Spanish troops in Iraq illegitimate. He pledged to bring home the 1,300 Spanish troops stationed in Iraq and to reorient

Spanish foreign policy away from the pro-war stance of Washington and London, and toward the anti-war position of Paris and Berlin.

The Zapatero campaign was also helped immeasurably by the blunders of the Rajoy campaign, and none more obvious than the PP's clumsy management of the investigations into those responsible for the terrorist attack. As reported by Woodworth (2004: 20), "what destroyed the party's prospects over the next few drop was not the attack, but the government's response to it." Until the eve of the elections, Aznar kept insisting that the bombings were the handiwork of homegrown ETA terrorists. PP officials vigorously defended this view and spared no resource to promote it. Aznar himself phoned the directors of the main television channels and the editors of the main papers to communicate the message that "ETA was certainly responsible for the attacks on Atocha." He also instructed Ana Palacio, the Minister of Foreign Affairs, to spread the news abroad of ETA culpability and to petition the United Nations to issue a resolution specifically condemning ETA. The day after the attack, the state's television channel dropped an evening viewing of the film *Shakespeare in Love* in favor of a documentary on ETA's killings.

The PP, however, had no evidence to back up its claims about ETA's involvement in the Atocha massacre; more importantly, it was clear from the onset that the bombings themselves bore little resemblance to ETA's terrorist activities and in fact were suspiciously similar to the work of radical Islamic terrorists. More troublesome yet, while busy pointing the finger at ETA, the government was blatantly ignoring mounting evidence suggesting strong links to Islamic radicals. Not surprisingly, the PP's candidate spent the last days before the elections fending off accusations that his party was engaged in a cover-up operation. Such charges carried a special sting, given the PP's prior history of misleading the public. For instance, in 2002 the oil tanker *Prestige* got stuck and eventually broke apart off the Galician coast, creating the worst environmental disaster in Spain's history. At that time, the PP faced allegations of having done little to avert the crisis and of misleading the public about the magnitude of the *Prestige*'s ecological disaster.

Allegations of a cover-up by the government brought out anti-PP voters who had previously decided to sit out the elections. There was an almost 8 percentage point increase in turnout in the 2004 elections over those of 2000 and the bulk of that increase in votes (1.6 million), according to polling data, went to the PSOE. The PP's behavior during the last days of the campaign also worked to unify the left. It motivated many IU voters to shift their support to the PSOE to ensure a Socialist victory. This explains the drop in support for the IU from 5.5 percent of the vote in 2000 to 5.3 percent in 2004 (about 105,000 votes) and the decline in its parliamentary representation. Last but not least was the young vote (530,000), half of the new votes cast in 2004, which went overwhelmingly for the PSOE.

Going back to being an opposition party, with the sense that it had been robbed of re-election, has not been easy for the PP, and this in turn has had a very detrimental effect on party relations. Since leaving office the PP has behaved more like "a government in exile than a loyal opposition" (Woodworth 2005: 71). Certainly, it has not helped that the parliamentary report on the terrorist attacks of March 11, 2004 was scathing. Signed by all the parties represented in parliament except for the PP, it charges the Aznar administration with distorting information, deliberately misleading the public, and behaving in a manner unbecoming of a democratic society. Such findings trashed Aznar's reputation in both Spain and Europe and in effect dashed any hope he may have entertained of attaining a high international post, perhaps EU Commissioner or head of an international body such as the International Monetary Fund or the United Nations (Woodworth 2005: 71).

But the fall of Aznar's reputation hardly excuses the behavior of many PP leaders. Some have discredited themselves by peddling conspiracy theories, such as the one that has left-leaning police members leaving the nation vulnerable to a terrorist attack around the time of the elections in order to facilitate a socialist victory (*El País*, July 1, 2005). Or the argument that, although there is no evidence linking ETA to the terrorist events, the PP was right in pointing the finger at Basque terrorists because ETA is the "intellectual author" of the attacks (Woodworth 2005: 71). Many PP leaders have continued to promote these stories even after the trial of the 27 Muslim men suspected of the attack found no link to ETA whatsoever.

CONCLUSION

Parties have been among the most important (perhaps *the* most important) political institutions in post-Franco politics. They organized the public for a peaceful transition to democracy in the wake of nearly four decades of Francoism, and anchored the political and constitutional compromises that facilitated the consolidation of democracy. While in government, parties from the center, the left, and the right have contributed immeasurably to democratic stability in Spain by advocating pragmatic policies in keeping with the public's desire for moderation in politics. This strong performance of the party system in Spain during the process of democratization powerfully brings to mind the pivotal role that political parties can play in the success of democracy at a time when cynicism about their importance in democratic politics is commonplace in both emerging and mature democracies. Indeed, parties are increasingly seen as secondary to the rise and maintenance of democracy, after a vibrant and robust civil society (see Encarnación 2006). But only parties have the institutional capacity to organize political competition effectively at the national level and channel citizens' demands through the political system.

Ironically, as the Spanish party system has gradually evolved into a two-party model – the quintessential party infrastructure for democratic performance and stability – relations between the dominant parties have never been worse. Whether this is a bump on the road or the new norm in party politics in Spain remains to be seen. However, unlike other periods in Spanish history marked by political acrimony (such as the interwar era), there is today an important tradition of political cooperation in interparty relations that serves as a counterbalance to an equally important legacy of political polarization.

THE DARK SIDE OF SUCCESS?
A CIVIL SOCIETY DEFICIT

If the passion of the Americans for joining and forming organizations of almost any kind and purpose makes them "a nation of joiners," as famously contended by Alexis de Tocqueville in *Democracy in America* (1835), the Spaniards may well deserve the title of "a nation of loners."[1] Among developed nations, Spain has one of the lowest aggregate percentages of the population that belong to a voluntary association, be it a union, a religious group, or a political party. Only about a third of Spaniards claim membership in at least one of these organizations. This places Spain far behind the United States, at the bottom among EU members and other Iberian–Latin nations, and roughly in the same vicinity as post-communist Europe, where communist rule is thought to have obliterated any traces of an independent civil society.[2] Not surprisingly, some scholars have observed with great worry that "civic anemia appears to be endemic in Spain" (McDonough et al. 1998: 1).

What explains the weakness of Spanish civil society? Why are Spaniards so disinclined to organize themselves politically and otherwise? Is this an unintended consequence of the tactical demobilization of the public demanded by the consensus-driven nature of the democratic transition, as some suspect? "The participatory deficit in Spain is a by-product of the ethos of tolerance and bargaining that pervaded the transition from Francoism. The viability of democracy has been achieved at some cost to its quality," note McDonough et al. (1998: 1). Addressing these assumptions and the questions that prompt them is the purpose of this chapter. It argues that the negotiated fashion of the Spanish political transition did play a role in shaping the post-transition civil society. It did so primarily by demobilizing civil society at the very juncture when its expansion seemed most promising. This can be attributed principally to the actions of the Spanish Communist Party (PCE), whose shift in political strategies in the mid-1970s from confrontation toward collaboration with the Francoist state dealt a devastating blow to many social movements that the party had nurtured in its struggle against the Franco regime.

This chapter, however, cautions against drawing too much of a causal connection between the dynamics of the transition to democracy and the weakness of civil society in Spain. Indeed, it is questionable that the so-called civil society deficit, especially the dearth of associational ties prevalent in Spanish society, has anything to do with the nature of the political transition in Spain. Comparative data from other newly democratic states suggest that civil society tends to retrench, not expand, following the transition to democracy (especially a successful one) and regardless of the type of transition. On the other hand, there is a host of compelling factors behind the weakness of Spanish civil society that has little to do with the transition. This chapter unpacks the legacies of Francoism, especially the "corporatization" of society that took place after the end of the civil war. The attempt by the Franco regime to create an artificial civic life through compulsory participation of the citizenry in state-sanctioned organizations, the co-opted collaboration of the labor movement with the government, and the de facto incorporation of the Catholic Church into the structures of the state severely weakened civil society's autonomy and compromised its development in the post-transition period.

A broad overview of the composition of Spanish civil society in the democratic period opens the chapter. It showcases a marked civil society deficit when data from other countries are taken into consideration. The chapter then examines the multiplicity of factors that have shaped the evolution of Spanish civil society in the post-transition period, beginning with the impact of the democratic transition. That discussion is followed by a consideration of the legacy of the Franco regime in shaping civil society, especially the labor movement and the Catholic Church. An examination of the consequences of the civil society deficit for the development and future of democracy in Spain concludes the analysis. It cautions against presuming that the chronic weakness of organized groups has lowered the quality of democracy in Spain by depressing participation in politics, or that it poses much of a risk to its future. These claims do not take into account other means of social bonding and organization in Spain, such as a strong culture of popular protest and public demonstrations.

SPANISH CIVIL SOCIETY: A SNAPSHOT

Contrary to what one would expect, the advent of democracy in Spain did not prove especially auspicious for the rise of a vibrant civil society, a point tellingly illustrated in the dearth of associational ties among the Spaniards. Survey data from a variety of outlets has consistently portrayed the Spanish people as one of the least inclined on the planet to join or support voluntary associations. The World Values Survey (WVS), which provides the richest data for contrasting levels of associational density across national boundaries, first revealed in broad comparative terms the overall weakness of associational activity in Spain (Inglehart 1997). As seen in table 5.1, in a sample of 20 nations, Spain falls at the bottom or near the bottom of every major category polled by the survey. Overall, according to the survey, less than one-third of Spaniards report membership in a voluntary association compared with between one-half and three-quarters of respondents in the United States, Sweden, the Netherlands and Norway, the countries leading the survey.

More recent studies confirm the weakness of Spanish civil society first reported in the WVS. The most comprehensive, by McDonough et al. (1998: ix), sets out to

Table 5.1 Membership in voluntary associations in selected countries (%)

Country	Religious	Trade union	Recreational	Cultural	Political
United States	27.9	1.7	8.3	9.9	4.7
China	2.5	0.8	6.7	8.2	19.3
Finland	6.4	8.0	15.9	8.5	6.8
Canada	15.5	3.6	12.3	9.2	3.7
E. Germany	8.5	10.3	11.2	3.6	5.7
Sweden	2.8	6.3	17.1	3.2	4.0
Norway	5.9	6.1	13.9	5.4	3.6
Netherlands	9.9	1.3	9.0	9.5	2.7
W. Germany	7.1	1.7	10.5	4.1	2.8
Chile	11.9	2.1	6.5	6.2	2.3
Belgium	6.8	1.9	6.1	7.4	1.6
Italy	7.4	2.3	7.4	9.3	4.2
Mexico	9.5	1.9	4.5	5.2	3.1
Brazil	12.6	1.7	3.6	2.8	2.3
France	4.8	2.4	6.2	4.6	1.6
Russia	4.8	2.4	6.2	4.6	1.6
Hungary	2.4	4.4	3.6	2.7	4.6
Argentina	2.6	4.6	1.7	1.9	1.2
Japan	2.5	1.4	2.8	3.0	1.4
Spain	2.1	0.7	1.3	1.3	0.5

Source: World Values Survey, 1991–3

investigate what is described as "the striking deficit in political participation and civic engagement across the Spanish public." The authors find that civic engagement – defined as closeness to neighbors, membership in voluntary associations, and conventional political participation – has held steady at a low level from the onset through the consolidation of democracy. The percentage of Spaniards claiming no affiliation to an organized group went from 64 percent in 1978 to 65 percent in 1980 and to 69 percent by 1990 (McDonough et al. 1998: 16). To illustrate how exceptionally low Spain's level of civic engagement actually is, the study incorporates comparative data from two other newly democratic nations: Brazil and South Korea. It finds that in Spain only about one-third of the public belongs to any voluntary association. In Brazil, by contrast, only about one-third of the citizenry fails to belong to voluntary associations. The comparison with South Korea is even harder on Spain. Nearly nine out of ten South Koreans claim to be members of some sort of voluntary organization.

A second study of associational patterns in Spain can be found in the Comparative National Elections Project (CNEP), which examines electoral politics in nineteen newly democratic states. As reported by Gunther (2007: 30), this study paints an even bleaker picture of associational life in Spain than depicted in previous studies. It concludes that the lack of organizational affiliation has actually worsened in Spain in recent years, having soared to 80 percent of all Spaniards by 2004. This figure is 11 percentage points higher than the one reported by McDonough et al.

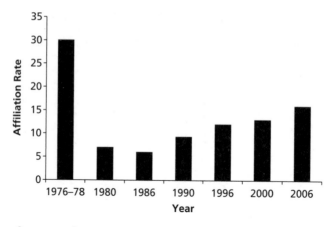

Source: various

Figure 5.1   Trade union affiliation rate in Spain (%), 1976–2006

The constitution of non-governmental organizations (NGOs) and interest groups provides another example of the weakness of civil society in Spain. A 2006 report by Lealtad, an NGO watchdog, provides a distressing view of the state of NGOs in Spain decades after the transition to democracy. Perhaps the most striking finding is the excessive dependence on public funds, especially those involved in the social action sector. Of the nation's 100 leading NGOs, a full third lack any significant private support. Private funding only reached 50.9 percent for all NGOs combined. This excessive dependence on public funds, the audit concludes, threatens the viability of some NGOs and undermines their capacity to act independently from the state. The report also criticizes the internal governance of Spanish NGOs by noting that they often fail to observe self-established rules of operation, such as annual meetings of the board of directors and/or steering committees.

As for interest groups, nothing suggests their travails in the post-transition period better than those of the labor movement, the most resourceful and best-organized sector of civil society in Spain during the transition to democracy. Spanish workers began to flee the trade unions almost as fast as they had joined them. The membership of CCOO, the largest trade union during the democratic transition, fell from 1.6 million in 1978 to 500,000 by 1985, while that of its main rival, the socialist UGT, dropped from 1 million in 1978 to 663,000 by 1985 (Encarnación 2001a: 348). This precipitous decline in membership is reflected in the declining rates of affiliation that unions experienced in the post-transition period. As seen in figure 5.1, having reached almost 30 percent during the late 1970s, the peak years of political liberalization, the national union affiliation rate experienced a dramatic collapse during the early 1980s, descending to less than 10 percent. This rate is the lowest level recorded among southern European societies, traditionally the lowest in western Europe. Comparative data for the late 1980s show a national union affiliation rate of 39.9 percent for Italy, 35.0 percent for Greece, and 28.6 percent for Portugal (Visser 1990: 173–4). Around that time, only post-communist countries, whose transition to democracy brought down state-sponsored labor unions altogether, had national union affiliation rates similar to Spain's.

Since the late 1990s, membership in Spanish unions has partly recovered but it remains among the lowest in the industrialized world. According to one study (European Industrial Relations Observatory 2003), "crude union density figures" for Spain hover between 10 and 19 percent. This is the lowest within the EU and about the same as that of new EU members, such as Poland and Latvia.

FROM BOOM TO BUST

As in many other newly democratic nations, civil society was the political celebrity of the transition to democracy in Spain. During the twilight of the late Franco period, Spanish civil society experienced a veritable renaissance. As seen shortly, multiple forms of political activism by trade unions, student groups, neighborhood associations, and dissent groups – to name just a few – accompanied the transition to democracy in Spain. These groups went on to play an important role in the democratization of the country by pressuring the authoritarian elite to open the political system, in extricating the legacies of authoritarian rule, and in constructing a new democratic public sphere (Maravall 1978; Pérez-Díaz 1980; Fishman 1990). This robust civil society revival, however, was a short-lived phenomenon. By the time democracy made its triumphant return to Spain with the 1977 elections, civil society had gone into a precipitous decline as once thriving social movements collapsed and others experienced a wrenching process of reorganization.

Among the first developments that signaled the awakening of civil society in Spain as democracy approached was the emergence of an agitated urban grassroots movement. Anchored upon a vigorous network of neighborhood associations (the so-called *Comisiones de Barrio*), this social movement began appearing in major working-class enclaves of Madrid and Barcelona in the early 1970s, encouraged by the reformist currents of the late Franco period and the sense that the end of the authoritarian regime was imminent.[3] It is reported that in one Madrid shantytown the neighborhood association grew from only six residents in 1970 to over 1,400 families in 1977 (Hipsher 1996: 288). The movement's agenda was initially limited to improving living conditions (housing, in particular) but was quickly expanded to include the liberalization of the political system.

An arguably more important development in the awakening of civil society was the re-entry into the political scene of organized labor. By the time of the legalization of independent unions in 1976, an outcome of the Law of Political Reform enacted that same year, the art of association among Spanish workers was in full bloom.[4] In 1977, more than 400 national and about 2,400 regional unions registered during the euphoria that surrounded the legalization of trade unions (Zufiaur 1985: 206). By far the best organized workers' organization was the Comisiones Obreras (Workers' Commissions, CCOO), a trade union illegally formed in the early 1960s to fight the Franco regime from within its very structures. In a relatively short period of time from its founding site at La Comocha, an Asturian mine, in 1956, the CCOO grew into a critical force in the struggle against authoritarian rule in Spain. This was largely due to the control exerted over the organization by the Spanish Communist Party, which assumed control of CCOO cells soon after their creation.

Table 5.2 Strikes during the democratic transition, 1975–1982

Year	Number of strikes	Workers involved	Working hours lost
1975	855	556,371	10,355.120
1976	1,568	3,638.952	110,016.240
1977	974	2,317.026	92,522.050
1978	1,356	3,633.004	128,738.478
1979	1,789	5,752.304	171,067.049
1980	1,669	2,461.061	108,625.662
1981	2,556	3,358.214	74,559.793
1982	2,582	1,634.062	57,834.829

Source: Comisiones Obreras (1989)

Beginning with the Barcelona transportation strike of 1951, and lasting through the early 1970s, rising workers' militancy began to make its presence felt in Franco's Spain. It made strikes an everyday occurrence in the life of ordinary Spaniards. Indeed, so common were strikes during the late Franco period that, by the early 1960s, Spanish strike rates usually exceeded those of any European nation except the United Kingdom and Italy (Malefakis 1995: 73). The highlight of workers' mobilization during this era was a landmark 1967 demonstration that drew some 100,000 workers to the streets of Madrid demanding authentic labor unions and chanting "Franco no, democracy yes" (Gilmore 1985: 105). It launched a vigorous resurgence of the labor movement as democracy began to approach and despite the move by the state to impede the movement's political activities. In the early 1970s, when the CCOO began to openly demand the end of the Franco regime, the state declared the organization illegal, and began to arrest its leadership and curtail the ability of the workers to strike.

Table 5.2 demonstrates that the years of democratic transition were an especially intense period of workers' mobilization in Spain, as strikes once motivated primarily by economic reasons (this was the only type of strike allowed under Franco) began to take on a distinctively political character. It is estimated that between 1967 and 1974, the percentage of strikes that involved some type of political demand stood at 45.4 percent (Maravall 1982: 8–10). In 1976, 3.6 million workers participated in strikes, in the biggest wave of workers' mobilization since the end of the 1930s. That same year, strikes turned deadly in the Basque city of Vitoria, where the police opened fire on a demonstration, killing five workers. This mobilization of the working class was critical in pushing democratization along in Spain. More than any other action of civil society, strikes convinced the Francoist leadership of the unfeasibility of "Francoism without Franco," the strategy designed by Franco himself before his death to prolong the life of the authoritarian state under the tutelage of King Juan Carlos.

There were political and economic pressures at work in the manner in which the strikes affected the Franco regime's future plans. The workers' mobilization sent the unambiguous message to Francoist officials that mere tinkering with the authoritarian regime would not be enough to pacify the masses. Only a full transition to democracy was capable of achieving that. As noted by Maravall (1982: 10), "The strategies of mere liberalization could have little chance of success." Pérez-Díaz (1993: 51) is more to the point when observing that "what decided the situation was the agitated response of the masses in the spring of 1976." Generally less noticed is the economic toll that the strikes took on the economy and the impact this had in accelerating the coming of the democratic transition. In the industrial belt of Barcelona, the country's economic engine, relentless striking by the workers basically shut down industrial production. As reported by Balfour (1989: 220), this mobilization not only had a destabilizing effect upon the Franco regime, it also posed a direct threat to business profits, thereby pushing business elites into joining other sectors of society in demanding the country's return to democracy.

The expansion and mobilization of civil society in Spain during the transition to democracy, however, proved to be an ephemeral affair limited largely to the period of political liberalization (1975–7). Perhaps the most dramatic illustration of this was the almost sudden collapse of the neighborhood association movement. Despite its auspicious beginning, it did not live to see the success of the democratic transition. Immediately before the 1977 elections, most neighborhood associations went into a period of crisis and eventual decline. It is reported that after the elections of 1977, the neighborhood movement "abandoned its former tactic of confronting the authorities directly through street protests and demands" (Hipsher 1996: 291). Other social movements met a similar fate of decline and demise, such as students's groups and feminist organizations, which like the neighborhood associations, had been active in the fight against Francoism (see Maravall 1978).

A watershed moment in the demise of the "movement" society of the democratic transition was the decision by the Spanish Communist Party (PCE) to abandon its plan to topple the Franco regime through a revolutionary overthrow, which had been the Communists' main strategy for regime change in Spain since the end of the civil war in 1939. While the Spanish Socialist Party (PSOE) chose to go into exile in western Europe, hoping to defeat the regime from the outside by organizing the exile community and putting pressure on foreign governments to press Franco into liberalizing his regime, the PCE went underground and began to organize civil society in opposition to the dictatorship. Accordingly, to a significant extent, the anti-Franco civil society that formed in Spain during the 1960s and early 1970s was a direct by-product of the activism of Spanish Communists, who began to organize students, workers, and neighbors, years before the formal collapse of the Franco dictatorship.[5]

The 1970 *Pacto por la Libertad* (the Pact for Freedom) signaled a dramatic change in political tactics for the PCE. The party agreed to work with other political forces, including its political rival, the PSOE, and representatives of the old regime, to bring about a peaceful end to the Franco dictatorship. This pact, in effect, ended the PCE's perception of itself as a source of revolutionary change and opened the way for a transition out of Francoism anchored on reform rather than rupture. In 1976, the Communists, together with the Socialists, accepted the reestablishment of the Spanish monarchy, in exchange for a speedy return to democracy. The political mainstreaming of the PCE was accelerated with its legalization in 1977, just in time for its participation in the 1977 elections, and was consolidated with the party's participation in the negotiation of the Moncloa accords, the political agreements negotiated by the leading political parties to stabilize the economy and facilitate a consensus-driven approach to enacting a new constitution.

Paradoxically, what was good for the institutionalization of democracy was not necessarily good for the expansion and diversification of civil society. A side-effect of the proliferation of political pacts around the time of Franco's passing in 1975 was putting nascent social movements on a course of rapid decline. On the one hand, by propelling the political parties to the forefront of the democratization process, the political pacts of the democratic transition simultaneously relegated civil society groups to a secondary plane. It is telling that only the heads of the political parties were invited by the government to negotiate the Moncloa accords. This decision vividly underscored the rising fortunes of the political parties vis-à-vis those of civil society organizations (such as the unions), as well as the shift in venue for effecting political change from the streets to behind-closed-doors inter-party bargaining. As explained by a senior official in the Suárez administration (the first of the post-transition period), although the government wished to be as inclusive as possible, in the end only the parties possessed the capacity, skills, and political framework required to integrate society and ensure that whatever compromise was agreed would be realized.[6]

On the other hand, the political pacts of the transition served to demobilize the popular sectors, an act that the political class deemed necessary for implementing the agreements of the transition and preventing political polarization. As part of the process of political accommodation triggered by the Moncloa accords, Communist and Socialist leaders began to discourage social protest and organization outside of the party structure. Among the first casualties of this was the neighborhood association movement, which the PCE began to disarticulate after 1976, together with the students' movement. The PCE and the PSOE also moved to restrain the nation's leading trade unions from excessive striking. This deliberate attempt by the left to demobilize the workers explains not only the sharp decline in the number of strikes in Spain between 1976 and 1977 but also the absence of general strikes in the country throughout the entire process of democratic consolidation (1977–82), a significant development considering the popularity of general strikes during the Second Republic.

Finally, it is worth noting that the willingness of the left-wing parties to enter into political compromises with the government exacted a price on the morale of many union leaders. This must be taken into consideration in understanding the failure of the unions to sustain the relatively high rates of union affiliation that accompanied the birth of democracy. For some union leaders, political pacts amounted to class betrayal. Emblematic of this perspective was the opinion offered to El País (May 21, 1976) by Nicolás Sartorious, a noted labor leader during the transition. Around the time when Prime Minister Adolfo Suárez began to talk about a social pact, Sartorious warned that the labor movement should oppose such a pact because accepting a pact "would hurt the process of democratization by diminishing the [movement's] role of agent of political change for the working class."

Beyond regime change

Although compelling, the notion that the weakness of Spanish civil society in the contemporary period resides primarily within the dynamics of the democratic transition is very problematic. For starters, the demobilization of civil society that accompanied the transition to democracy in Spain is not unique to the country. Comparative studies of civil society in newly democratic nations (Diamond 1999; Encarnación 2006) make note of what has been referred to as the "post-transition civil society recession," a common phenomenon in virtually all transitions to democracy, which entails the weakening and gradual passing of citizens' groups and social movements once their main objective, the defeat of an odious regime, has been accomplished. Such "civil society recessions" have been spotted in places as diverse as Latin America, South Africa, and the former communist world. Moreover, other countries that underwent a transition to democracy similar to that of Spain (anchored on elite pacts and the tactical demobilization of the masses) do not exhibit the civil society deficit prevalent in Spain.[7]

A case in point is Chile, whose civil society, according to the WVS data, is far denser than Spain's, and is in fact one of the most vibrant in the Iberian–Latin world (see Encarnación 2003: 180). As in Spain, a "pacted" transition in Chile had a tremendous effect in demobilizing the public. Prior to the transition to democracy, Chile witnessed the rise of a massive urban movement that rose around the shantytowns of Santiago, and whose agenda included the defeat of the Pinochet regime, together with better living conditions and respect for civil and human rights. But all this came crashing down with the 1987 democratic plebiscite that ushered in the transition to democracy. By 1987 only a minority of shantytown residents in Santiago were either organized or active. In Chile, as in Spain, inter-party bargaining accelerated the weakening of social movements. It is reported that the 1989 electoral triumph of the multi-party alliance Concertación, which signaled the end of the Pinochet regime, "put the nail in the coffin of the shantytown protest and organization" (Hipsher 1996: 283).

Further weakening the claim that the transition to democracy is responsible for the civil society deficit in Spain is the fact that a weak civil society was long thought to be a "problem" well before the democratic transition. Not surprisingly, explanations for this phenomenon abound. A time-honored explanation is the proverbial individualism of the Spanish people, which is believed to cause an aversion to joining voluntary associations of almost any kind. The most popular and influential theory behind this aversion toward associations is what has been termed "amoral familism," an unhealthy tightness of family connections (Banfield 1958). This characteristic of the Spanish people (which has also been observed in other Latin–Catholic societies, such as Italy and Argentina) has long been regarded as the root cause behind the incapacity of citizens to develop social ties and interpersonal trust, and their unwillingness to join groups outside of the nuclear family. In discussing these issues in reference to Spain, it has been noted that "excessive individualism, a narrow radius of trust and the centrality of the family have long been characteristic of Spain" (Fukuyama 1995: 56).

Spain's agonizing process of state building and economic development provides another compelling explanation. Juan Linz (1981: 365) has argued that Spain's failure to generate the moderate and well-organized social movements that emerged in western Europe prior to World War II is rooted in the country's historic economic backwardness. With the exception of a few areas, such as Catalonia and the Basque Country, industrialization would not arrive in Spain until the early 1960s. Consequently, for much of the twentieth century, Spain lacked the conditions that are thought to have facilitated the growth of organized groups in other European countries, including the "Western urban social structure of professional and bureaucratic middle classes, and of commercial activity and incipient industrialization." In its place, the nation developed into "a large agrarian and under-developed society in which organized interest groups were less important than the personal and family links between the political class and large landowners, bankers, railroad magnates and many new industrialists."

THE LONG SHADOW OF FRANCOISM

Finally, there is the issue of the complex legacy for civil society of the Franco regime. Most obvious are the lingering effects of the elaborate effort to create a state-sponsored civil society following the end of the Spanish Civil War, with the intention of depoliticizing the citizenry. Due to the influence of fascist organizations, such as the Falange, the Franco regime enacted a complex corporatist scheme for organizing society that incorporated students, workers, employers, and housewives, among others. This meant that around the time of the transition to democracy the experience of ordinary Spaniards with organizations that were truly autonomous was "scanty"; "this was true not only for those connected with industrialists and workers, but also for those representing the interests of farm-workers, consumers, professionals, cadres, students, etc." (Pérez-Díaz 1986: 6). Just as important is the apathy toward social organizations engendered by the state's efforts to organize a state-mandated civil society. For many Spaniards, living under democracy has come to be seen "not only as being free to join voluntary associations but, perhaps more important, as being able to choose not to join them" (Encarnación 2006: 362).

Less obvious is the legacy of incorporation by the Franco regime of many societal actors that in other countries have played an important role in mobilizing and organizing the public against the authoritarian order and in organizing citizens' associations during the transition to democracy. By far the best example of an incorporated social actor under the Franco regime is the Catholic Church, which became a partner of the state in the consolidation of authoritarian rule. Indeed, the Spanish Catholic Church became in effect a branch of the Francoist state and this remained the case until the early 1970s. This had a twofold consequence for the development of civil society. On the one hand, it meant that in Spain, in stark contrast to Latin America and some post-communist countries, the Catholic Church would play no significant role in rallying the masses against dictatorship. It had neither the desire nor the legitimacy to undertake this project. On the other hand, the eventual rejection of Francoism would go hand in hand with the wholesale rejection of the Catholic Church, as expressed most tellingly in the deep process of secularization of Spanish society, a key cause behind the exceptionally low percentage of Spaniards who belong to a religious organization.[8]

The corporatization of society

General Francisco Franco came to power with a resolute will to reconstruct Spanish society from top to bottom. Seeking to cure what he referred to as the "familiar demons" of Spanish society, "individualism, lack of solidarity, and extremism," the

Franco regime rejected pluralist forms of interest representation and organization (Amodia 1976: 26). Instead, it embraced a project of social integration as dictated by the rigid doctrine of "organic-corporatism" in an attempt to control and integrate society. It afforded the state the right to grant legitimacy to social organizations, political and otherwise, or to withhold it from them. This, in turn, meant the sudden death of the flourishing but problematic civil society of the Second Republic. During this period, civil society in Spain was dominated by organizations prone toward extremism and often violent political strategies. Most notable among them was the anarchist Confederación Nacional del Trabajo (CNT), an organization that effectively marshaled its 1-million-plus membership into conducting labor warfare and terrorism in the countryside (the fields of Andalusia, most prominently) and major Spanish cities (Barcelona, most notably).

After the end of the Spanish Civil War in 1939, the Franco regime banned all political parties and jailed, murdered, or sent into exile many of their leaders. It also passed a number of laws aimed at regulating associational life. In 1945 the state recognized "the right of all Spaniards to associate freely for licit purpose," but the limits of the law were "so narrow as to make the creation of any political organization unthinkable" (Amodia 1976: 137). Strict restrictions were also placed upon the media. Franco expropriated private and political party publications and placed them under the control of the government; in all, 100 publications, including 39 newspapers, and several radio stations were taken over (Roldán Ros 1985: 255). The few newspapers that remained in private hands, *ABC* of Madrid and *La Vanguardia* of Barcelona, for instance, survived by collaborating with the government and never criticizing its policies. Their collaboration with the regime entailed a marriage of convenience. In exchange for their collaboration, the government protected these publications by denying publishing licenses to would-be competitors.

The Franco regime also undertook to impose an ambitious, state-sponsored project of civic organization. Much of this task fell upon the Catholic Church, a pillar of support for the Franco regime that yielded enormous influence over education and social policy. The main task of the Catholic Church during the period of "Catholic Triumphalism" (1945–57) was to "re-Catholicize" Spanish society following the Republican assault on Spanish Catholicism (Linz 1984: 164). To execute this mission, the Church organized a broad universe of organizations, such as the Hermandades Obreras de Acción Católica (HOAC), Juventudes Católica Obrera (JCO), and Vanguardias Católicas Obreras (VCO), which carried out pastoral activities amongst the students and the workers. The explicit intent of these organizations was to depoliticize the masses and eradicate any lingering anarchist and socialist influence among the population. This mission gave these organizations the privileged status of being among the very few that the Franco regime permitted to organize the workers and students outside of state-sanctioned unions. Because of their affiliation with the Church, a key ally of the Franco regime, none of them was in a position to defy the regime and question its policies.

Another institution heavily involved in promoting civic organization in Franco's Spain was the Falange, a fascist party. Its main job was the "Spanishification" of society, a mission that included honoring and promoting the memory of Franco's nationalist crusade and commemorating sacred anniversaries such as July 18, 1936, which marked the day of "National Liberation," and May 2, 1808, which paid tribute to the memory of the Madrid uprising against the French invaders. The Falange carried out its patriotic work through a variety of civic, educational, and recreational organizations. Until 1965, all university students in Spain were compelled to belong to the Sindicato Español Universitario (SEU), a Falangist union founded in the late 1930s as a means of controlling and indoctrinating the Spanish youth. Among its core missions was promoting awareness of the sacrifices of nationalist leaders. The Falange also assumed a central role in the organization and socialization of females under the Franco regime. The organization's Sección Femenina (SF) was devoted to teaching domestic sciences and enforcing the regime's program of *Servicio Social*, a compulsory and unpaid form of community service. Targeted at women between the ages of 17 and 35, the program encouraged service in schools, hospitals, orphanages, and nurseries. This form of free labor allowed the state to meet many of its social obligations, especially in the countryside.

The work of the SF reinforced the gender policies of the Franco regime. The state (acting mainly through the Catholic Church) was especially attentive to female education, ensuing from the belief that "woman's entire being was conditioned by motherhood, and her destiny was to live for home, husband and family" (Alted 1985: 198). This led to the abolition of coeducation for moral and pedagogical reasons, the inclusion of domestic service in the curriculum, and the restriction of teacher training for women to primary and technical (i.e. non-academic) education (Alted 1985: 198). There was a larger political project at work behind these policies, aimed at keeping women divorced from society. As explained by Helen Graham (1995: 184), the attention that the Catholic Church devoted to the education of females echoed "the primacy of the patriarchal family in Francoist social policy." The family was seen as representing "the corporate order of the state in microcosm." It was envisaged by the Franco regime as "unthreatening because it connected vertically with the state rather than horizontally within society. Thus it reinforced the unity and power of the state, rather than challenging it, as did the horizontal solidarities of civil society (other sorts of 'family'/affective ties, political parties, trade unions and the traditions of civic associationalism)."

A decimated labor movement

Given the fact that class warfare was a central component of the Spanish Civil War, the state's attempt to "corporatize" society under the Franco regime reached its apex in the realm of labor and industrial relations. Upon usurping power, the Franco regime declared illegal the independent syndicates of the Second Republic, and attempts by the socialist UGT and the anarchist CNT to mobilize the workers against the Franco regime were severely repressed by the state. After 1939, the Franco regime also shut down the Unión Nacional Económica (UNE), the country's first ever national employers' association, created in 1931. This act of aggression against the employers probably meant little for them, given the privileged position that they occupied within the Franco regime; they reciprocated by becoming "a source of passive, non-ideological support for the Franco regime" (Martínez 1993: 172).

In place of independent trade unions, the Franco regime created a vast and complex system of 24 compulsory "vertical syndicates" grouped around the Organización Sindical Española (OSE), which united workers by profession and occupation, and also incorporated the nation's employers. The OSE's chief purpose was to create a harmonious environment of labor and industrial relations based on the corporatist idea that there is no inherent conflict in the relations between capital and labor. In reality, however, the organization's principal task was to "subjugate, domesticate and depoliticize the Spanish working class" (Foweraker 1987: 60). This mission remained the OSE's *raison d'être* until it was dismantled in 1976. Key to its operation was co-opting collaboration from the workers. Although illegally formed, the Ministry of Labor tolerated the existence of the CCOO, the grassroots union movement born in the early 1960s, until the organization began to use strikes to demand political freedoms. Indeed, the CCOO enjoyed the ambiguous designation of "semi-official" within the Franco regime, a status that entitled it to receive direct financing from the state (see Foweraker 1987).

Unsurprisingly, by the time of the transition to democracy the Spanish labor movement, although highly mobilized, was, organizationally speaking, in shambles. The once vigorous trade union movement of the Republican years "had declined to the point of relative insignificance" (Fishman 1990: 97). Of the UGT, it is reported that at the inception of democracy this organization stood for little more than "some historical initials" with a few thousand members concentrated in the Basque Country and Asturias (Burgess 2000: 4). In better shape was the CCOO, but only by comparison. Despite its impressive mobilizing capacity, the CCOO operated in the new democracy more as a movement than a formal union. Coming out of the democratic transition, the CCOO experienced a wrenching period of reorganization in which many of its early leaders abandoned the organization once the decision was made to become a conventional union. Many CCOO leaders would further fragment the labor movement by creating new unions, thus making collective action among the various unions more difficult to attain.

The labor movement in Spain also entered the democratic period financially strapped, and direct financing from the government kept many unions from folding while simultaneously compromising their independence from the state. Official financing of the unions by the state began in 1982, with the infusion of 800 million pesetas (5 million US dollars), a practice that would become a fixture in the national budget. The labor movement's financial troubles were exacerbated by internal competition, since the unions kept affiliation dues artificially low as a way to attract new members. For example, in 1986, nearly ten years after the democratic transition, the required monthly contribution by UGT members was eight-tenths of 1 percent of the minimum monthly wage, a very low subscription by European standards (McElrath 1989: 114). This problem was compounded by the high incidence of non-payment among union members. It is reported that in 1983 only 58 percent of the membership of the UGT was paying dues and 34 percent for CCOO (McElrath 1988: 114).

Several unusual features of the Spanish industrial and labor relations regime inherited from the Franco era have also worked to the detriment of the organizational development of the unions in the democratic period. A surviving institution of the Francoist vertical syndicates is a system of works councils, which plays a pivotal role in organizing collective bargaining in firms employing more than 100 workers. This system was created by the Franco regime in the early 1960s to facilitate the introduction of collective bargaining (a rarity for an authoritarian regime), in an effort to liberalize the economy and to make independent unions redundant. The system allows for the election of those who will represent the workers in negotiations with management. Therefore, whether they belong to a union or not, Spanish workers have the means to influence who represents them in such negotiations. This provides little incentive for the workers to join the unions and in fact encourages a lot of "free-riding."

The Catholic Church: a compromised actor

Another factor distinguishing the Spanish case, which is significant to the development of civil society in the democratic period, is the behavior of the Catholic Church during the years of regime change. While in many societies in Latin America and the formerly communist world the Catholic Church was a source of political dissent and opposition to the authoritarian order, in Spain the situation was considerably different. As seen previously, seeking to legitimate itself in the eyes of the Spanish public at the end of the civil war, the Franco regime had recognized Catholicism as the official religion of the state and the Catholic Church was given a very prominent role in shaping social policy, particularly education. The Catholic Church was a de facto component of the state in Spain through the direct subvention that the Franco regime offered to cathedrals and parishes, and the salaries paid to the clerics. Prominent Catholic organizations, most notably the Opus Dei and the ACNP, also played a pivotal role in shaping the structures of the Franco regime and providing some of its leaders.

Coming on the heels of the attacks on the Church during the Republican period, to say nothing of the anti-clerical violence witnessed during the civil war, such as the burning of churches and the killing of thousands of priests and nuns, the Catholic Church eagerly embraced Franco's pro-Catholic policies. They essentially restored the Concordat of 1851, which stressed Catholicism as the official religion of the Spanish state, something the Catholic Church secured in the new Concordat of 1953. This official recognition of the Church, however, came at a hefty price, for it granted the Franco regime the privilege of appointing the diocesan bishops.

It was only in the early 1970s that the Catholic hierarchy in Spain formally disassociated itself from the Franco regime.[9] On January 13, 1973, less than three years before Franco's death, the Church released a statement with the provocative title of "The Church and the Political Community," which announced a formal split between the Franco regime and the hierarchy of the Catholic Church. Drafted by the Spanish Conference of Bishops, it declared the Church to be politically neutral, independent from the state, and committed to political pluralism. This statement of withdrawal of support for the Franco regime by the Catholic Church, however, did not explicitly call for the country's return to democracy. Nonetheless, it was a watershed in the relationship between the Catholic Church and the Franco regime with important political implications for the state, the Catholic Church, and Spanish society at large.

Two factors conditioned a change of heart in the hierarchy of the Spanish Church about its connection to the Franco regime. The most obvious was the social transformations within Spanish society set into motion by the social and economic advances of the late Franco period. In the face of a relentless process of modernization and secularization, the Church rapidly began to lose whatever influence it had over its flock. In the mid-1960s, about half of the men in rural Spain went to church regularly, but only 5 to 10 percent of the workers in the cities (Herr 1971: 11). This led the Church between 1966 and 1968 to formally dissolve many of the popular organizations that tied it to the Franco regime. Although independent from the state, these organizations were part of a state-sanctioned project of civic development born with the consolidation of the Franco regime in the 1940s. Its intention was to create a society that was subservient to the commands of the state and that embodied its core values. More often than not, these values were essentially Catholic in nature and emphasized that devotion to the evangelical work of the Church and allegiance to Franco went hand in hand.

Church leaders also began to realize that in the new liberalizing climate of the late Franco period its association with the regime was alienating the public, pushing even the highest authority figures in the Church to distance themselves from the authoritarian state. More worrisome yet, the Church's association with the state was propelling a growing dissent movement within the Spanish clergy. During the 1970s, younger priests began to embrace opposition groups and to call for a more open and tolerant society, thereby signaling to other groups in civil society the willingness of the Church to embrace the country's transition out of authoritarian rule. For instance, by the late 1960s, sections of the Church began to encourage strikers and support their economic and political demands even if it meant having to openly contradict the state (Herr 1971: 12). These actions reflected a dramatic transformation of political attitudes within the Spanish clergy. A 1970 survey that covered 85 percent of the total Spanish clergy revealed that the political preference that received the most support was "socialism," which was endorsed by 25 percent of the survey participants; "workers' movement" ranked third with 14 percent (Gunther et al. 2004: 75).

So strong was the dissatisfaction of some clergy with the Church's hierarchy that they effectively became radicalized. Nowhere was this more evident than in the Basque Country, historically Spain's most religiously devout region. The Franco regime's attempt to eradicate Basque nationalism, which by the late 1960s had turned the Basque provinces into the epicenter for large-scale violations of human rights in Spain, prompted many Basque priests to openly disobey the government. Taking advantage of the Church's independence from the civilian government, priests in the Basque Country (and Catalonia) often conducted services in the local language, directly violating the Franco regime's official linguistic policy of "one nation, one language" (Castilian). In 1960, 350 priests in the Basque country wrote a letter to their local bishop protesting the Franco regime's policies in the region. It led to the trial of several Basque priests in Madrid on charges of insubordination to state policy. Priests in the Basque Country are also reported to have been active in the formation of ETA (Herr 1971: 12).

Much of the dissent within the Catholic Church was being promoted by new trends in Catholic theology that were dramatically transforming the Catholic world, including Spain. The Second Vatican Council, convened by Pope John XXIII in 1962, acknowledged that the Catholic Church had not always been on the side of the poor, human rights, and democracy. Accordingly, Vatican II committed the Catholic Church to a social and economic agenda that stressed equality, freedom, and justice. This new orientation did not radicalize the Catholic Church in Spain, as was the case in several Latin American countries, where it inspired the rise of Liberation Theology, a militant type of social activism among the clergy in Chile, Brazil, and several Central American nations. Liberation Theology sought to wed Marxist economic ideas with the Vatican's newfound emphasis on democracy and social justice.

Nonetheless, the postulates of Vatican II had a profound impact on church–state relations in Spain. Above all, Vatican II undermined the nationalist–Catholic dogma upon which Franco's support of the Catholic Church rested and that saw the Spanish state and the Catholic Church as sharing a symbiotic relationship ensuing from the Catholic Church's historic role in informing Spanish national identity. This view of church–state relations contradicted the emerging desire among many priests in Spain, triggered by the encyclical letters of Vatican II, to put some distance between themselves and the state. Only then could the Church fulfill its role as a promoter of democracy and human rights, and an advocate for the poor and the disfranchised. After all, the principles of Vatican II stood in striking contrast to the very nature of the Franco regime.

The Catholic Church's policy of neutrality with respect to the transition to democracy had enormous political ramifications. It dealt a final blow to Francoism, albeit a rather symbolic one, given the already decaying state of the Franco regime. A more important legacy, however, was the effect of the Church's position on the texture of mass politics. After withdrawing its support for the old regime, the hierarchy of the Church made no effort to mobilize the masses against the authoritarian order. To be sure, the Catholic Church did not oppose democratization and it facilitated some of the contacts that developed between the old regime and the democratic opposition. But no concerted effort was made by the Church's hierarchy to mobilize the faithful against the authoritarian state, either by organizing the citizenry to demand the liberalization of the political order, or by building bridges between the various pro-democracy social movements. As a consequence of the Church's "neutral" stance toward the change in political regime, Spain did not develop during the transition to democracy the kind of "movement" civil society generated by the Catholic Church across Latin America and the former communist world. As reported by the cross-national study on political participation by McDonough et al. (1998: 157), "Spain stands out among recently democratized countries for the absence of religious sentiment in the rallying of mass support . . . the result was to leave the link between popular devotion and political abstention intact."

A DEMOCRACY AT RISK?

Should the weakness of civil society in Spain be a cause of concern for the future of the country's democracy? According to the prevailing conventional wisdom, the answer is a resounding yes. A strong civil society is widely regarded as essential to the maintenance of a democratic public life. Behind this notion are two influential arguments inspired by Tocqueville's theorizing about the democratic virtues of voluntary associations. The first one contends that civil society greases the wheels of democracy by furnishing the "social capital" that makes democratic institutions work (Putnam 1993).

"Social capital" is generally referred to as a culture of social trust and reciprocity. In its absence, apathy, cynicism, and indifference (a negative form of social capital) prevail and democracy is likely to wane as citizens find it difficult to connect with one another and realize common goals. The second argument sees civil society as critical to democracy by serving as a democratic watchdog whose functions include keeping the state's authoritarian tendencies under check and promoting transparency in government, among other "advocacy" functions (Diamond 1999). All this attention to civil society explains the widespread view that a vibrant and robust civil society is the bedrock of democracy.

There are reasons to be skeptical of the view that the weakness of civil society in Spain poses a serious risk to its democracy. On the one hand, there is the relevant fact that a very successful new democracy has been consolidated in Spain in the last three decades despite the absence of a strong civil society. Moreover, Spanish democracy shows none of the political pathologies that we have come to associate with late-democratizing societies. Interestingly enough, many new democracies where a democratic constitution co-exists with rampant human rights violations (several Latin American countries, for instance) have a denser universe of associational life than Spain (Encarnación 2003: index). Not surprisingly, the case of Spain has been used to challenge the perceived importance of a vibrant and robust civil society to the functioning of democracy, and to argue that what matters most to the functioning of democracy is not the composition of civil society but rather the stability and efficacy of the political system (Encarnación 2001b).

On the other hand is the provocative argument that the civil society landscape in Spain may not be as weak as it is purported to be due to biases in how the strength of civil society is conventionally calibrated. Indeed, the so-called civil society deficit in Spain may well be something of a mirage or at least nowhere near as acute as generally presumed. For starters, the image of Spain as a nation of loners, provided by cross-national surveys like the WVS, is certainly at odds with what any visitor to Spain is likely to encounter. It is a well-documented fact that Spaniards spend more time than probably any other people on earth "schmoozing" – talking to friends in bars, casual (not to say anarchic) socializing, "Mediterranean" lounging, and so on (McDonough et al. 1998: 203). This is hardly surprising considering that, according to Eurostat, which collects European statistics of almost any kind, Spain has the highest ratio of bars to population in Europe with almost six bars per thousand inhabitants (3 times the UK's ratio and 4 times Germany's).

Of course, neither bar hopping nor clubbing is recognized as civic activity likely to have salutary effects on democracy. Yet, civil society advocates such as Putnam (1992) have famously regarded recreational activities such as bowling and bird watching as acceptable measures of civic engagement and sources of social capital because they allow citizens to socialize with one another as equals. Perhaps the Spanish case suggests the need for more expansive criteria for gauging what constitutes civil society across cultures. This point is underscored by research by a number of sociologists who have found that Spaniards have in fact substituted membership in organized groups for informal means of socializing outside the home, such as bar hopping and clubbing (Requena and Benedicto 1988; Requena Santos 1994). Whether the Spanish people derive trust and reciprocity from clubs and bars is, of course, questionable. But, as seen in figure 5.2, the data on comparative social trust do not reveal Spain to be especially weak in this category, certainly not as weak as its low levels of associational density would suggest.

Protest and political participation

Another interesting insight is that surveys like the WVS fail to take into consideration Spain's vigorous culture of mass mobilization and protest. Yet, as seen shortly, in the post-Franco era, participation in mass demonstrations has become one of the most important modes – perhaps *the* most important mode – of citizens' engagement in politics. A cross-national study drawing on data from 1990 to 1995 places Spain third among western European nations according to the yearly mean of protest events (Nam 2007: 108). The data give Spain an annual average of protests of 554.17 versus 1,253.67 for France and 718.67 for Germany. These data, however, are not standardized on the size of the population, an important point considering that Germany's population is almost double that of Spain, and France's population is about a third larger than Spain's. More recent data from the Spanish Ministry of the Interior provide a finer-grained view of how prevalent demonstrations are in Spanish life. Between 1996 and 2001 the number of demonstrations averaged 9,611 per year, with the lowest figure of 8,004 in 1999 and a peak of 11,186 in 1996 (Casquete 2006: 49).

The propensity of the Spaniards to take to the streets en masse has been especially notable whenever the public perceives that democracy is under threat. The first sign of this came with the massive rallies staged against the military coup attempt of February 23, 1981, including the main demonstration in Madrid in February 27, 1981, which drew over 1 million people. During the 1990s, anti-ETA rallies became common occurrences in major Spanish cities, especially in the Basque Country. Nothing, however, provides a better sense of how much non-institutionalized expression of political sentiments has become a part of the political culture in Spain than the demonstrations that followed the terrorist bombing of Madrid's Atocha train station on March 11, 2004 (usually referred to in Spain as "M-11"). According to an account by the daily *El Mundo* (March 12, 2003), 11.4 million people participated in public demonstrations in the day that followed the attacks. For a country of just over 44 million inhabitants, this amounts to a staggering 25 percent of the population. Leading the demonstrations were marches in Madrid and Barcelona that drew 2.0 million and 1.5 million people respectively. The numbers are even more striking for mid-sized cities like Valencia and Seville (both with a population of under 1 million), where more than 700,000 people took to the streets. This amounts to an astonishing 75 percent of the population for each city.

The vibrancy of Spain's protest culture gives rise to a set of compelling questions; first among them, what makes it possible? Alternatively put, why is there so much political activity on the margins in Spain? Surprisingly, this question remains relatively unexamined by scholars. Certainly, the propensity of Spaniards to try to influence policies by taking to the streets rather than through activism in formal organizations fits well with the characterization of the Spanish people as anarchic and individualistic. Another obvious factor is the longevity of the Franco regime and the very prominent

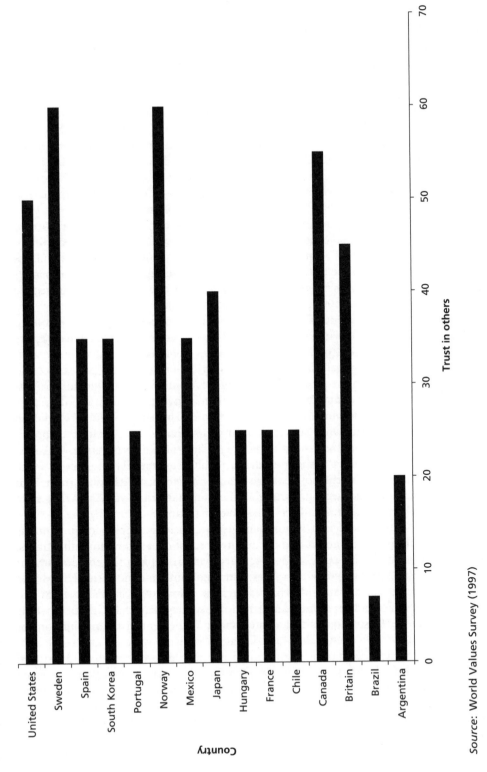

Source: World Values Survey (1997)

Figure 5.2 Trust levels in selected democracies (%)

role that protests played in the effort by civil society to uproot the dictatorship. The fact that strikes began to be tolerated by the Franco regime in the early 1960s while formal political organizations were still banned certainly helped to consolidate the practice of spontaneous demonstrations as a primary means for citizens to express their political sentiments.

A more fundamental concern, however, is whether Spain's lively protest culture contributes to the quality of democratic life. Does it influence the political behavior of the political elite and the course of policy making, or does it simply channel the public's discontent? Robert Fishman (2007) has compellingly argued that Spain's protest culture is a vital component of the country's democratic culture, a point often obscured by the overwhelming emphasis that elite action is given in some of the most influential narratives of Spanish democratization (Gunther 1992; Linz and Stepan 1989, 1996). Fishman's point is broadly supported by the fact that from the very inception of democracy in Spain, protests have significantly influenced the direction of the country's politics. As seen already, it is virtually impossible to divorce the willingness of the Francoist state to reform itself from the pressure exerted by the public through mass demonstrations and strikes. Almost every step in the liberalization of the authoritarian regime was preceded by a massive public demonstration or a strike.

Since the consolidation of democracy in Spain, mass demonstrations have continued to influence politics, often with dramatic results. The weakening of ETA during the 1990s cannot be fully understood without considering the effect generated by the anti-terrorist demonstrations staged throughout Spain by NGOs like Gesto por la Paz and Elkarri, which have taken the lead in denouncing ETA violence (MacDonald and Bernardo 2006: 191). The massive demonstrations that followed M-11 played an important role in determining the winner of the 2004 elections. The demonstrations weakened the government's candidate while simultaneously drumming up support for the opposition. Public rallies accusing the governing Popular Party of a cover-up after it blamed the attacks of M-11 on ETA without evidence to back up this claim, dealt a severe blow to the credibility of the party just days before the elections. Many of those who took to the streets, young people in particular, had not planned to vote until they were enticed to do so by participating in the mass demonstrations.

Less obvious is the manner in which demonstrations helped Spain cope with the trauma of M-11. Research conducted by team of scholars at the University of the Basque Country (Páez et al. 2007: 332–3) reveals that participation in the demonstrations that followed M-11 generated values and emotions that most scholars would easily recognize as "social capital." The researchers interviewed Spanish college students and their relatives from five Spanish regions and eight universities to test how participation in demonstrations affected their emotions, one, three, and eight weeks after the bombings. They found that "participation in demonstration and communal coping indirectly reinforced a positive emotional climate (perceived hope, solidarity and trust) 2 months later by (1) reinforcing the perception of social integration (perceived social support and positive affect) at the three-week period; and (2) reinforcing beliefs regarding positive life changes in response to trauma (post-traumatic growth)."

Finally, it is worth noting the synergy that exists between, on the one hand, Spain's culture of protest and demonstrations, and on the other, organizations from civil society and the political system. One of the puzzles of political participation in Spain is that trade unions and political parties, which are weak and generally held in low esteem by the public, are actually very effective at mobilizing the public. For all of its organizational woes, the labor movement has repeatedly demonstrated its fabled *poder de convocación*, or ability to send the workers into the streets to influence pending legislation or government action. This suggests that civil society groups have successfully tapped into the culture of protest and made it a central component of the repertoire of political strategies. The first general strike in the democratic period took place on December 14, 1988 against a youth employment program introduced by the Socialist government of Felipe González, which the unions argued would weaken labor laws because of its reliance on temporary employment. The most recent one took place in June 20, 2000 against the conservative government of José María Aznar, in protest against a plan that called for the trimming of unemployment benefits. In both cases, the government was forced to withdraw or modify its policy.

Political organizations have followed suit in incorporating protest as a means of connecting to the masses. The PSOE played a leading role in organizing the massive public demonstrations that followed M-11. More telling still is that the March 12, 2004 demonstration in Madrid was especially notable for the participation of virtually the entire political class, which was joined by the prime ministers of France, Italy, and Portugal. For the first time in its history, the Spanish royal family participated in a public demonstration. More recently, the PP has rallied Catholics and Conservatives against the policies of the Zapatero administration, which the party has branded as "rabidly anti-Catholic." On June 18, 2004, the leadership of the PP and the Spanish Conference of Bishops, for the first time in the democratic period, organized an anti-government demonstration in the form of a "pro-family" rally, intended to derail the legislation that eventually legalized homosexual marriage; its organizers estimated that the rally drew a crowd of 500,000 people.

CONCLUSION

"Spain is different" was Franco's justification for the absence of democracy in Spain. Clearly, this claim is no longer valid with the country having secured a stable democratic regime. But the weakness of associational ties in Spain suggests that the country remains somewhat distinct from other mature democracies. The underlying causes of this condition are numerous and complex, and, contrary to the conventional wisdom, connected only tangentially to the negotiated route to democracy that the country adopted after the demise of Francoism. More important, perhaps, is the apparent challenge that the case of Spain poses to popular assumptions about the critical importance of a vibrant and robust civil society to the well-being of democracy. While democratic institutions and practices have consolidated their position in Spain, the growth of civil society organizations appears to have stagnated.

Yet, the contradiction of Spain – a successful democracy lacking a vibrant and well-organized civil society – may seem less puzzling if we go beyond conventional means of calibrating the strength of civil society. Surveys such as the WVS have been rightly criticized for providing a western and especially America-centric approach to understanding the composition of civil society, since they rely almost exclusively on a set of categories that may be irrelevant to countries outside of the traditional cultural, economic, and political milieu of the western experience. This criticism resonates loudly with the Spanish experience. Certain aspects of civic and political life unique to Spain, including an intense social life outside the home and a vigorous protest culture, appear to have been left out of the equation of what makes for a strong civil society. These appear to have filled the void left behind by the weakness of formal associational connections.

6

A NATION OF NATIONS:
DECENTRALIZING THE STATE

In his *Handbook for Travellers in Spain* (published in 1845), the English writer Richard Ford referred to Spain as the land of the *patria chica* (small fatherland) for the extent to which people are innately attached to their region or province of birth.[1] Spain, Ford argued, was "a bundle of local units tied together with a rope of sand." Over the course of centuries, rulers in Spain have sought with little success to erase regional differences by pursuing state-sponsored projects aimed at strengthening a national sense of identity; none more so than General Franco, whose regime was explicitly devoted to the promotion of a monolithic Spanish identity, going as far as using force to repress regional cultures. Predictably, the end of the Franco era brought about a robust revival of regional nationalisms across Spain, especially in Catalonia and the Basque Country, two regions with longstanding historic claims to "nationhood" based on the conviction that their culture is distinct from that of Spain. Accommodating this claim has proved to be the most difficult of all problems faced by the country in the post-Franco era. Two interrelated reasons made meeting regionalist demands especially taxing.

One the one hand, the right and the military have historically opposed any scheme to decentralize the Spanish state by granting the regions some control over their own affairs. The extension of self-governance to Catalonia, the Basque Country, and Galicia during the interwar years was a key factor behind Franco's 1936 military uprising, the prelude to the Spanish Civil War. On the other hand, by the time of Franco's death in 1975 it was clear that decentralizing the state would probably not be enough to satisfy the demands of regional nationalists. Franco's attempt to eradicate regionalism by banning local languages and symbols, and repressing regional–nationalist groups, had the unintended consequence of radicalizing Basque nationalism during the late 1950s and giving birth to the Basque terrorist organization Euskadi Ta Askatasuna, ETA (Basque Homeland and Freedom). Franco's actions thus ensured that by the time of the transition to democracy in the mid-1970s Spain would be gripped by a full-blown civil conflict between ETA and the military. On the surface this conflict seemed intractable. As an ultra-conservative institution, the military was committed to the idea of a centralized and culturally homogeneous Spain. ETA, for its part, sought nothing short of outright independence for the Basque Country.

Shedding light on how Spain negotiated the challenges posed by regional nationalist movements in the democratic period is the central purpose of this chapter. Inevitably, this requires delving into the process of devolution of powers from the central state to the regions, the most politically sensitive and organizationally complex outcome of the politics of compromise that accompanied the transition to democracy in Spain. It resulted in the creation of the *Estado de las Autonomías* (State of the Autonomies), a system of 17 self-governing regions, each with its own president and elected parliament. This system subscribes to the doctrine of "consociationalism," a process by which multi-ethnic nations agree to decentralize the state by allocating decision-making power according to cultural or linguistic boundaries (Lijphart 1968). As institutionalized in Spain, consociationalism resulted in a hybrid system of regional governance that combines aspects of federalism with those of a unitary state, and therein reside its virtues as well as its problems. This marriage has fashioned a workable dispersion of power between the central state and the regions, and has promoted a new identity for the country as a "nation of nations," which is nowadays taken for granted by ordinary Spaniards. It has not, however, satisfied all the regions.

The chapter first examines the underlying causes behind the rise of powerful regional nationalist movements in Spain, especially in the Basque Country and Catalonia, two of Europe's best-known stateless nations. A secondary purpose of this section is to shed light on the puzzling question of why Basque nationalism is exclusionary and violence-prone, while Catalan nationalism is politically inclusive and accommodating. As shown shortly, a central distinction between the two is that whereas in Catalonia identity is based on language and culture, in the Basque Country it is anchored upon ethnicity and race. The second part of the chapter examines the institutional nature of regional self-governance in Spain, and whether it has entailed the creation of a de facto federal state, a development not foreseen in the 1978 constitution. The third and closing section of the chapter discusses the legacy of state decentralization in Spain, especially its inherent tension, a reflection of the delicate balancing act faced by the architects of Spain's new democracy: decentralizing without altering Spain's basic constitution as a unitary state.

PERIPHERAL NATIONALISMS IN SPAIN

The absence of a cohesive national identity across the Spanish territory is generally seen as a legacy of the country's early process of state building (Linz 1973). From the onset of its consolidation in 1492, with the unification of the kingdoms of Castile and Aragón, the legitimacy of the Spanish state has been challenged by a number of regions whose culture and language developed in the periphery of Castile, Spain's dominant regional power. Over the years, the attempt by the central state to consolidate power across the Iberian Peninsula served to generate significant protest, instability, and even violence, and never quite succeeded in erasing regional distinctiveness. The last political regime to seek to impose a policy of cultural homogeneity was the Franco dictatorship, which was built upon the idea that Spain's ethnolinguistic differences made the country unsuitable for democracy, given an inherent proclivity toward anarchy and separatist violence. In Franco's view and that of his sympathizers, only an authoritarian government could keep the nation together and at peace with itself.

Franco had no use for the claim of the Basques and the Catalans that they were "nations" different from Spain and that their local languages deserved state recognition and protection. *Habla cristiano* (speak Christian) was Franco's admonition to the Basques and the Catalans as he proceeded to cancel the autonomy charter granted to them by the Second Republic and to prohibit the use of any language other than Castilian in both public and private spaces. Not surprisingly, the democratic transition brought to the surface the resentment toward the central state accumulated over four decades of Francoism, as the political opening created by the transition served as a useful vehicle for regional nationalists to assert their demands for self-governance. Yet, in the democratic period the politics of regional nationalism have played out quite differently across Spain. As will be seen, in the Basque Country ETA's violent struggle on behalf of Basque independence made Spain the epicenter of terrorism in the whole of western Europe. In Catalonia, by contrast, a tense but workable arrangement between the central state and regional nationalists emerged. In Galicia, Spain's third "historic" region, as in the other regions, peace prevails.[2]

The Basques and the politics of violent nationalism

The Basque Country, whose provinces straddle the Spanish/French border, is the vortex of ethnopolitical conflict in Spain.[3] At the center of the maelstrom is ETA, created in 1959 by middle-class university students frustrated with the passivity toward the Franco regime of the Partido Nacionalista Vasco (PNV), the historic advocate of Basque nationalism. For ETA's founders, the PNV was "a collaborationist organization of Francoism" (Muro 2005: 579). ETA's early ideological orientations were rooted in Catholic social radicalism, a reflection of the Basque Country's deeply entrenched Catholic traditions.[4] Over time this orientation has experienced many permutations, including anti-colonialism, Marxist-Leninism, and ultimately Basque independence and socialism. A constant feature of ETA, however, is its commitment to violent action against the state. The driving goal is to create a cycle of "action–repression–action," a classic strategy of insurgencies, designed to provoke the state into all-out repression, which in turn would lead to a mass-based revolutionary upheaval.

ETA's terrorism grew lethal after 1968, when it attacked a train full of soldiers and civil war veterans. Until then, the organization's violence had been limited to acts of vandalism, such as blowing up monuments and setting off bombs in front of Guardia Civil (National Police Corps) stations. In 1973, ETA committed its most spectacular act of terrorism to date with the assassination of Admiral Luis Carrero Blanco, Franco's alter ego and apparent political heir. The opening up of the political system paradoxically provided little relief from ETA's terrorist activities. Quite the contrary: as democratization progressed, so did the scale of ETA's terror. Between 1973 and 1982, the critical years of democratic transition and consolidation, ETA was responsible for 371 deaths, 542 injured, 50 kidnappings and hundreds of bomb explosions and other acts of violence and terror (Maravall and Santamaría 1986: 105).

Figure 6.1 traces ETA's killings since 1968. The vast majority of those killed (approximately two-thirds) have been members of the Guardia Civil and military personnel,

Source: Muro (2008)

Figure 6.1   ETA's killing campaign, 1968–2006

often high-ranking officials. The toll of ETA's terror on the civilian population, although small when contrasted to that of public officials, has left an indelible mark on the nation's collective consciousness. In 1987, 21 people were killed as a consequence of a bomb planted in the garage of a Barcelona supermarket. That same year, five children were killed in Zaragoza, the capital of the Aragón region, in a bombing of a Guardia Civil family complex. Figure 6.1 also suggests that since the late 1980's, ETA's violence has ebbed significantly, a telling sign of the organization's recent decline. Twice in the last ten years (1998 and 2006) the organization has declared "an indefinite and uni-lateral truce" only to break this pledge and renew the violence. The first one, inspired by Northern Ireland's Good Friday Agreement, lasted fourteen months. The second one was in place for only nine months. It ended on December 30, 2006, when ETA planted of a bomb in a parking lot of Madrid's Bajaras airport that killed two immi-grants from Ecuador.

But even if the worst of ETA's violence is effectively over, the organization remains a potent threat to Spanish society due to its ever-expanding repertoire of terrorist activi-ties. From its inception, ETA has relied upon extortion schemes (a so-called "revolu-tionary tax") imposed upon Spanish and especially Basque businesses to underwrite its activities. After the arrest of many of its leaders in the early 1990s, ETA developed a strategy of "socialized suffering" designed to extend the terror beyond state targets (most notably military officers and installations) and into society by singling out for attack ordinary civilians, journalists, academics, business leaders, judges, and celebri-ties. According to the Spanish NGO Gesto por la Paz, ETA's list of potential targets in the Basque region alone exceeds 42,000 people, including 200 teachers and intellectuals, over 1,200 politicians and party officials, approximately 15,000 entrepreneurs, over 25,000 policemen, 350 judges and attorneys, 400 journalists, and 800 prison officers (Mata 2004: 76). These individuals are forced to live their lives in perpetual fear, careful to avoid company and crowds, constantly changing their itineraries and checking their vehicles for bombs, and even having to resort to hiring bodyguards.

Less known (at least outside of Spain) about ETA's repertoire of terrorist activities is the so-called *Kale borraka* (street struggle), bands of hooded youth out to terrorize and vandalize the streets of major Basque towns on both sides of the border. They are blamed for millions of dollars in damage to private and public property. The goal of the *Kale borraka* is twofold: to sustain an environment of terror and destruction and to serve as a foundation for the recruitment of new ETA members. Both of these goals are critical to ETA's survival, given the successes of the government in recent years in capturing some of the organization's leadership as well as the overall decline in support for ETA's terrorist campaign among the Basque people.

ETA has also used the political arena to discredit Spanish democracy. Since its formation in 1977, Herri Batasuna (HB), ETA's political wing, has been a constant source of irritation for mainstream political organizations. In striking contrast to most of the Spanish political establishment, HB has traditionally refused to criticize ETA and its terrorist activities, which the party regards as critical to the struggle for Basque independence. In the view of its members, "ETA terrorists are soldiers fighting for their country's freedom, and their victims are either fascists or representatives of a repressive foreign power" (Coverdale 1985: 231). HB has also shunned participation in the institutions of the new democracy. In 1978 it opposed the ratification of the new democratic constitution and in 1979 the party refused to occupy the seats that it had gained in the national parliament in that year's elections, in protest against the new political regime.

ETA has also affected Spanish politics by helping to radicalize other Basque institutions, including the historically moderate PNV. This party has traditionally made no demands for pardon for ETA terrorists, nor has it insisted that the neighboring region of Navarra be incorporated into the Basque region, positions associated with ETA and HB. Moreover, as the architect of the Basque autonomy charter, the PNV accepted Basque and Castilian as co-official languages of the Basque region. Yet, as both ETA and HB have grown more strident in their criticism of Madrid, and their political demands have become more extreme, the PNV has been put on the defensive, which explains the many ambiguous positions that the party has taken in the post-Franco era. The PNV joined HB in boycotting the parliamentary vote on the 1978 constitution, resulting in a rate of abstention from the constitutional referendum of more than 50 percent in two Basque provinces. While the majority of political institutions in Spain have unambiguously condemned ETA's terrorist activities, the PNV has been more guarded. A statement from the PNV in the 1980s reveals the party's ambivalence towards ETA:

We must bear in mind that ETA was born out of the violence of the Franco regime, but this very clearly is not a sufficient excuse for their present acts. Nevertheless, as long as the Spanish state does not take effective and clear steps designed toward reversing discrimination against Basque culture, it will be difficult for us to explain to ETA why they should lay down their guns. (Gunther et al. 1980: 186)

The roots of ETA terrorism

The reasons behind the persistence of the Basque conflict are not self-evident. Conventional explanations, such as ancient hatreds and rivalries, religious differences, or economic deprivation or exploitation, the kinds of factors generally thought to have generated violent and seemingly intractable ethnic conflict in places as varied as the former Yugoslavia, Northern Ireland, India, and Palestine, do not apply to the Basque Country. The struggle for Basque independence is a relatively new phenomenon. Its roots are generally traced to the founding of the PNV in 1895. Religion is not a source of conflict within Spain, a predominantly Catholic country. ETA followers are drawn largely from the middle class, and the Basque Country is a bastion of Spanish finance and industry. In the early 1970s, when ETA terrorism began to explode, Vizcaya, home to Bilbao, the Basque capital, enjoyed the highest per capita income of any of Spain's 50 provinces, and the next two positions were occupied by Ávala and Guipúzcoa (Coverdale 1985: 227). On the other hand, of the three ethnic groups with claims to "nationhood" in Spain (the Basques, the Catalans, and the Galicians) only the Basques have resorted to violence against the state in the democratic period.

What then explains the violence in the Basque Country? State repression of Basque culture is the most commonly offered explanation. The rise of Basque nationalism is often traced to the nineteenth century when the central government in Madrid withdrew the so-called *fueros*, special social and economic rights accorded for centuries by the Spanish crown to the Basques. The *fueros*, formally abrogated in 1876, were especially cherished in the Basque countryside, which eventually emerged as the principal repository of Basque culture, identity, and nationalist fervor. Further impetus for the growth of Basque nationalism came with the advent of the Second Republic (1931–9). Its anti-clericalism (the Second Republic's constitution recognized freedom of religion, ended financial support for the clergy, and nationalized the Catholic Church's vast property holdings) shocked conservative Basques in historically the most devoutly Catholic region in Spain. Indeed, Basque support for regional autonomy during the interwar years was rooted not in cultural and racial uniqueness (as is the case today) but in the hope "that an autonomous Basque region might be able to follow a religious policy more favorable to the church than that of the rest of the Republic" (Coverdale 1985: 231).

Basque nationalism consolidated during the Spanish Civil War, in which the Basques found themselves on the losing side. An emblematic event of the war, and a defining moment in the development of modern Basque nationalism, was the bombing of the village of Guernica by Franco's Nazi allies in 1937. It involved the massacre of Basque nationalists and socialists defending the region from fascism and the killing of some 1,500 civilians in a territory traditionally regarded as the ancient capital of the Basque Country.[5] Attacks on Basque culture intensified after the end of the war in 1939 with the advent of the Franco regime and its attempt to impose a homogeneous cultural identity. Under Franco, Basque nationalist symbols were under constant threat, thereby creating the impression that the Basque region was under foreign or colonial occupation. A case in point was the banning of the public use of Euskera, the Basque Country's ancient language. The Franco regime also instituted a ban on the public display of the

Basque flag as well as the very intrusive and seemingly incomprehensible policy of forbidding parents from giving their children Basque names. These policies resulted in thousands of Basques being arrested, tortured, or forced into exile by the Franco regime during the years leading to the democratic transition. In so acting, the Franco dictatorship created an environment of societal resistance and resentment highly conducive to the founding and flourishing of groups such as ETA.

Of course, under Franco all regional cultures in Spain were under attack, since the old regime's policy of cultural homogeneity applied to the nation at large, but only in the Basque Country did ethnopolitical conflict give birth to terrorism. This suggests the need to account for the peculiarities of Basque nationalism and their interaction with Franco's repressive policies. A prominent one is the fragility of Basque culture, which gives life to the argument of Basque nationalists that their culture is under mortal threat and rapidly fading away. This, in turn, has given way to ETA's claim that cultural genocide is presently taking place in the Basque Country. Under this calculus, the democratic nature of the state in Spain is irrelevant, as is the strong recognition of minority cultures guaranteed by the 1978 democratic constitution, since only complete independence can guarantee the survival of Basque culture. Certainly, claims of cultural genocide are exaggerated, since the central government no longer imposes a national policy of cultural homogeneity in Spain. Since the transition to democracy, Basque culture is recognized as unique within the Iberian context and Euskera is taught in schools and widely used in the affairs of the Basque regional government.

Nonetheless, several factors permit the argument about cultural genocide to resonate powerfully with the Basque people, even among those opposed to ETA's violent political strategies. Basque culture, as will be seen shortly, lacks the confidence of Catalan culture. It is telling that Euskera is spoken by only about 30 percent of the Basque population, with 53 percent only speaking Castilian (Roller 2002: 279). Spanish is the language of the Basque economic and political elites. Some of the better-known Basque intellectuals, such as Miguel de Unamuno and Pio Baroja, towering figures of twentieth-century Spanish literature, wrote exclusively in Castilian. The reasons behind the semi-obscurity of the Basque language include its origins in the Basque countryside, where it is most frequently encountered, and the absence of ties to Latin. This makes acquiring fluency in the language exceptionally difficult for the Basques themselves and especially for the thousands of immigrants who over the years have arrived in the Basque Country in search of economic opportunities.

Another peculiarity of Basque nationalism concerns the core issues that animate it, key among them nostalgia about the past. "Very few other regions in Western Europe have a nationalist movement that yearns for the past more intensively than the Basque one," observes Diego Muro (2005: 576). Part and parcel of the appeal of the past is the strong mythical component underpinning Basque nationalism, such as the assertion of the Basques as Europe's oldest indigenous ethnic people and the continued habitation of the Basque territory by the Basques for at least 2,000 years. This, in turn, has made the cause of maintaining the ethnic purity of the Basque people a central purpose of Basque nationalists. Indeed, the intellectual father of Basque nationalism, Sabino de Arana y Goiri (1865–1903), defined Basqueness primarily in racial terms, as something that cannot be acquired but rather is inherited. This type of race-based nationalism has been tied to the use of violence in the Basques' struggle for independence (Conversi

1997). Terrorism is the most obvious expression of this violence. Less visible, but more widespread, is the exclusionary treatment of immigrants to the Basque Country from other parts of Spain. Since Arana's days, radical Basque nationalists have regarded immigrants from other parts of Spain as carriers of the culture of the colonial power (Madrid) and thus impossible to assimilate into Basque culture and society. For Arana, immigrants were "a new Spanish invasion" by a people who were "racially inferior" (Muro 2005: 577). Such attitudes suggest that some Basques "envisage an autonomous Básque state that would be as intolerant of non-Basques as the Franco regime was intolerant of Basques" (Meisler 1977: 204).

The state's response to ETA terrorism

Under Franco, the military spared no effort in attempting to repress the onset of ETA terrorism. So pronounced was the militarization of the Basque Country after 1968 that the region gained the appearance of being an occupied territory. This had the unintended consequence of making real the stated claim of Arana that the Basque Country was a nation militarily occupied by Spain. Underscoring the "occupation" were anti-terrorism laws that applied exclusively to the Basque provinces and that produced some of the most emblematic episodes of political repression of the late Franco era. In the 1970 Burgos trial, 16 ETA members, including two women and two Basque priests, were collectively court-martialed and nine of them were sentenced to death. International pressure spared them their lives. In 1975, despite pleas from the international community, including the Vatican, the Franco regime executed two ETA members and three Communist leaders.

After the transition to democracy in 1977, an amnesty law granted a pardon to all Basques imprisoned for political crimes committed under the old regime. The government also enacted programs for the reintegration into society of ETA members ready to renounce their association with the organization's terrorist activities. These early overtures of reconciliation from the government failed to appease ETA and ushered in the first anti-terrorist legislation of the democratic period. Following the enactment of a new constitution in 1978, laws were passed that expanded the powers of the Guardia Civil to detain and arrest anyone suspected of involvement with terrorism, even if peripherally. This was made possible by the adoption of the very expansive and highly ambiguous definition of terrorism articulated in the 1981 "Law for the Defense of the Constitution." It defined terrorism not only as "any attack on the integrity of the Spanish nation" but also as "any effort to secure independence of any part of the territory, even if non violent" (Clark 1990: 39–47). This led to the arrest and eventual conviction of virtually the entire leadership of HB.

During the 1980s, under the Socialist administration of Felipe González, the government adopted extra-judicial measures to battle ETA, organizing death squads, the Grupos Anti-terroristas de Liberación (GAL), whose main job was to target for assassination ETA's leaders. Interestingly, the GAL's activities tellingly mirrored ETA's own, including placing bombs in commercial establishments used by ETA members, leading to the charge that "in going after the terrorists the Spanish government itself became a terrorist organization" (Encarnación 2007: 969). Over the course of its life (1983–7), the GAL was responsible for 27 assassinations and three times as many injured. About a third of those killed (nine) and an even higher proportion of those injured had no connection to ETA at all. As would be expected, the exposure of the existence of the GAL by the media in the late 1990s created one of the biggest political scandals in Spain's history. The ensuing investigations absolved Prime Minister González of any direct involvement with the GAL's extra-judicial killings, but established clear links between his administration and the death squads. They resulted in the conviction and sentencing in 1995 of several government officials, including two of González's ministers, José Barrionuevo, the Secretary of State for Security, and Rafael Vera, Minister of the Interior.

The discovery of the "dirty war" against ETA brought a new era of counter-terrorism strategies focused mainly on restricting civil and political rights. In 2002, the conservative administration of José María Aznar outlawed any organization that espouses violence, leading to the banning of HB. In 2003, a national court banned *Euskaldunon Egunkaria*, the only newspaper published entirely in Euskera, on grounds that the paper contributed to "the Basque-language information structure, which facilitated the dissemination of terrorist ideology" (MacDonald and Bernardo 2006: 184). Both actions led to denunciations from international human rights organizations, such as Amnesty International (2003), which criticized the Spanish government for restricting freedom of political speech and organization.

The Catalans and the politics of civic nationalism

Notwithstanding the disturbing headlines that it generates, the Basque situation provides a somewhat distorted view of ethnopolitical conflict in Spain. The rest of the Spanish regions have successfully advanced their own project of regional autonomy with Madrid without a single shot being fired. Paradoxically, this is the case of Catalonia, the Spanish region with the longest and most legitimate claim of constituting a nation separate from Spain.[6] Since Catalonia was granted autonomy in 1979, the region has been successfully "re-Catalanized." Nothing suggests this better than the revival of the Catalan language. Once moribund under Franco, today Catalan is a constant presence in the region's media, education, commerce, and, most notably, government. In the view of some scholars, this success makes Catalonia "something of a role model" for other European stateless nations (Crameri 2000: 146).

The successful revival of *Catalanisme* that followed the Franco regime was led by organizations emphasizing autonomy over independence. The most important Catalan party in the post-Franco era is Convergència i Unió (CiU), arguably western Europe's most powerful regional party. Not only does CiU, a center-right party, reject violence as a means of dealing with the central state, but its discourse over home rule is usually couched in the context of greater autonomy for Catalonia vis-à-vis the central state rather than outright independence. "Catalan nationalism is fundamentally different from Basque nationalism. There will never be an ETA associated with our movement," remarked a CiU official around the time of the political transition (Gunther et al. 1980: 188). Accordingly, the Catalans have chosen not to provoke a confrontation with Madrid by demanding outright independence, for fear of inciting a nationalist response from the Spanish state or from the thousands of non-Catalan residents of Catalonia.[7] Instead, they have invested in attaining an ever-escalating degree of local autonomy within the political framework of Spain and the European Union. These strategies are in keeping with the moderate and very pragmatic form of nationalism that consolidated in Catalonia during the nineteenth century and that stands in striking contrast to the radical form of nationalism adopted by the Basques.

The Catalan claim for nationhood is based on the region's proud history as an autonomous principality of the kingdom of Aragón during the Middle Ages and a long history of battling the Spanish central state for independence.[8] In 1640, Catalonia, together with Portugal, declared its independence from Spain. Portugal, aided by its traditional allies, France and England, successfully kept the Spaniards at bay, but Catalonia was reincorporated into the Spanish crown in 1652. Catalan nationalism, however, was hardly squelched, although in the ensuing centuries the goal of Catalan nationalists shifted from outright independence to some type of compromise on home rule from the central state. This change in tactics responded to the recognition by the Catalan political elite of the role of Catalonia in the history and development of Spain (especially its industrial and commercial infrastructure), the very sizable non-Catalan population of Catalonia, especially in Barcelona, and the advantages that accommodation poses to the advancement of the project of Catalan autonomy.

The pragmatic brand of nationalism that developed in Catalonia flourished between about 1840 and 1880, when the region experienced a *Renaixença* or a rebirth of all things Catalan. It saw Catalan emerge as a vehicle for the expression of both high and popular culture as well as the dominant language of the political elites and an expansive bourgeoisie. Even immigrants to Catalonia began to adopt the Catalan language (a process facilitated by the similarities between the Catalan and Castilian languages), if only as a means of advancing social mobility. All of this allowed Catalan nationalism to remain "moderate and broadly united around a cultural platform," much in contrast to the situation in the Basque Country, where a weakly developed and rooted Basque culture encouraged Basque nationalism to keep its "radical separatist posture and its internal fragmentation" (Conversi 1997: 158).

Around the same time that *Catalanisme* was being consolidated, Catalan politicians began to devise ways to transform Spain in a fashion that would accommodate Catalonia's desire for autonomy, leading Catalan politicians to become major figures in national politics in Madrid. Thus, while in the Basque Country the nationalist project was anchored upon attaining independence from Spain, in Catalonia it depended upon gaining control of Spain. During Spain's First Republic, 1873–4, led by its Catalan President Pi Margall, plans were drawn up to turn Spain into a confederation of 13 peninsular and four overseas states, each with its own constitution and with significant control over its own political and economic affairs. This first attempt to federalize Spain never actually got off the ground, since it met with immediate, strong resistance from the military.

In the twentieth century, right-leaning and left-leaning Catalan political parties pursued Catalan projects of autonomy of their own by actively participating in national politics. During the first decades of the twentieth century, the main objective of the Lliga Regionalista, the bourgeois party that dominated politics in pre-Republican Catalonia, was to secure autonomy for Catalonia by allying itself to right-wing, anti-democratic national regimes. The Lliga's involvement in national politics included its support for the dictatorship of General Miguel Primo de Rivera, which ruled Spain during the 1920s and which tolerated the Catalans' aspirations for autonomy, and its active support for the establishment of the Franco regime in 1939. This problematic history, to say nothing of the overt hostility that Lliga leaders demonstrated toward the Second Republic, made it all but impossible for the Lliga to revive itself in Catalan politics in the post-Franco era. Those who revived Catalan nationalism during the 1940s and 1950s viewed the Lliga as "a party that had betrayed Catalonia and its ideology" (Dowling 2001: 19).

During the left-leaning Second Republic, Catalan politicians wasted little time in securing autonomy for their region. In 1931, Esquerra Republicana de Catalunya (ERC), the party that represented the Catalan Republican left and which had replaced the Lliga as the dominant political force in Catalan politics during the Republican era, drew up a statute of autonomy. This document was overwhelmingly approved by the local electorate and by the central government in 1932. Under the stipulations of the statute, the Catalan people were entitled to elect their own president, prime minister, and parliament (the Generalitat). The Catalan language, together with Castilian, was made an official language of the region. This movement toward regional autonomy started by the Catalans inspired similar initiatives by the Basques and the Galicians, but only in Catalonia was home rule fully realized.[9]

Franco's right-wing coup in 1936 dealt a severe blow to the left-wing Calatan project of autonomy erected during the Second Republic. The advent of the Franco regime meant the sudden death of Catalan political institutions such as the Lliga and ERC, and the banning of Catalan language and symbols, including *la senyera*, Catalonia's historic flag. Ironically, sectors of Catalan society such as the Catalan Catholic Church and the business community were critical in facilitating the imposition of authoritarianism in Catalonia by actually supporting Franco's rule. When the Francoist rebellion erupted in 1936, the choice of the Catalan bourgeoisie was "between fidelity to the Catalan nation and its struggle for self-governance and fidelity to class" (Marsal and Roiz 1985: 212). Their decision decisively favored class interests. However repugnant the Catalan bourgeoisie may have found Franco's nationalist *Españolismo*, his regime represented "the restoration of bourgeois order to a society that had become incomprehensible to them" (Dowling 2001: 19). The Second Republic's secular constitution and the regime of terror and assassinations imposed by communists and anarchists had quickly soured Catalan conservatives against the Republican project. In essence, the Catalan bourgeoisie and Catholic Church were willing to sacrifice their autonomy aspirations for the sake of safeguarding their economic and religious interests, which under the Second Republic had come under mortal attack.

Under the auspices of the relative openness of the late Franco period (1959–77) Catalan nationalism began to re-emerge. It rejected the tame, conservative nationalism associated with the Lliga as well as the left-wing, anti-clerical nationalism of the ERC. Instead, it promoted the kind of nationalism associated with Convergència. Anchored on the mobilization of the public on the basis of pride in Catalan culture, this party has been hailed by some as a symbol of "civic" nationalism for the absence of violence in its pursuit of a nationalist identity (Conversi 1997), and derided by others as "banal" for the extent to which nationalist symbols are manipulated for political benefit

(Crameri 2000). Jordi Pujol, President of the Catalan autonomous government from 1980 to 2003, is the architect of modern-day Catalan nationalism. He used his post as head of the Generalitat to promote Catalan culture and language as a means of strengthening Catalan identity. He also endeavored to advance his region's economic position within Spain and the European Union. Especially notable was Pujol's leadership in promoting regional rights within the EU, such as having the organization declare regional languages like Catalan official EU languages, which requires the publication of EU documents in Catalan. And like the pragmatic nationalist leaders who founded modern Catalan nationalism, Pujol used the national political arena to pursue Catalan autonomy. This he did most blatantly and effectively between the years of 1993 and 2000, when he became the ringmaster of Spanish politics by providing support to the two major national political parties: the PSOE between 1993 and 1996, and the conservative PP between 1996 and 2000.

Decentralizing Spain

Spain's first democratic government in the post-Franco era came into office believing that both the survival of democracy and the nation's geographic integrity were contingent upon the successful decentralization of the state. But Prime Minister Suárez made it clear that only a properly constituted democratic political system, anchored upon the enactment of a new democratic constitution, could legitimately deal with the task of reforming the state. To signal his commitment to regional governance, and by extension to the decentralization of the state, immediately following the 1977 elections, Suárez authorized the restoration of the Catalan parliament (the Generalitat). Although the powers granted to this body were very limited (in fact, they were largely symbolic), its resuscitation represented a huge first step toward advancing regional autonomy in Spain. The Catalans presented an ideal scenario for the introduction of regional home rule because, as seen already, in contrast to the Basque Country, violence is not an important component of Catalan nationalism. During the democratic transition this legacy of political pragmatism was fully embodied in the figure of Josep Tarradellas, the president-in-exile of the Catalan government. A politician whose political background dated back to the Second Republic, Tarradellas represented continuity with Spain's democratic past and Catalonia's history of accommodation with the central state.

Among the many virtues of Suárez's approach to handling the complex issue of regional autonomy – especially his insistence that elections and the writing of the constitution precede the decentralization of the state – was ensuring that by the time the nation undertook the process of devolution of powers to the regions, the authority of the central state was legitimized by a popularly elected government and a new constitutional framework, thereby ensuring that democratization and decentralization would prove mutually reinforcing. In this way, Spain averted a Yugoslavia-type scenario in which regional agendas, elections, and institutions were allowed to submerge and undermine national institutions and political processes. By contrast, in Spain, by the time regional identities and institutions began to assert themselves politically and challenge the new political regime, the country had successfully created "legitimate state power with the authority and capacity to restructure the polity" (Linz and Stepan 1996: 99).

A federal or unitary state?

The new democratic constitution of 1978 opened the way for the creation of Spain's system of regional governance. Article 2 of the constitution allows for the possibility of regional autonomy, a first in Spanish constitutional history, in accordance with a process requiring a region-wide referendum and the negotiation of an *estatuto de autonomía* (autonomy charter) between the central government and the region clamoring for self-rule. It is important to note that the constitution does not include a list of the regions entitled to self-governance, although it makes reference to Catalonia, the Basque Country and Galicia as constituting "nationalities" within the Spanish national territory. This, in essence, introduced the novel and radical conception of Spain as a "nation of nations." The constitution also offers broad protection to symbols of regional culture – regional languages in particular. Recognition of a distinct linguistic heritage is, after all, at the center of the argument of the "historic" regions for having a different nationality from the rest of Spain.

Article 3 of the constitution declares Castilian the official language of the Spanish people but acknowledges the existence of other Spanish languages. The use of the word "Castilian" rather than "Spanish" in the constitution is very studied, since it is ostensibly meant to convey the sense that Castilian is just one among other Spanish languages. The constitution, however, does not aspire to give regional languages the same status as that granted to the Castilian language. This gives rise to the argument that "Spain could be considered to be closer to a monolingual nation-state than to a proper multilingual state" (Costa 2003: 416). The Spanish constitution notes the "duty" of all Spaniards to know Castilian and specifies that the status of "official" language for the regional languages is limited to the region's own territorial space, and not the nation as a whole. In effect, this ensures a dominant status for the Castilian language within the Spanish territory as well as a minority status for the regional languages.

The system of regional governments created in Spain is unusual in many respects. Although it looks strikingly similar to federalism, in reality it is not. This accounts for descriptions of Spain as "an imperfect and incomplete federation," "a hybrid system of regionalism and federalism," a "covertly federal state," "a state based on the right of self-government for which time alone will provide the final definition," and "non-institutional federalism" (Encarnación 1999: 96). Certainly, federal states come in a variety of institutional guises, but Spain does not meet the most important criteria found in federalist systems generally regarded as prototypes. This was no accident, since the architects of the new democracy, very mindful of Spain's explosive history with federalism, studiously avoided constructing a federal system of governance (see chapter 3). Indeed, references to the nation as a "federation" or a "confederation" appear nowhere in the new Spanish constitution. The main objective of this purposeful omission of the terminology associated with federalism was to avoid offending or antagonizing the political forces that have historically opposed the federalization of the country, especially the military and other allies of the Franco regime.

More important, key institutional features of federalism are conspicuously absent from Spain's system of regional governments. In the first place, the new constitution does not afford the regions direct participation in decision making at the central level. Unlike the situation in most federal states, such as the United States, Germany, Mexico, and Brazil, Spain's autonomous communities are not constitutionally empowered to reform the constitution. Nor do they have control over so-called remaining powers, as is customary in federal states. Spain's taxation system is also at odds with that usually found in federal states. The central state in Spain collects nearly all taxes and then distributes the revenue to the regions according to a complex formula that takes into consideration the size of the region, its per capita income, the number of provinces included in the region, and the range of responsibilities delegated by the central government to the region. This type of tax collection and distribution stands in contrast to the norm in federal systems, where spending by each state is financed by the taxes it collects from its own residents.

Another feature of federalism missing from the Spanish model is an elected chamber (usually the Senate) with political representation based on the regions' territorial boundaries. Instead, political representation in the Spanish Senate is assigned according to provinces. Conservative politicians worked hard to make this a part of the nation's electoral law before the formal dismantling of the Franco regime, with the intention of undermining the development of regional identities in Spain. This representational scheme continues to give Spain a strong unitary character despite the significant degree of state decentralization experienced by the nation in the post-Franco years. Also peculiar to the Spanish experience is that the distribution of powers among the regions (quite in contrast to federalism) is highly asymmetrical in structure. The 17 regions of Spain do not enjoy the same degree of self-government, as some have been granted special privileges by the central state that are denied to others. An autonomy charter negotiated directly between the central state and each individual region rules the relationship between Madrid and the regions. It stipulates the scope of self-rule authorized by the central government and allows for periodic revisions as petitioned by regional authorities. As would be expected, the "historic" regions (Catalonia, the Basque Country, and Galicia) enjoy the highest degree of autonomy whereas the new regions generally tend to possess the least. Among the historic regions, the Basques are accorded special privileges such as the right to have their own police (*ertzaintza*) and collect taxes. These provisions have endowed the Basque Country with "the highest level of regional self-governance in the European Union" (Mata 2004: 82).

The asymmetrical nature of regional governance in Spain is owed to the fact that it did not develop in any kind of coherent fashion. Mindful of history's lessons, there was no master plan or philosophy to guide the politicians as they undertook to decentralize the state, as had been the case during the First and Second Republics. Instead, they made it up as they went along. The decentralization of the state evolved over a number of years beginning with the granting of self-governance to Catalonia, the Basque Country and Galicia. These regions gained home rule in 1979 through the "fast-track" route because of the speediness with which their autonomy charter with the central government was negotiated. The rest of the regions were created via the "slow-track" route.[10] This process entailed a local referendum, approval by the national parliament, and a gradual transfer of administrative powers.

The granting of self-governance to the historic regions (Catalonia, the Basque Country, and Galicia) unleashed multiple regionalist projects from regions of Spain that lacked any history of nationalism, such as Andalusia, Murcia, and Valencia. Such projects have involved not only seeking autonomy, as in the case of the historic regions, but also turning dialects into languages ("Valencian" in Valencia, "Asturian" in Asturia, and "Aragonese" in Aragón) and creating newly minted nationalist symbols, most notably a regional flag (see Gimeno Martínez 2006). Other regions were created as some provinces chose to pursue autonomy projects by breaking away from their traditional cultural–historical regional environment. Cantabria, La Rioja, and the capital city of Madrid, which today functions as some sort of federal district, are all historically parts of Castile.

ASSESSING THE "STATE OF THE AUTONOMIES"

Judging by the degree to which the state has been decentralized, it is easy to declare Spain's *autonomías* system a success. By 1982, the right to petition for regional self-government had led to the establishment of 17 autonomous communities in Spain.[11] This process of devolution of powers to the regions has left a detectable impact on the structure of the central state. It is estimated that, by 1985, 300,000 functionaries of the central government had been transferred to the regions, and that by the end of that year all but a few regional governments had received the full measure of the competencies granted to them by the central state (Shabad 1986: 112).

Another measure of success of the *autonomías* system is the palpable effect it has had in shaping the dynamics of the politics of terrorism. To be sure, home rule has not satisfied ETA, which demands nothing short of outright independence from Spain, but it has undermined ETA's campaign to portray the Spanish state as a colonial oppressor (a goal of ETA since its inception) and to turn the Basque people against Spain. This, in turn, has prevented the conflict in the Basque Country from becoming one between the central government and ordinary Basque people, rather than a conflict between the central state and radical Basque nationalists. A majority of the Basque electorate approved the autonomy statute in 1979 and public opinion data suggest that the Basque public has remained supportive of the statute ever since. This point is highlighted in the data from the Euskobarómetro, a polling survey at the University of the Basque Country that traces public opinion among the Basque population.[12] The 2003 data reveal that 30 percent of Basques say that they are "satisfied" with the present stipulations of the statute, 40 percent are "partially satisfied" (and presumably would like to see it expanded), and 25 are "dissatisfied." As to political status preferences, 32 percent express support for the status quo (autonomy), 35 percent prefer a federal state, and 30 percent prefer independence. Clearly, the preference of the Basque people for some sort of affiliation with Spain is overwhelming.

More important is the decline in popular support for ETA since the advent of self-governance. As seen in other countries, the success of terrorist organizations with respect to their longevity and ability to provoke the state into repressing society (and hence restricting democracy) is linked to their capacity to cultivate support among the public. When such support materializes, political loyalties shift away from the central state and toward the terrorist organization. But this has not been the case in the Basque Country. Quite the opposite: according to data from the Euskobarómetro, total rejection of ETA among ordinary Basques increased from 23 percent in 1981 to 60 percent by 2003. To be sure, multiple factors account for this significant decline in support for ETA, including, most notably, people's weariness with the violence being spewed by the organization, especially since the terrorist attacks on the United States in 2001 and Madrid in 2004 (see Encarnación 2007: 971). But self-governance has made a difference as well, as seen in the failure of ETA's political agenda to gain almost any traction with the Basque people. Total support for ETA's political agenda dropped from 8 percent in 1981 to 1 percent in 2000. It has remained stuck at 1 percent ever since.

The dark side of regional autonomy

Notwithstanding its contribution to democratic stability in the post-Franco era, the system of regional self-governance has not been a panacea. In the first place, there is the enormous expense involved in administering the additional layers of government created by the regional governments, including a dramatic increase in the number of civil servants. According to a report by the Real Instituto Elcano (Chislett 2002: 72), close to 120,000 fewer civil servants worked for the central government in 1999 than in 1990, while the number employed by regional and local governments increased by 165,000 and 125,000, respectively. This means that for every civil servant who stopped working for the central government, two posts were created at regional and local levels. The expansion of regional governments has also put a burden on the national debt. The debt of regional governments rose from 2.7% of GDP in 1984 to 9.8% in 2001. There has also been a sharp rise in extra-budgetary debt. While the number of state companies has fallen dramatically as a result of privatizations, hundreds of entities have been created by regional and local governments. The Elcano report notes that few of these entities respond to social needs; in many cases they only serve to cover a volume of extra-budgetary debt that represents more than 1.5% of GDP.

A more serious problem is the manner in which the advent of regional self-governance has hardened regional identities in Spain. As seen in figure 6.2, regional nationalism is pervasive in both the Basque Country and Catalonia, with the majority of Basques (52.5 percent) thinking of themselves as "Basque" first and foremost, and a minority (11.9 percent) as "Spanish" first and foremost. In Catalonia, the situation is more ambiguous, with 35.9 percent of Catalans thinking of themselves as "Catalan" first and foremost, and 24.9 percent thinking of themselves as Spanish first and foremost. To the extent that the viability of the modern nation-state depends upon the existence of a common set of values that comprise national identity, the prevalence of strong sub-nationalist identities in Spain poses an important challenge for the Spanish nation. These challenges were vividly displayed in the heated debate over the renegotiation of Catalonia's autonomy pact, approved by the Spanish parliament and the Catalan people in 2006. The new document now refers to Catalonia as possessing a "nationality," much to the chagrin of Conservatives and Spanish nationalists, who deem this a prelude to the eventual secession of the region from Spain.

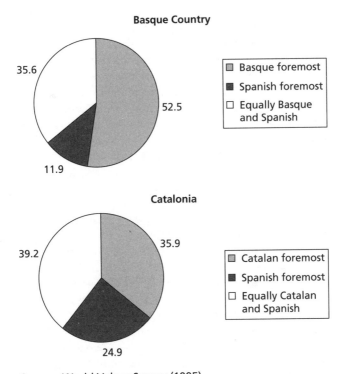

Basque Country

35.6

52.5

11.9

- Basque foremost
- Spanish foremost
- Equally Basque and Spanish

Catalonia

39.2

35.9

24.9

- Catalan foremost
- Spanish foremost
- Equally Catalan and Spanish

Source: World Values Survey (1995)

Figure 6.2 Identity in the Basque Country and Catalonia (%)

Another problem is the emergence of powerful regional parties, not only in the historic bastions of regional nationalism like Catalonia and the Basque Country, but also in Andalusia, the Canary Islands, and Galicia. This makes it difficult for any of the national parties to win a plurality of the vote to form a government without the support of another party. On the surface this appears quite harmless, especially considering how widespread and generally positive the phenomenon of coalition governments has been in the development of democratic politics in western Europe. But in the context of Spain, a coalition government involving regional parties has generally been a cause for concern. As explained by Gunther et al. (2004: 304–5), because of the "open ended nature of the decentralization process" in Spain (ensuing from the absence in the constitution of clear stipulations about the allocation of powers and financial resources between the central state and the regions), participation of regional parties in the national government has often resulted in very unhealthy politics.

Regional parties have often used their political clout to support the national parties and allow them to form a government in exchange for political and economic concessions designed to advance their autonomy projects. At times this has resulted in totally ironic (and almost comic) consequences, such as during the years 1996–2000, when the conservative and anti-regional PP was forced to rely on support from the Catalan, Basque, and Canary Islands nationalist parties to form a government. The PP, whose founding fathers actually opposed the 1978 constitution on the grounds that it was too liberal with respect to the issue of regional autonomy, ended up expanding regional rights in Spain more than any other party previously in government, due to the concessions extracted by the nationalist parties. This form of political blackmail practiced by the nationalist parties diminishes the capacity of the state to implement national policies and to reduce economic disparities among the regions.

Yet another problematic legacy of the advent of regional autonomy is the cultural policies that it has engendered in the various regions, especially those with a unique linguistic heritage. The recognition of regional languages such as Catalan, Galician, and Euskera (the Basque language) as co-official (together with Castilian) within their respective autonomous communities has been a stunning success, at least from the standpoint of reinvigorating moribund linguistic traditions. Most notable is the case of Catalan, the most widely used of Spain's regional languages. In Catalonia, around the time of Franco's death in 1975, 74.3 percent of the population claimed to understand Catalan and 53.1 percent to speak it; by 2001, those percentages had climbed to 97.3 percent and 78.4 percent respectively (Roller 2002: 279). This success in reviving the Catalan language reflects the success of the 1983 "Law of Linguistic Normalization," intended to revitalize the use of Catalan, which led to the creation of Catalan media, including newspapers published in Catalan and television stations broadcasting in Catalan, and a significant number of primary and secondary schools and universities offering instruction in Catalan. Television, in particular, has had a significant impact on the promotion of the Catalan language. It is estimated that by 1990, TV3, the Catalan government-run television station, had captured a 40 percent share of the entire Catalan audience, a big factor in increasing knowledge of Catalan in recent years (Fernández 1995: 344).

The 1983 legislation, however, has not really succeeded in making Catalan the most important language in Catalonia or even in giving it parity with Castilian. Most central government public services in Catalonia, such as judicial proceedings and administrative transactions, continue to be conducted in Castilian; foreign imports such as films largely continue to be shown in Castilian with only 2 percent shown in Catalan (Roller 2002: 280). To further advance the use of Catalan the regional government passed another law in 1997 (the Catalan Linguistic Law) which enhances the rights of individuals to communicate in Catalan with public administration and business, requires public servants working for the regional government to be knowledgeable of Catalan, and regulates the use of Catalan in all non-university institutions, the dubbing of films, television broadcasting, business conducted by subsidized firms, and the labeling of traditional products. With this law Catalan linguistic policy shifted "from an emphasis on education to promotion to regulation" (Roller 2002: 280).

Implementation of the 1997 law has generated a particularly rancorous debate in Catalonia that includes charges of linguistic discrimination and accusations that the regional government is behaving "like Franco but the other way around: persecution of the Spanish in Catalonia" (Costa 2003: 421). The debate has included arguments over the extent to which regional governments in Spain are constitutionally empowered to enforce usage of regional languages. Andalusians residing in Catalonia, for instance, have challenged the constitutionality of the Catalan government's requirement that fluency in Catalan be a condition for employment with the regional government.

Catalan firms that do business all over Spain but also across Latin America have also balked at having to observe the stipulations of the new law. The same goes for powerful international companies active in Spain, such as Hollywood studios that see no point in dubbing their films in Catalan for the relatively small Catalan market. Not surprisingly, the Catalan government has shied away from implementing many of the stipulations of the law for fear of antagonizing powerful business interests. This stance may also reflect recognition of the reality that bilingualism is as much part of Catalan culture as *Catalanismo*, especially in Barcelona, the region's cosmopolitan capital, where Castilian and Catalan have for centuries co-existed with remarkable ease.

Finally, the uneven allocation of powers among the regions is a source of governmental inefficiency and constant aggravation in the relations between the central state and the regions. Duplication of government services is a big problem, since not all the regions are equipped to handle the full range of public services; hence central state agencies must be kept in place "in order to guarantee continuity in the provision of services, even though those services may already be reduced" (Gunther et al. 2004: 308). Understandably, over the years the central state has sought to devise ways of eliminating bureaucratic imbalances across the regions, as a means of facilitating the administration of the system, which was the intent of the ill-fated 1981 Law for the Harmonization of the Autonomy Process (LOAPA). An unexpected constitutional challenge to the law emerged from the historic regions, which contended that a wholesale revamping of the system diluted the special recognition granted to them by the constitution. The country's highest courts agreed with this argument and the LOAPA was never implemented. In the absence of the option of overhauling the system comprehensively, governments from both the left and the right have attempted to bring parity in the level of administrative responsibilities allocated to the regions by upgrading each one of the autonomy charters. Much has been accomplished thus far. At the present time, it is estimated that levels of autonomy are approximately the same across the regions except in the areas of health, security, and taxation (Gunther et al. 2004: 308).

CONCLUSION

Regional nationalisms have historically constituted the central dilemma in Spanish politics, and the transition to democracy has done little to change that. But in comparison to other states that in recent years have undergone democratization while contending with similar challenges, the picture looks decidedly brighter in Spain. Indeed, none of the dispiriting scenarios that we have come to expect when multicultural states undertake to democratize have materialized in Spain. Perhaps the most likely one is the break-up of the nation along ethnic lines once the grip of dictatorship is gone. This may occur through an amicable divorce, as was the case in the former Czechoslovakia, or through a bitter civil war, as was the case in Yugoslavia and more recently Iraq, where the American attempt to democratize the country has triggered a bloody civil war between Sunnis and Shiites. Another typical outcome is a democratic breakdown and the return to dictatorship, probably as a result of a military coup in reaction to the perception that the nation is falling apart. This was, of course, the case in Spain during the interwar years. A more recent common occurrence is the rise of an "illiberal democracy," the consequence of the state's attempt to stamp out the violence ensuing from separatist movements (see Zakaria 2003). The paradigmatic case is post-communist Russia, where the state's struggle against Chechnyan separatists has largely discredited the country's claim to be a democracy by fueling widespread human rights abuses and even attempts to restrict political competition.

Spain's avoidance of these scenarios is due in no small measure to the unorthodox decentralization of the state. The Spanish model of state decentralization stands in contrast to classic federalism characterized by, among other things, an equal distribution of power between the central state and the individual states. This has led, as we have seen, to many descriptions of Spain as an imperfect or incomplete federation. Such characterizations highlight the tension inherent in Spain's system of regional self-governance. But they should not detract from what has actually been accomplished in Spain. The admittedly awkward marriage of the ideology and structures of federalism to deeply entrenched traditions of unitary government has allowed the nation to retain its geographic integrity while providing effective institutional mechanisms for managing ethnopolitical conflict. Along the way, a viable multicultural state has emerged. As noted by Antonio Elorza (1995: 334): "the plural reality of Spain is now mainstream national political discourse."

7

GROWING PAINS: MODERNIZING THE ECONOMY

For good reasons, the post-transition era in Spain is associated with unprecedented economic prosperity and social progress. According to the World Bank, the Spanish economy is today the world's eighth largest, having surpassed Canada's in 2006. More gratifying for the Spaniards are the forecasts that put Spain ahead of Italy (its southern European rival in culture and sports) in per capita income by the year 2009 and perhaps sooner (*Economist*, November 4, 2006).[1] This is a stunning turnaround for a country that through the mid-1970s, and despite the considerable economic gains of the late Franco period, was, by western European standards, a byword for economic backwardness. Spain's rags-to-riches transformation, however, has not been a smooth one – far from it. Considerable "growing pains" have marred the Spanish economic miracle, with none more apparent than a dramatic spike in unemployment.

Under Franco, Spaniards had grown accustomed to near full employment. During the last nine years of the Franco regime (1965–74), the unemployment rate in Spain averaged 1.5 percent, one of the lowest in all of Europe.[2] Perhaps only communist countries had lower rates of unemployment than Spain. But just a few years after the transition to democracy in 1977, a jarring new reality set in with unemployment becoming a fact of life for millions of Spaniards. At the peak of the unemployment crisis in Spain, during the mid-1990s, unemployment reached 24 percent of the active population (more than twice the EU average and a record for an OECD country), or 3.7 million.[3] Such a radical transformation in the unemployment picture provides the impression that the Spaniards traded economic protections under the Franco dictatorship for political freedoms under the new democracy.

An extraordinary confluence of economic, social, and political factors accounts for the dramatic surge in unemployment in Spain, beginning with the fact that with the end of the Franco dictatorship the government was no longer compelled to use employment as a form of economic compensation for the lack of political freedoms. Economic realities rather than political concerns began to govern the labor market. Another culprit was the economic chaos created by the international energy crisis of the early 1970s, whose repercussions on the Spanish economy were nothing short of severe.

Rising oil prices sent hundreds of local firms into bankruptcy, which in turn left thousands of Spaniards jobless. This same reason prompted the return to Spain of hundreds of thousands of Spanish migrant workers from northern European countries, whose economies no longer had use for their services.[4] Structural social factors, such as the coming-of-age baby boomers and the late entry of females into the workforce, added to the rolls of the unemployed by significantly expanding the size of the population actively seeking employment.[5] Last but not least was the massive destruction of jobs occasioned by the program of economic modernization that became a requirement for Spain's admission into the European Economic Community (EEC), which the country joined in 1986. As will be seen later, this program entailed downsizing, selling off, or closing down numerous state-owned enterprises.

Surprisingly, the stratospherically high rates of unemployment prevalent in Spain throughout the consolidation of democracy did not bring about the most typical (and predictable) of political consequences: the erosion of democratic legitimacy. Across the democratizing world, especially in Latin America, Russia, and post-communist Europe, painful programs of structural economic reform similar to those implemented in Spain have taken a high toll on democracy by sapping people's faith in the capacity of democratic governments to improve the quality of their lives (see Przeworski 1991). Although *desencanto* (disenchantment) was widespread in Spain during the 1980s, support for democracy remained solid (see chapter 3). Nor did high unemployment radicalize politics in Spain by fueling the rise of extreme right-wing parties, as was the case across western Europe (see Betz 1995; Eastwell 2000; Encarnación 2004). As seen in chapter 4, extreme right-wing political movements have enjoyed very little electoral success in Spain in the post-Franco era. What explains these outcomes in Spain? As this chapter will show, the answer is to be found in the manner in which the program of economic reform was conceived and implemented.

Generally referred to as "social-democratic" (Bresser Pereira et al. 1993), the Spanish approach to economic reform emphasizes three components: (1) moderation in the introduction of structural change into the economy with the intention of protecting nascent democratic institutions; (2) compensation for those most directly affected by economic change by expanding the welfare state; and (3) "social concertation," or bargaining and consultation involving the government, the national unions, and the leading employers' associations. These orientations in policy making made economic reform in Spain "less of a bitter pill than in other democracies" (Bresser Pereira et al. 1993: 113). More importantly, as this chapter will suggest, they prevented the loss of democratic legitimacy while helping sustain societal support for reforming the economy.

The chapter begins with a review of the economic context of the political transition in Spain, which highlights some of the principal factors that made an overhaul of the economy imperative, including heavily protected state-owned companies, an aging and uncompetitive industrial complex, and a very rigid labor market. It continues with an overview of the implementation of structural economic reforms from 1984 to 2004, years of intense economic change, especially with respect to privatizations, under left-wing and right-wing governments. An analysis of the aforementioned "social-democratic" approach follows, which explains how it interacted with the process of economic reform. The aim is to demonstrate why in Spain radical economic change and its accompanying consequences, most notably high unemployment, did not disrupt the consolidation of democracy. The conclusion considers the challenges facing the Spanish economy, many of them created by its recent successes.

THE ECONOMIC CONTEXT OF THE POLITICAL TRANSITION

The boom years of the late Franco era (see chapter 2) were brought to a screeching halt by the international energy crisis of the early 1970s, thereby ensuring that during the transition to democracy Spain would be in the grip of a deep economic crisis. In 1974, as a consequence of the first oil shock, which saw the price of a barrel of oil quadruple, the nation's bill for imported oil and other sources of energy rose from 72.9 billion pesetas to 225.8 billion, while the share of energy in total exports soared from 13 percent in 1973 to an average of 27.4 percent during the period 1974–8 (Harrison 1993: 26). Rising oil prices sent shockwaves through the Spanish economy, driving hundreds of businesses into financial ruin. This is reflected in the sharp decline in GDP between 1973 and 1979. According to the Instituto Nacional de Estadísticas (INE), GDP fell from 6.7 percent in 1973, to −0.5 percent in 1975, to −1.0 percent in 1979. Other economic indicators further reveal the seriousness of the crisis. Unemployment soared from 2.6 percent in 1974 to 5.7 percent by 1977. Most worrisome was inflation, which in July–August of 1977 ran at an alarming rate of 42 percent.

There were also important domestic roots for the economic crisis, many of them exposed or aggravated by the international challenges that Spain was facing in the mid-1970s. The transition to democracy had complicated the state's management of the economy. As observed by Harrison (2006: 10), during the transition two attitudes toward the economy prevailed: denial – *aquí no pasa nada* (nothing is happening here) – between 1975 and 1976, followed by paralysis – *aquí no puede hacerce nada* (nothing can be done here) – between 1976 and 1977. This meant forgoing taking any aggressive stances on the economy for fear of aggravating a delicate political situation. Internal structural problems placed additional strains on the economy and complicated its recovery. Key among them was an outmoded tax system that gave Spain the lowest level of taxation in all of western Europe. In 1975, the year of Franco's death, tax revenues as a percentage of GDP stood at 19.5 percent, well below the OECD average for that year of 32.7, a performance exceeded by every other OECD member save Turkey (Gunther et al. 2004: 338). The national tax system was also highly regressive with the upper-income Spaniards paying as a percentage of their total income about 50 percent less in taxes than did those in the poorest income bracket (Gunther et al. 2004: 340). Tax evasion was also rampant among Spaniards and rarely prosecuted.

Coming out of the Franco dictatorship, the Spanish economy was among the least competitive and most isolated in all of western Europe; perhaps only Portugal had a more protected economy (Royo 2000: 146). External and internal factors had conspired to create these conditions. By the mid-1970s, the most important sectors of the Spanish economy (textiles, footwear, and shipbuilding) were facing stiff competition from other newly industrialized countries like Brazil and South Korea. These nations had begun to industrialize around the same time as Spain (during the 1960s) but enjoyed the advantage of having a larger and cheaper supply of labor. Keeping up with the likes of Brazil and South Korea, to say nothing of western Europe, would be a daunting challenge given the precarious health of Spain's industrial infrastructure. Notwithstanding the modernization of the state undertaken during the late Franco period, the management of state enterprises had been negatively affected by modes of decision making in which arguments about political interests often trumped economic realities (see Bermeo 1990). Employment in state companies, for instance, was used to keep economic conflict from threatening the stability of the authoritarian regime, giving rise to a tightly regulated labor market. Under Franco it was almost impossible for employers to get rid of anyone; only political reasons were deemed serious enough to merit a job dismissal.

A rigid labor market and a meddlesome state bureaucracy were just the tip of the iceberg of what was ailing Spain's industrial infrastructure. Under Franco, trade barriers in many economic sectors, including energy, banking, and manufacturing, remained high with the intention of protecting local businesses from foreign competition. Virtual state monopolies in the automobile, airline, and tobacco industries (to name just a few) were created. This was largely the result of the state-centered model of industrialization championed for decades by the Franco regime. Spain's engine of industrial production was the Instituto Nacional de Industria (INI), created in 1941 as the National Institute of Autarky, which was responsible for promoting capital formation and creating an industrial infrastructure.[6] By the early 1970s, the INI owned some 70 companies that employed over 215,000 people, primarily in the industrial enclaves of Barcelona, Madrid, and Bilbao (Aceña Martín and Comín 1991: 52). These companies were engaged in a variety of industrial pursuits including aircraft and automobile production, electricity supply, and shipbuilding.

REFORMING THE FRANCOIST ECONOMY

Under Spain's first democratic government of the post-Franco era, headed by Prime Minister Adolfo Suárez and his center-right party UCD (1977–81), the emphasis of economic policy was on firefighting (such as slowing down inflation and stopping the hemorrhaging of jobs) rather than on structural adjustment. In fact, under Suárez, not a single public enterprise was sold or dismantled and employment in the public sector actually expanded, as he generously used the state's economic resources to "mitigate political conflicts," especially those linked to rising unemployment (Bermeo 1994: 602). Suárez nationalized firms that were on the brink of collapse and negotiated directly with the unions and the employers ways to control inflation and promote employment. The 1981 Acuerdo Nacional del Empleo (ANE), signed by all the important economic actors, committed the government to creating 350,000 new jobs in the public sector in an effort to combat the loss of jobs in the private sector (Comisiones Obreras 1989: 103).

Structural reform intended to privatize state-owned enterprises, deregulate financial markets, and make the economy more competitive and capitalist-friendly did not arrive in Spain until the mid-1980s, courtesy of the Spanish Socialist party (PSOE). This was quite ironic. Until the 1977 elections, the PSOE incorporated the "Marxist" label as part of its official description, and, as recently as the 1982 elections, the party ran on a platform that articulated a radical reorientation of the economy. In 1982, the PSOE promised *El Cambio* (the change), an economic plan intended to replace capitalism with socialism in as short a period of time as possible. It emphasized an egalitarian reform of society affecting income distribution, education, health, social security, and housing policy. Its overall make-up largely reflected the influence of the UGT, the PSOE's sister organization within the labor movement. The UGT's most visible influence over the PSOE's electoral program was the promise to create 800,000 jobs during the legislative session, mostly in the public sector (Smith 2000: 121).

To the surprise of many, once in office the PSOE adopted an economic program that called for devaluing the peseta, imposing a tight monetary policy, and, most telling of all, executing an extensive program of industrial reconversion intended to modernize the country's economic infrastructure with an eye toward incorporation into the EEC. Therefore, rather than pushing *El Cambio*, the PSOE introduced an ambitious program of market-driven reform designed to strengthen, not weaken, capitalism in Spain. Structural economic reform in Spain got under way in earnest with the 1984 Law of Reconversion and Reindustrialization, which in a single legislative coup targeted 11 sectors for reconversion, entailing the elimination of 80,000 jobs. This meant laying off one-quarter of the workforce in the steel, shipbuilding, and textile industries (Bermeo with García-Durán 1994: 111). By 1986, the government had sold or dissolved more than 30 enterprises, mostly those belonging to INI, including banks, automobile manufacturers, utilities, energy concerns, and steel mills. Many of the companies sold by the government went to foreign investors eager to partake in Spain's newly liberalized economic environment. The most memorable sale was that of SEAT, the automobile company created by Franco during the heyday of the state's effort to modernize the country, which was sold to Germany's Volkswagen Corporation.

Liberalization of the labor market was another hallmark of the PSOE's plan of economic reform. The general aim was to do away with the job protections created by Franco, arguably the only legacy of the old regime that the Spanish working class truly cherished. This effort centered on passing legislation designed to create a more flexible environment for employers to hire and fire workers. Although stiff opposition from the unions prevented the advent of the dreaded *despido libre* (free dismissal), the PSOE nonetheless managed to alter the Spanish labor market dramatically (Bermeo with García-Durán 1994: 110). In 1984 the government introduced part-time and temporary employment, virtually a novelty in Spain at the time. Prior to the advent of the Socialist administration, temporary contracts were quire rare and part-time employment was ten times less frequent in Spain than in the EEC (López-Claro 1988: 26).

The most obvious reason behind the PSOE's about-face on the economy was to get the nation ready for integration into the EEC. Targeted for 1986, it gave the new incoming Socialist administration a relatively short time (four years) in which to modernize the Spanish economy and make it internationally competitive. Another important factor was the economic team that González put in charge of the economy. The new Minister of Industry, Carlos Solchaga, and the new Minister of the Economy, Miguel Boyer, were the intellectual engines behind the PSOE's new political economy. Their economic thinking, shaped largely by their training at the research tanks of Spain's leading private banks, reflected a decreasing faith in state-centered solutions for dealing with economic downturns. As explained by Solchaga: "no one in the PSOE today thinks that the state by itself can or should design an industrial profile which will bring us out of the economic crisis. This we can only do with more recourse to the market and its general laws" (Bermeo 1990: 149). In pressing these views, PSOE technocrats pointed to what they saw as the failure of France's nationalization policies of the early 1980s, under the Socialist government of François Mitterrand (see Maravall 1997: 148).

In executing its ambitious economic agenda, the administration of Felipe González relied heavily on its institutional strengths. The PSOE enjoyed a clear parliamentary majority (57 percent of seats in the Congress of Deputies) when it enacted legislation that made economic reconversion a reality. This strength was enhanced by the control that González exerted over the PSOE, which became essential for imposing discipline within the party and its allied groups in civil society, such as the labor movement, which only reluctantly agreed to support the government's economic plans. By 1982, it is reported that González had consolidated his control over the party thus allowing for the "subordination" of the party to the government (Gillespie 1989: 420). Also critical to the implementation of the new economic plan was the tenacity and coherence of the economic team behind it. Both Solchaga and Boyer ruled their respective ministries with an iron hand, convinced that Spain's poor economic performance reflected structural problems such as a lack of competitiveness.

A second wave of reforms

Building on the foundation laid down by the PSOE, the Popular Party (PP), which gained control of the government in 1996, introduced a second wave of economic reforms. Arguably the most important area of reform was monetary policy. Under the PP, Spain was made a founding member of the European Monetary Union (EMU), which led to the introduction of a single currency, the euro, in 2002. Although this has entailed the loss of economic sovereignty, and with this the ability to adjust monetary policy to confront local economic crises (a currency devaluation is no longer an option), Spain has benefited greatly from belonging to the "euro zone." With Brussels now dictating monetary policy, the Spaniards have been forced into greater fiscal responsibility (Chislett 2002: 70–1). Spain's general government deficit averaged 4.1 percent of GDP during 1980 and 2000, compared with an OECD average of 3.1 percent. The government's financial balance went from a deficit of 6.6 percent of GDP in 1995 to a balanced budget in 2001 for the first time since democracy had been restored. Over the same period, the average for the euro zone went from a deficit of 5.8 percent of GDP to a deficit of 1.3 percent. "Without the fiscal discipline imposed by Brussels, it is quite likely that such progress would never have been made" (Chislett 2002: 71).

To ensure future fiscal prudence, the PP introduced in 2003 a law of fiscal stability, which abandons deficit financing as one way of paying for public expenditure and seeks to ensure that government accounts always balance or show a surplus. This law is actually stricter than the rule imposed by the EU's Stability and Growth Pact, which allows for a maximum deficit of 3 percent of GDP. The PP also moved aggressively to complete the privatization of the economy begun by the Socialists in 1984. The main target was what remained of the INI, which was tagged for wholesale dismantling. Unlike the first wave of privatizations that took place under the PSOE, which mainly targeted inefficient and/or antiquated companies, the PP sold the jewels among state-owned companies.

Table 7.1 Main macroeconomic indicators in Spain and the EU, 2001–2006

	2001	2002	2003	2004	2005	2006
GDP growth						
Spain	3.6	2.7	3.0	3.2	3.6	3.9
EU	2.0	1.0	1.0	2.0	1.5	3.1
Inflation						
Spain	2.8	3.6	3.0	2.5	3.1	3.4
EU	2.2	2.0	2.2	1.8	1.9	1.9
Unemployment						
Spain	11.8	14.0	13.0	12.0	11	8.6
EU	10.0	8.0	9.0	8.0	8.1	7.0

Sources: OECD, INE, and *The Economist*

Between 1996 and 2004 the PP sold 43 companies, including Telefónica (telecommunications), Endesa (electricity), Repsol (oil), Tabacalera (tobacco) and Argentaria (banking) and 48.5 percent of Iberia, the national airline. Relatively little remains to be privatized in Spain, including Hunosa (coal), RTVE (television and radio), EFE (news service), RENFE (rail), and the postal service. At present the 30 Spanish companies listed in the 2006 *Financial Times*' Top 500 European Companies are in private hands.

Undoubtedly, the balance of Spain's experience with economic reform is positive. For much of the democratic period, the Spanish economy has remained one of western Europe's most vibrant with annual growth rates often outpacing the EU average. GDP growth between 1986 and 1990, during the first phase of reform, averaged 4.5 percent, making the Spanish economy the fastest growing within the EU. Between 1995 and 2000, during the second phase of reform, GDP growth average 3.42 percent, lower than during the late 1980s but significantly higher than the EU average of 2.3 percent. As noted in table 7.1, between 2001 and 2006, while the economy stagnated across the EU, it experienced a boom in Spain with the annual GDP growth rate averaging more than 3 percent. Economic reforms have also increased the competitiveness of the economy, as can be seen in international assessments of "economic freedoms." Arguably the best known is the Heritage Foundation's "Economic Freedom Survey." It ranks countries according to such things as "business freedom," "trade freedom," investment freedom," and "property rights." The 2007 report ranks Spain sixteenth among 41 European countries, well ahead of major economic powers such as France (26), and other southern European nations, such as Portugal (24), Italy (28) and Greece (36).[7]

Severe unemployment, however, remains the dark spot in Spain's economic record in the post-Franco era. As indicated in figure 7.1, the trend in rising unemployment that began in Spain with the democratic transition in the late 1970s had by the mid-1990s reached nearly 25 percent of the active population. The main response of Spanish governments to the unemployment crisis has been to continue to liberalize the labor market in the hope of enticing employers to create more jobs. This strategy has generated mixed results. Although the unemployment rate has decreased significantly since its strato-

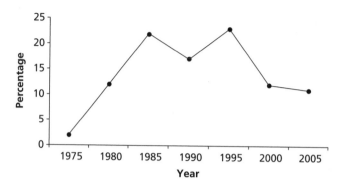

Sources: Instituto Nacional del Empleo (1975); *Anuario El País* (1980–95); *The Economist* (2000–5)

Figure 7.1   Unemployment in Spain, 1975–2005

spheric high in the mid-1990s, coming down by 2006 to within shooting distance of the EU average (8.6 percent for Spain compared to 7.2 for the EU average), this has come at a cost. Liberalization of the labor market has created a second type of employment crisis in Spain: a dramatic rise in the number of people working part-time or on temporary contracts. Temporary and part-time employment in Spain stands at nearly 30 percent for 2004, by far the highest within the EU (*Economist*, June 24, 2004).

The political consequences of economic reform

Structural economic adjustment appears to have had little, if any, negative impact on the process of democratic consolidation in Spain. An extensive study of the government's economic performance and people's sentiments about democracy by Maravall (1997: 95) found that in Spain, "citizens believed that, regardless of the state of the economy or the government's policies, democracy still represented the best political system." Variables like unemployment, personal economic conditions, and the general economic situation accounted for only 1.6 percent in assessing the legitimacy of democracy. Maravall's conclusion (1997: 97) is that in Spain "the legitimacy of democracy was autonomous of efficiency, as citizens considered democracy to be a value in itself and not just a means to an end." More surprising, perhaps, is that the Spanish electorate appears to have exonerated the government responsible for the unemployment crisis created by the restructuring of the economy.

The PSOE, which introduced structural economic reforms in Spain in 1984, repeatedly won national elections between 1982 and 1996, and retained an absolute parliamentary majority until 1993. And even when the PSOE lost vast numbers of votes, the party managed to hang on to its parliamentary majority. This was the case in the 1986 elections, when the unemployment rate had already passed the 20 percent mark. That year the PSOE lost more than 3 million votes but still managed to attain an absolute majority of parliamentary seats. Also revealing is that while in power, and even in defeat in 1996, the PSOE retained significant support from those who one might think would be most likely to defect from the party: the unemployed. According to a study of voting patterns among the unemployed in Spain, during the 1986 elections there existed no difference in the level of support for the PSOE among employed and unemployed, with 48 percent voting for the party in both cases (Maravall 1997: 95). In the 1993 elections, 40 percent of the employed and 35 percent of the unemployed voted for the PSOE, but support for the PSOE was always higher than for the opposition, the conservative PP. During the 1996 elections, the winning party (the PP) received 30 percent of the unemployed vote as against 30 percent for the PSOE.

To be sure, the PSOE's embrace of neoliberal reforms did not come without a political price. The party's about-face on its economic program put the party on a collision course with the national unions that led to a formal split between the UGT and the PSOE in 1988, a terrible blow to the party's social-democratic identity. This high-profile divorce within the socialist family ended more than a century of official affiliation between the Socialist party and the labor movement (see Gillespie 1989). The straw that broke the camel's back was a government plan designed to create 800,000 temporary jobs under a youth employment program, which was opposed by the unions on the grounds that it increased workers' vulnerability and reduced job security. This employment scheme generated calls from union leaders for an all-out assault on the government, which succeeded in bringing the UGT closer than ever to its long-time rival, the CCOO. Both unions joined forces for the first time in the post-transition period to organize the 1988 general strike, an event notable for its anti-government nature. In the aftermath of the strike, the UGT joined the CCOO in calling for a *giro social* (social turnaround), a fundamental reorientation of the government's economic program that demanded the extension of social protections, and a new focus on wealth redistribution and job creation. These actions, coupled with intense strike activity, made Spain one of the most contentious industrial settings in Europe during the late 1980s.

A SOCIAL-DEMOCRATIC APPROACH TO ECONOMIC REFORM

Unique aspects of Spanish society that have traditionally mitigated economic downturns help explain why the high cost of economic reform (especially a record-breaking unemployment crisis) did not complicate the consolidation of democracy by undermining the faith of the public in democratic institutions and practices or by propelling the rise of extremist politics. The most obvious is the vast size of the informal economy. Traditionally one of the largest and most diverse in western Europe, the informal economy in Spain was able to absorb hundreds of thousands of those being pushed out of the "formal" economy.[8] Further softening the blow of high unemployment was the family, which research shows that in Spain, as in other southern European countries, "has a welfare function that works to the benefit of the unemployed" (Bermeo 2000: 274). In Spain, as in Italy, Greece, and Portugal, households embracing several generations are not uncommon, family members tend to live within close proximity to each other, and pensions and other economic resources are often pooled to benefit the entire family. Surely, were it not for these two factors, the unemployment crisis would have been a far more severe hardship than it actually was.

What is most revealing and instructive about the Spanish experience of consolidating democracy while restructuring the economy, however, is how economic reform was designed and managed. This contention echoes the argument that policy-making styles and the intellectual references that guide them matter to the success of economic reform (Maravall 1997: 127). As seen next, two broad factors gave shape to the political economy of democratization in Spain. The first was the highly consensual nature of the democratic transition (see chapter 3), which infused policy making with a significant degree of cooperation between the government and the opposition. This was in keeping with the desire by all the politically significant actors to avoid the divisiveness of the past. The second factor was the economic philosophy of those in charge of the economy. The architects of Spain's post-transition economy shared a strong Keynesian background inherited from the late Franco era (see Gunther 1980; Encarnación 1997), which, combined with the social-democratic orientations of the PSOE, the party that implemented economic reform, made cross-class consensus, the expansion of the welfare state, and direct state investment in the economy policy priorities for the government in the new democracy.

Protecting democracy

The first component of the Spanish approach to economic reform was a concerted effort to protect nascent democratic institutions. As contended by Bresser Pereira et al. (1993: 89), the reason why structural economic reform was delayed under the Suárez administration was the sense that the new democracy was fragile and therefore "not ready to undertake serious economic reforms." This realization translated into a gradual, moderated, and sequenced approach to economic reform. As seen previously, no significant changes were introduced into the Spanish economy until the mid-1980s, nearly a decade after Franco's death. The aim of moving cautiously on the economy was twofold: to allow democracy to gain its institutional bearings and to use economic policy making as an arena to facilitate democratic consolidation.

In shaping his response to the economic crisis that accompanied the transition to democracy, Prime Minister Suárez rejected the advice of many local economists who advocated a comprehensive overhaul of the economy implemented by decree (Encarnación 1997: 406). He also turned down offers of assistance from international financial organizations, like the IMF, because the political price of meeting their demands "might be too high" (Bermeo with García-Durán 1994: 92). Instead, Suárez deferred to the advice of his Vice President for the Economy, Enrique Fuentes Quintana, a highly respected economist with significant credibility with both the left and the right, having influenced an entire generation of Spanish economists from his teaching post at Madrid's Complutense University and as former director of the Bank of Spain. Fuentes Quintana was also an old economic hand from the late Franco era and a leading figure among the cadre of technocrats credited with the economic boom of the 1960s. As such, he was a direct heir to the technocratic tradition of the late Franco period, especially a strong Keynesian orientation that Spanish technocrats borrowed from their counterparts elsewhere in Europe. Keynesianism emphasized a strong role for the state in managing the economy and manipulating state budgets to finance social services and employment, and favored "social contracts" with the labor movement to secure "cross-class" compromises.

The first recommendation that Fuentes Quintana offered to Suárez was that the government's economic program should stress first the most immediate and urgent problems (economic stabilization) and delay structural change (such as industrial reconversion) until a new democratic constitution was comfortably in place.[9] The second recommendation was that economic decision making be backed by a broadly based political consensus. Thus, he impressed upon Suárez the overall utility of a political pact with the opposition while discouraging the imposition of an economic adjustment program by decree. In a policy paper entitled "A Program of Recovery and Economic Reform," Fuentes Quintana warned that only a negotiated approach to economic management could prevent a situation of economic collapse with serious consequences for democracy.[10] Specifically, this position paper highlighted a broad political agreement with the opposition simultaneously to consolidate democracy and stabilize the economy. Fuentes Quintana argued that the complexity of the economic crisis, its political ramifications, and the configuration of political forces that emerged from the elections of 1977 made ordinary adjustment programs either ill suited or inefficient. In his own words (Fuentes Quintana 1980: 155): "it was imperative that the economic program pursued by the government was supportive of the consolidation of democracy and that it possessed a critical quality: it had to be pacted."

Fuentes Quintana's policy advice led to the signing of the Moncloa pacts on October 21, 1977. Brokered by Suárez with the opposition parties outside of parliament to deal with the most pressing economic problems of the democratic transition, these agreements incorporated all the electorally significant parties. In reality, however, the Moncloa pacts were an agreement between the two parties that really mattered in Spain in 1977: the center-right UCD, the governing party, and the PSOE, the leading opposition party. These accords have been described as having "a social democratic quality" (Encarnación 2001a: 363) because they combined economic sacrifices with increases in social protections. The most important component of the Moncloa pacts was a global wage band that dictated salary caps for the nation as a whole as a means of curbing inflation. This practice of tying wages to predicted inflation contrasted with the previous practice of decentralized collective bargaining where past inflation plus productivity was the norm. The wage band incorporated into the Moncloa pacts was rapidly translated into law. It was made obligatory for public enterprises and suggested for the private sector. To compensate for the moderation in wages, the government increased spending on education and housing. To pay for these additional expenses, the pacts introduced a series of tax reforms, such as the elimination of secret bank accounts, increased penalties for tax evasion, and a new wealth tax.

The Moncloa accords and subsequent ones did little to ameliorate the unemployment crisis, but they (as well as subsequent ones) had a very positive impact on the economy, especially in taming inflation. The annual rate of inflation fell from almost 25 percent in 1977 to 14 percent by 1982, and the rate of wage inflation was reduced from 30 to 15 percent (Bermeo with García-Durán 1994: 94). The Moncloa pacts also succeeded in containing industrial conflict in a nation long known for its combative labor politics. Although the number of strikes in Spain remained one of the highest in Europe for the period of 1977 and 1986, the number of days lost to strikes dropped from 16,641.7 in 1977 to 2,279.4 by 1986 (Royo 2000: 103). Another contribution of the Moncloa pacts was a positive impact on business profits. Labor costs have always been an important component of total costs for Spanish business (no less than 60 percent in the 1970s), but as a consequence of the wage moderation scheme built into the Moncloa pacts, that figure had been reduced by 6.4 percent by 1986, and this coincided with the recovery of profits (Royo 2000: 103).

The success of the Moncloa pacts mirrors the support they enjoyed from the left-wing parties and their allies in the labor movement. Although they complained of being blind-sided by the accords, and accordingly declined to sign them, the unions played a significant role in ensuring that the workers adhered to the wage mandate of the accords (see Encarnación 2001a). The socialist UGT and the communist CCOO refrained from mobilizing the workers against the Moncloa agreements, and in the case of the CCOO it agreed to participate in the tripartite commission comprised of representatives from government, the unions, and the employers, which oversaw the implementation of the pacts.[11] This helps explain the extraordinary degree of societal compliance that accompanied what was agreed to by the bargaining agents, especially in regards to wage policy. For instance, in 1978, the first year the Spanish economy operated under the Moncloa pacts, 1,838 collective agreements were signed covering nearly 70 percent of the salaried population. Only in a few isolated cases did these agreements break the wage ceiling imposed by the Moncloa pacts (Encarnación 1997: 411).

The stabilizing effects that the Moncloa pacts brought to the economy meant that in Spain the task of consolidating democracy would not be complicated by the loss of governmental credibility. In 1978, just months after the signing of the Moncloa pacts, the country enacted a new constitution (which, after all, was the primary political goal of the Moncloa pacts, see chapter 3), noted by an extraordinary level of compromise across political lines, and began to undertake the arduous process of decentralizing the state along ethnic and linguistic lines (see chapter 6). Both of these tasks would have been extraordinarily difficult to execute had Spain fallen into hyperinflation during the transition, as was the case in countries like Argentina and Russia. As for economic reform, a legacy of the Moncloa pacts was that by the time the PSOE got around to tackling the reformation of Franco's outmoded economic structures, democracy in Spain was basically on a firm footing. This significantly lowered the political risks of structural adjustment, since the PSOE was not burdened with "the uncertainties of the transition to democracy itself" (Bermeo with García-Durán 1991: 122).

Expanding the welfare state

Coinciding with the beginning of democracy in Spain was a dramatic rise in social spending, which in turn fueled an unprecedented expansion of the welfare state. Both of these developments are critical to understanding why governments in Spain were on the whole spared the voters' wrath at election time, and why the disenchantment with politics experienced during the 1980s did not translate into open disdain for democracy. Despite the significant social and economic progress of the late 1960s and 1970s, spending on education, housing, and public health under Franco as a percentage of GDP remained at third-world levels. As seen in figure 7.2, in 1975, only 9 percent of GDP was devoted to social services in Spain as compared to an EEC average of 24 percent. This meant that critical areas of social services, like education and healthcare,

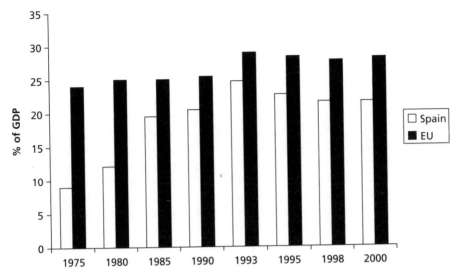

Sources: 1975–85: Gunther et al. (2004); 1990–2000: Ministry of Labor and Social Services

Figure 7.2 Social spending in Spain and the EU, 1975–2000

went largely neglected. By 1977, the Spanish government was still incapable of providing free elementary education for all children (Gunther et al. 2004: 339). Through 1982, an estimated six million Spaniards had no access to public health (Kennedy 2001: 55).

By the mid-1990s, two decades after Franco's death, government spending on social services had been significantly transformed. In 1995, public sector spending in Spain was almost 50 percent of GDP, of which outlays on the welfare state (pensions, unemployment benefits, health, education, housing, and other services) accounted for around half, in line with the European average (Kennedy 2001: 55). This translated into free healthcare for everyone and the extension of minimum pension rights to the entire Spanish population. The effect of this dramatic expansion in the welfare state in Spain is most strikingly suggested by looking at the number of people benefiting from it. In 1992, the national healthcare system covered 9,644,000 more people than it did in 1977, and 1,885,507 more students received secondary or higher education in 1992 than in 1975 (Maravall 1997: 98).

A desire to catch up with the rest of Europe, a stance shared by centrist (UCD), liberal (PSOE), and conservative (PP) administrations, is the most obvious explanation behind the expansion of the Spanish welfare state in the post-transition era. Although correct, this explanation obscures a close connection between social spending and the willingness of the government to compensate those most adversely affected by the radical changes being introduced into the economy. This point is underscored by looking closely at social spending under the PSOE between 1982 and 1996, when policies of economic restructuring were taking a huge toll on the national unemployment picture. The amount spent on unemployment benefits by the PSOE more than doubled to 4.8 as a percentage of GDP between 1983 and 1994 (Kennedy 2001: 55). This expansion in unemployment benefits served to underwrite the creation of "elaborate compensation schemes" specifically designed to ameliorate the effects of economic modernization (Bermeo with García-Durán 1994: 113). Workers who lost their jobs because of industrial reconversion were, under some conditions, given three years of unemployment subsidy; those who lost their jobs after age 55 were given benefits indefinitely. The parts of the country hardest hit by the closing or selling of state-owned firms were given tax deductions, investment subsidies, and special assistance to help out the unemployed population, including job training and retraining.

Social spending under the PSOE, especially in connection to the creation of compensation programs for the unemployed, is a telling reminder of the party's ideological roots. Clearly, the PSOE's embrace of economic neoliberalism did not imply a rejection of the welfare state. Nor did this embrace dampen the party's commitment to wealth redistribution. PSOE leaders, especially those with links to the unions, were convinced that those most directly affected by the transformation of the economy deserved something in return for their sacrifices. These perspectives are often overlooked by the more dramatic and sexier story of a Socialist administration embracing economic policies usually associated with conservative parties. But, as contended by Maravall (1997: 127), the program of economic reform implemented in Spain by the PSOE "is clearly distinguishable from non-socialist ones."

The PSOE's commitment to the expansion of the welfare state was felt well beyond Spain's national boundaries, a remarkable happening given that for much of the 1980s and 1990s such policies were either unpopular or in retrenchment elsewhere. The dramatic expansion in social welfare that took place in Spain was financed largely by González's skillful diplomacy within the EEC, which translated into billions of ecus and euros for Spain. González was the biggest proponent of the creation of a new European cohesion fund designed to promote social spending and economic development in the less developed parts of Europe. According to a study by Kennedy (2001: 53–4), in the year of its inception (1992), Spain obtained over half of the 15 billion ecus initially slated for the fund, with the remaining moneys going to Portugal (18 percent), Greece (18 percent), and Ireland (9 percent). In the same year the cohesion fund was established, the EU doubled the money going to the structural funds, of which Spain also received the lion's share, almost 35 million ecus, between 1994 and 1999, over half as much as the second recipient, Germany, which received almost 22 million ecus to support reunification efforts. In all Spain obtained 27 percent of the EU's aid programs between 1994 and 1999, making it the largest recipient during this period.

Engaging civil society

Building upon the cross-class cooperation embedded in the 1977 Moncloa pacts, democratic governments have developed a regime of "social concertation," or consultation and negotiation between the state and economic actors in society, to give an aura of consensus to Spanish public policy. It is a hallmark of policy making in the post-Franco era. Whereas the various accords of the Moncloa pact were negotiated among the national political parties, hence the usual description of this pact as "political,"

Table 7.2   Social pacts in Spain, 1977–1986

Agreement	Duration	Participants	Content
Moncloa accords	1977–8	Government and leading opposition parties	Wage policy, social policy, tax reform
Basic Inter-confederate Agreement (ABI)	1979	CEOE, UGT	Labor relations
Framework Inter-confederate Agreement (AMI)	1980–1	CEOE, CCOO, UGT	Wage policy
National Employment Agreement (ANE)	1982	CEOE, UGT, CCOO, government	Wage policy
Inter-confederate Agreement (IA)	1983	CEOE, UGT, CCOO	Wage policy
Social and Economic Agreement (AES)	1985–6	CEOE, UGT, government	Wage policy

Table 7.3   Social pacts in Spain, selected, 1994–2005

Agreement	Duration	Participants	Content
Inter-confederate Agreement to Regulate Labor Ordinances	1994	CEOE, UGT, CCOO	Labor relations
Agreement for the Resolution of Labor Conflict	1996	CEOE, CCOO, UGT	Labor relations
Agreement on Pension Reform	1996	CEOE, UGT, government	Pension reform
Tripartite Agreement for Professional Training	1996	CEOE, CCOO, UGT	Professional training
Inter-confederate Agreement for Employment Stability	1997	CEOE, UGT, CCOO	Reduction of temporary contracts
Inter-confederate Agreement on Collective Bargaining	1997	CEOE, UGT, CCOO	Collective bargaining regulations
Agreement to Increase Minimum Social Security Pensions	1999	CEOE, UGT, government	Pension reform
Pact for the Prevention of Labor Risks	1999	CCOO, UGT, government	Workplace safety
Agreement on Pensions and Social Protection	2001	CCOO, UGT, government	Pension reform
Inter-confederate Agreement for Collective Bargaining	2001–5	CEOE, CCOO, UGT	Wage bargaining

subsequent pacts have involved direct participation by the nation's leading unions and employers, and are therefore generally referred to as "social." Tables 7.2 and 7.3 detail the social pacts generated by the process of social concertation in Spain from 1977 to 2004. They reveal that despite the often-volatile relationship among the main social actors, especially between the government and the labor movement, these social agreements have succeeded in bringing a strong sense of cross-class cooperation to Spanish labor and industrial relations, as suggested by the dazzling array of social and economic matters that they have covered, including incomes policy, labor and industrial policy, and pensions systems. Not surprisingly, the social pacts are generally credited with aiding the governing of the Spanish economy in multiple ways (Encarnación 1997; Maravall 1997; Royo 2000).

One of the earliest contributions of the process of social concertation was the normalization of industrial and labor relations following the dismantling of Franco's vertical syndicate. This was the subject of the 1979 *Acuerdo Básico Interconfederal* (ABI), which established the basic legal framework for the enactment of a Workers' Charter, something akin to a bill of rights for Spanish workers. Subsequent accords intensified labor's participation in social concertation and, by extension, in the national policy-making process. As a result of this, the labor movement, an actor that has traditionally remained on the margins of Spanish politics, has been given an official platform from which to influence policy. Indeed, elevating the role of the labor movement in Spanish politics is one of the most significant developments to come out of social concertation. As noted by one analyst, through the social pacts the unions "have been granted a degree of power in the realm of government policy formulation that would generally not evolve from the normal collective bargaining process" (McElrath 1989: 170).

Social concertation can also be credited with facilitating the market-oriented economic reforms introduced in the mid-1980s, even though the social pacts themselves had little to say about such things as privatizations. The closest that any social pact negotiated by the PSOE came to dealing with economic reform was the 1985 *Acuerdo Económico y Social* (AES). Negotiated with a view to getting the economy ready for incorporation into the EEC, it dealt primarily with how to mitigate the adverse consequences of economic reform, such as unemployment. However, the impact of social pacts in facilitating the acceptance and implementation of the various reforms should not be dismissed. They were crucial for attaining the goals of economic reform by creating a climate of negotiation with representative institutions that made more acceptable the measures adopted unilaterally by the government (Przeworski 1991: 187; Encarnación 1997: 405). This point is recognized even by those opposed to the policies of the Socialist government. José M. Zufiaur, a noted UGT labor leader, has observed that: "The social pacts served to blunt the impact of reform since the rhetoric of negotiation and pact-making served to convey the message that the government and the unions were in agreement on the subject of economic reform."[12]

Despite the organizational weaknesses of the social partners, especially the national unions, which historically have been fractured by ideological differences (see chapter 5), social concertation in Spain has shown remarkable resilience. Although the system of social pacts collapsed altogether in 1986, it was revived a decade later; more significant, perhaps, is that the social pacts span political administrations from the left and the right. The return of social concertation in the mid-1990s under the Aznar administration is especially surprising, since conservative or right-wing parties are not known for their affinity toward concertation, usually due to their aversion to having to negotiate with the unions. Yet in Spain social concertation enjoyed a robust run under the PP. Among the reasons that can be cited for Aznar's support of social concertation is the value that politicians of all political stripes have placed on consensus in the making of public policy in the post-Franco era. Of course, while implementing its controversial policies of economic modernization, the PSOE had just about done away with consensus altogether, which explains the absence of social pacts in Spain from 1986 and 1996. But for the upstart PP, skirting consensus was probably not an option. The right regained power in Spain in 1996 with an obvious "democratic legitimacy deficit," given the close association of so many of its leaders with the old regime (Hamann 2005: 70). Thus, once in power again the right was careful not to appear extremist in any of its political or economic policies, for fear of being branded authoritarian.

Whatever the case, social concertation under a conservative government in Spain evolved in interesting ways. First, there are significant similarities between the ways in which social concertation has been organized under the PSOE and the PP. The most obvious is the non-institutionalized nature of the bargaining process. From its very inception with the Moncloa accords, social concertation in Spain has lacked much of an institutional framework. There is no formal bargaining institution in which to organize participation of the unions and the employers in the policy-making process. The Social and Economic Council, envisioned in the 1978 constitution to organize cooperation among the state, capital, and labor, has never been fully articulated due to a seeming lack of interest from all parties concerned. The absence of a formal bargaining framework makes for a very unpredictable and unstable bargaining process. This means, for one, that social pacts take place sporadically: in some years there are social pacts, in others there are not. Participation in the agreements also tends to vary. In some instances the government chooses to sign the accord, while in others it is just as happy to stay behind the scenes and leave the unions and the employers to sign the pact.

Among the differences, the most obvious is the broader range of subjects negotiated by the social partners under the PP. The social pacts negotiated under the PSOE focused largely on wage policy; under the PP, by contrast, they covered pension reform, part-time employment, professional training, and workplace safety. Under the PP, the bargaining process also appears to have developed greater coherence and stability, at least as suggested by the larger number of social pacts negotiated. Finally, it could be argued that the social pacts negotiated after 1996 have been more successful than those of the early democratic years, at least from the perspective of contributing to the social peace. There is less complaining from the unions about unkept promises, a central reason for the collapse of social pacts in the mid-1980s.

Spain in the Global Economy

Having overcome decades of backwardness and isolation, Spain seems poised to take its place as one of Europe's economic engines. Indeed, Spain's climb to the rank of the world's eighth largest economy has generated calls for Spanish membership into the "Group of Eight," the exclusive club of the world's leading industrial powers. Significant challenges loom ahead, however. For all of the progress that the Spanish economy has made since the democratic transition, important questions about economic sustainability and disparities with other EU countries remain outstanding. Most notable are the very shaky foundations underpinning economic growth in Spain. The vibrancy of the Spanish economy in recent decades is owed largely to a construction boom, an inflated housing market, and extraordinarily high levels of private consumption (110 percent of the available income) (Royo 2007: 10). Spain lags the EU average in a variety of key indicators, from spending on research and development (1.05 percent of GDP, less than half of the European average), to a productivity rate that from 1994 to 2003 placed the country next to last among OECD countries (Royo 2007: 10).

Less evident about Spain are the problems posed by the unintended consequences of its economic success. The most obvious is the shifting economic position of Spain within the EU. Since its accession into this body, Spain has been the principal beneficiary of its structural and cohesion funds, moneys allocated to the poorest regions in Europe for the purposes of evening out economic disparities across Europe. By 2006, Spain's annual share of structural funds had reached 8.4 billion euros, making a total of more than 65 billion euros since 1986 (*International Herald Tribune*, December 6, 2006). The impact of European aid on the overall well-being of the Spaniards is hard to ignore. Spanish GDP per capita is currently 98.2 percent of the EU average compared with 74 percent when it joined in 1986 (*Economist*, June 24, 2004).

The full incorporation of new members from eastern and central Europe is likely to have a deep impact on Spain with the country becoming for the first time a net contributor rather than a net beneficiary of European regional funds. The combined GDP of the first ten new members, with a total population of 105 million (two and a half times that of Spain and 28% of the EU-15), is not much larger than Spain's, but their per capita GDP, in purchasing power parity terms, is only 34% of the EU average – much lower than Spain's when it joined the EU (Chislett 2002: 75). If there is no change in the current eligibility criteria, after the incorporation of eastern and central Europe, Spain is likely to have only three regions (Andalusia, Extremadura, and Galicia, "by the skin of their teeth") that will qualify for European funds (Chislett 2002: 76). No longer Europe's poor man, Spain will now have to learn to do with less help and with a lot more sharing.

A more dramatic consequence of Spain's economic success is immigration. In the last two decades, the country has become a magnet for immigrants, encouraged largely by a booming economy and a relatively open-door policy (see chapter 9). This is quite a novelty for Spain, which historically has been an exporter rather than an importer of migrants (see Encarnación 2004: 175). Spain's emergence as a major gateway for immigrants has been quite fast, as suggested by the data from the Migration Policy Institute (2003).[13] During the early 1980s, the increase in the number of immigrants was rather moderate, averaging 2 percent annually. Between 1985 and 1991, however, the foreign population of Spain soared, rising on average 7 percent per year, and by 1992 annual increases had jumped to over 10 percent. By the early 2000s, as seen in figure 7.3, Spain was outpacing other industrialized nations in the annual growth of its immigrant population. The most recent figures from the OECD (2006) put Spain's foreign-born population at 11 percent of the country's 44 million population, one of the highest proportions in western Europe, and quite close to the American rate of 12.9 percent. Between 25 and 35 percent of Spain's immigrants are estimated to be living and working in the country illegally, with the majority of them coming from Ecuador, Morocco, and Romania, representing, respectively, the three main exporting regions of immigrants to Spain: Latin America, North Africa, and the former Soviet bloc.

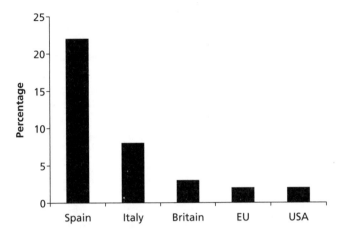

Source: OECD as reported in *Business Week* (May 21, 2007)

Figure 7.3 Annual growth in Spain's immigrant population, 2000–2005

Thus far, immigration has been a boon for the Spanish economy. As seen previously, economic growth in the last few years has outpaced that of other EU economies. As would be expected of a country receiving mass migration for the first time in the midst of an economic boom, most immigrants in Spain work in areas of the economy for which there is very little local labor: agriculture, domestic service, and construction. Interestingly enough, Spaniards generally perceive employment in these areas as reserved almost exclusively for foreigners. This is especially true of returned Spanish immigrants who once toiled at precisely the same kinds of jobs as immigrants in northern Europe. The fact that immigrant labor is almost exclusively tied to low-skilled jobs also explains why in Spain, in contrast to other European countries and the United States, "the government faces a limited amount of resistance to undocumented migration by its citizens due to perceived job competition" (Sammers 2001: 140). Immigrants are doing all the jobs that the Spaniards are simply unwilling to do. As the American business magazine *Business Week* (May 21, 2007) put it, "besides providing muscle for construction, immigrants care for children and the elderly, allowing more Spanish women to take jobs outside the home. They do backbreaking agricultural work and take minimum-wage positions in restaurants and hotels."

As long as the economy continues to grow and migrant labor is restricted to low-skilled and low-paying jobs, immigration in Spain is unlikely to pose much of a problem. But what is likely to happen in the event of an economic downturn and as immigrants begin to compete with native Spaniards for better-paying jobs is a cause for concern. Anxiety about immigration is already bubbling in Spain. Public opinion surveys conducted by the Centro de Investigaciones Sociológicas (CIS) reveal that 53.8 percent of Spaniards think there are already too many foreigners in Spain, and almost 60 percent believe that immigration and insecurity are closely related. Not surprisingly, anti-immigrant violence is already a reality in Spain (see Encarnación 2004).

One of the most disturbing incidents of anti-immigration violence in recent memory in western Europe took place in 2000 in the small Andalusian village of El Ejido. Reports that a Moroccan immigrant with a history of mental illness had stabbed a Spanish woman to death unleashed a wave of reprisal violence against the local Moroccan immigrant community that left some 50 people injured. Local gangs also torched the homes, bars, and mosques of immigrant workers and vandalized the office of the local NGO that provided legal and social services. More disturbing still, the local police and governments stayed on the sidelines as immigrants were attacked and their property was looted allowing the violence and unrest to persist for days.

Conclusion

Seen from a global perspective, the most striking thing about the Spanish political economy of democratization is how radically it departs from the "Washington Consensus," the policy framework designed by Washington-based organizations (the IMF, the World Bank and the US Treasury) to advise countries on how to deal with the conundrum of consolidating democracy while attempting to restructure an outmoded and stagnant economy (see Williamson 1994). Relying on "shock therapy," a "big bang," or a "sneak attack" in the implementation of such policies as fiscal discipline, financial and trade liberalization, and the privatization of state-owned companies, this approach requires the government to adopt quasi-authoritarian powers to see the reforms executed and to exclude actors from society (the unions, for example) from the decision-making process, for fear of corrupting its coherence. Underpinning the logic of the architects of the Washington Consensus is that democratic transitions create a unique political environment for introducing bold and comprehensive economic change. As seen already, little of what the Washington Consensus recommends was part of the Spanish experience with economic reform. In fact, Spain's "social-democratic" approach stands in almost complete opposition to what the Washington Consensus recommends.

Time has proved the Spanish approach right, and the Washington Consensus, if not wrong, highly problematic. In recent years, Washington Consensus prescriptions have become a byword for political discontent and economic trauma.[14] Not surprisingly, the "new" consensus, the "Santiago Consensus," named after the Chilean city where it was forged in the late 1990s, advises a policy-making style strikingly similar to that adopted by the Spaniards. It acknowledges the importance to the success of economic reform of stable governance, the rule of law, and direct engagement of representative institutions and civil society organizations. These strategies are seen as critical for safeguarding the stability and legitimacy of democracy, and for guaranteeing that the economic reform effort will itself gain traction within society.

8

Awakened Ghosts: Memory and Politics

"The past is never dead; in fact, it is not even past" is a famous saying by the Nobel prize-winning American novelist William Faulkner that perfectly suits the current state of the politics of memory in Spain.[1] Nearly three decades since the Spaniards consciously sought to bury the memory of past political excesses with the so-called *Pacto del Olvido* (Pact of Forgetting), one of the pillars of the democratic transition, in a sort of poetic justice the past has come back to haunt them by becoming one of the most contentious issues in Spanish politics. The "return" of the past is intimately associated with the Socialist administration of José Luis Rodríguez Zapatero. Upon entering office in 2004, Zapatero authorized funds for the exhumation and reburial of thousands of bodies of individuals killed by Franco's Nationalist army in the civil war, giving literal meaning to the phrase "digging up the past." Legislation approved by the Spanish parliament on October 31, 2007 calls for the investigation of all claims of human rights violations by victims and survivors of the Spanish Civil War. This law also offers compensation for those exiled, jailed, and forced into labor camps by the Franco regime, and sets guidelines for the removal from public view of monuments honoring Franco and the "heroes" of his nationalist crusade.

The aptly named Law of Historical Memory appears to have opened a Pandora's box of troubles. Rhetorically speaking, it has unleashed a civil war all of its own. The conservative opposition has attacked the law as a ploy to incite old resentments and disturb memories that everyone has already overcome. "For no reason at all, Spain is being forced to relive all the conflicts of the last two centuries," complained a spokesman for the conservative Popular Party to the *Wall Street Journal* (December 4, 2006), a point echoed in the Spanish right-wing media. An editorial in the daily *ABC* (August 25, 2006) accuses the government of "distracting the nation" and "opening old wounds that could only destabilize the country." "Democracy requires that its rulers devote their time to solving problems not creating them," the editorial admonishes. The left has fought back with its own political vitriol, accusing Zapatero's right-wing opposition of wanting to keep a veil over the horrors of the "Spanish Holocaust" and demanding from the government a policy of "de-nazification" to erase all traces of Francoism (*El País*, August 25, 2006).

Following the lead of the politicians, the general public is conducting its own war of words over the past. Obituaries (so-called *esquelas*) are the weapon of choice. In recent years, ordinary Spaniards have taken to publishing these memorial notices about their relatives killed during the civil war in local and national newspapers to remind the nation of who did what to whom. The incendiary language employed by the obituaries speaks volumes about how sensitive (and divisive) the memory of the civil war remains to this day. Those from the Republican side invariably tell the story of someone killed by "fascist insurgents" for standing up for democracy. Those from the Nationalist side commonly make reference to a murder by "vicious Marxist hordes."

Why are the Spaniards coming around to confront the legacy of a painful past that many thought had been dealt with so efficiently during the democratic transition? What has changed in the national political landscape to prompt the desire to overturn the terms of the pact to silence the past? The 1996 arrest of Chilean strongman Augusto Pinochet on charges of crimes against humanity is generally considered the catalyst behind the return of the past in Spain.[2] Two prevailing theoretical explanations have been offered to suggest how the "Pinochet affair" upset the consensus about the past that solidified with the democratic transition. One draws heavily upon political psychology and sees it as a veritable case of "collective recovery of political memory." According to this explanation, Pinochet's arrest (which came on orders from a Spanish court) shattered the collective amnesia created by the Pact of Forgetting, as Spaniards began to "project" their desire to punish Pinochet for the crimes committed by Franco (Davis 2005). The other explanation relies upon the theory of "political opportunity structure," that standby of the social movement literature, which emphasizes how changes in the political environment affect the possibility for collective action (Tarrow 1994: 18). According to this view, Spanish society was galvanized by the international effort to bring Pinochet to justice, and this collective energy was eventually diverted toward upsetting the political settlement of the Pact of Forgetting (Blakeley 2005).

This chapter explores a third dimension of the impact of the Pinochet affair: the end of the complicity of society with the Pact of Forgetting. It is unlikely that the elite consensus to voluntarily repress the past would have emerged in the first place, and much less endured for nearly 30 years, without the support of ordinary citizens. Among other things, the Pinochet affair sensitized the public about the artificial line that the democratic transition had drawn between the past and the present. It also highlighted the hypocritical situation of Spain, the only case of contemporary democratization not to have undertaken any kind of self-examination about the crimes committed by the pre-democratic regime, in taking the lead in indicting another country's dictator. Finally, it made people aware that Spanish democracy no longer depended for its stability on the political compromises upon which it was built, a point driving Zapatero's ongoing project to force Spain to deal with its past.

The first part of the chapter discusses the origins of the Pact of Forgetting as a component of a broader set of political compromises secured around the time of the democratic transition. That discussion continues with an examination of the reasons behind the complicity of civil society in Spain with the pact to silence the past, including the fear of another civil war and/or another dictatorial regime. A discussion of the consequences of Pinochet's arrest follows, suggesting how this event upset the consensus about the past that had consolidated after the change in political regime, and how the current debate over the historical memory is shaping a new public memory about the past. The chapter closes with a summary of the lessons of the Spanish case for the comparative study of how nations cope with a difficult and painful past.

SEALING THE PAST WITH A PACT

Spain's Pact of Forgetting was institutionalized with the Amnesty Law of 1977, the same year that the country formally became a democratic state. This law guaranteed, in the expressive words of one parliamentarian from the Basque Country, "amnesty from everybody to everybody and forgetting from everybody to everybody" (Davis 2005: 863). The willful decision of the Spanish political elite to deal with the past by choosing simply not to deal with it meant an almost complete silence over the human cost of the Spanish Civil War and the political crimes of the Franco dictatorship (see chapter 2). Amnesty was followed by a very limited compensatory scheme for those victimized by the Franco regime, such as pensions to Republican civil war veterans and the reinstatement of civil servants dismissed from their jobs. In keeping with the desire to "forgive and forget," this was the extent of reckoning with the past during the transition.

The political dynamics of the transition to democracy in Spain shaped the deliberate attempt to create a consensus about the historical memory based on forgetting. In Spain, the authoritarian state did not collapse; instead it was reformed from within through complex negotiations between the reformist elements of the Franco regime and its democratic opposition (see chapter 3). Ensuring the success of these negotiations demanded a concerted effort by the political class to avoid resuscitating old political quarrels, such as who was responsible for the civil war and the advent of the Franco regime. Thus, silencing the past in exchange for a safe and speedy transition out of authoritarianism was the lesser evil, especially for the left, which had been demonized by Franco as the culprit behind the bloodshed and chaos of the interwar years. This point was underscored by the intense parliamentary debate that preceded the vote on the 2007 Law of Historical Memory, in which many parliamentarians made the argument that "forgetting" the past was necessary to advance the political transition. Ramón Jáuregui, a Socialist parliamentarian from the Basque Country, noted that "The transition to democracy demanded that we overlook thousands of memories and claims that weren't convenient to bring up because they could endanger the pact of the transition" (*New York Times*, October 8, 2006).

Interestingly, the left remained unwilling to make the past a political issue well beyond the point when democracy had gained a firm footing. It was not until the thirty-sixth Socialist Congress held in July 2004 that the Spanish Socialist party (PSOE) approved a resolution endorsing recovering the historical memory and addressing the injustices of the past committed against "fellow Socialists." More telling still, the "golden era" of Spanish socialism, 1982–96, which saw the PSOE win impressive parliamentary majorities, has been characterized as "the years of the great silence and of no memory" (Gálvez Biesca 2006: 33). Nothing suggests this better than the strange manner in which the country marked the fiftieth anniversary of the beginning of the civil war, which fell in 1986, in the middle of the first administration of Felipe González, who governed Spain from 1982 to 1996. The central conundrum for the González administration rested on how to observe the occasion in the absence of an appropriate monument to the victims of the civil war without having to acknowledge the obvious need for such a monument. The *Valle de los Caídos*, Franco's megalomaniac memorial to the civil war on the outskirts of Madrid, and his final resting place, is widely recognized as a one-sided monument to his Nationalist cause.

In 1985, on the occasion of the tenth anniversary of the restoration of the Spanish monarchy, King Juan Carlos inaugurated a memorial to those who had perished during the civil war. But no new monument was built; instead an existing monument to the heroes of May 2, 1808 (which marks the Spanish resistance to the French occupation) was altered by the addition of the inscription "Honor to all those who gave their lives for Spain." The point of recycling the May 2 monument had two purposes: to tie the memory of a very controversial event within Spanish society (civil war) to one that is universally cherished (May 2), and to observe the fiftieth anniversary of the war with a monument that is barely there. Aguilar and Humlebaek (2002: 126) underscore this point about the new civil war memorial by noting that "Being merely an addition to an existing monument, it does not even alter the landscape of the city." On the actual anniversary of the start of the war, in 1986, González declared that the civil war "was finally history" and that "it is no longer present and alive in the reality of the country" (Garton Ash 1998: 35).

Among the reasons that can be cited for the PSOE's apparent disinterest in confronting the past, the most compelling is the very ambitious project of political reinvention that the party undertook following the transition to democracy. The last thing the party needed, as it sought to shed its identity as a Marxist institution and appeal to the voters as a forward-looking and "catch-all" political organization, was a discussion of the party's role during the days of the Republic and the civil war. Among other things, this would have reminded voters of the role the Socialists played in radicalizing the working class, antagonizing the Catholic Church, and terrorizing the business community. More generally, it would have awakened the memory of the political crimes committed by the Republican leaders during the war. The Republican side was hardly an innocent bystander in this conflict. In the exhaustive accounting of the killings of the civil war by the historian Gabriel Jackson (1965: 526), the Republican side is responsible for some 20,000 deaths as a result of political reprisals.

Why the public went along with the elite consensus to forget the past, however, is harder to comprehend. In other nations, vigorous civil society organizations were key in pressuring the political elites not to forget the past as they were conceiving the future, including some countries with negotiated transitions like Spain's – Uruguay, Chile, and South Africa, to name only the most prominent. But this was not the case in Spain, where civil society was a willing participant in silencing the past. The complicity of society with the *Pacto del Olvido* is powerfully suggested by the "absence of a social demand" on the issue of the past around the time of the transition (Gálvez Biesca 2006: 33). Such demands from society did not arise in Spain until the year 2000, 25 years after Franco's death, when the first national human rights organization devoted to recovering the historical memory emerged. More telling still in underscoring the voluntary acceptance of the politics of no memory by the public is that following Franco's

Table 8.1 Citizens' attitudes toward the future in Spain, 1975–1976 (%)

Looking toward the future	March 1975	June 1975	January 1976
With worry	58	57	54
With tranquility	39	31	34
Don't know	3	12	12

Source: Adapted from Wert Ortega (1985)

death a whopping 61 percent of the population approved of the idea of a blanket amnesty (Wert Ortega 1985: 75).

SOCIETY'S COMPLICITY WITH FORGETTING

There is no shortage of compelling reasons for the willingness of Spanish society to go along with the elite consensus to let bygones be bygones. Elite political discourse about the need to set the past aside certainly played a central role. In justifying the 1977 amnesty law, the government and the left-wing opposition argued, rather convincingly, that setting the past aside was actually a stand against Francoism, given the Franco regime's long history of abusing and manipulating the history of the civil war for partisan political purposes. For instance, Franco was in the habit of exaggerating the number of casualties of the civil war as a means to promote his claim of having saved the nation from ruin. The Franco regime's official tally of the human toll of the civil war (1 million dead) stands in striking contrast to the more conservative estimate of historians, who put the number of people who died as a direct consequence of the war at 300,000, with an additional 200,000 who either were executed by Franco after the end of the war or perished in his jails and concentration camps (see chapter 2).

Elite political discourse also emphasized the argument that forgetting the past was in the interest of advancing democracy, by avoiding the possibility of opening old wounds, a point that played on widespread fears within the public about the future. Fear in the aftermath of Franco's demise had a twofold dimension. Foremost was the fear to engage in anything that could remotely aggravate an already delicate situation and trigger another civil war and/or a military rebellion. The polling data from the early 1970s suggest that the Spanish public anticipated the transition to democracy as a "harsh and frightful experience, a sort of ordeal" (Wert Ortega 1985: 74–5). As revealed in table 8.1, during the key years of democratic transition, the majority of Spaniards remained "very worried" about their political future. Fueling their worries was the violence that accompanied the end of the Francoist era. ETA's assassination of Prime Minister Carrero Blanco in 1973 eerily suggested the rash of political assassinations that ushered in the civil war. Fears of another civil war were further stoked by the outbreak of a left-wing revolution in neighboring Portugal on April 25, 1974, following the fall of the Salazar dictatorship. It generated workers' rebellions and land seizures not seen in western Europe since the outbreak of the civil war in Spain.

There was also fear about what a full exposure of the past could reveal. An important reason for the state's success in institutionalizing its repression under Franco was the often willing participation of individuals and groups that fervently believed in Franco's cause. There was also the shame of those victimized by Franco. The bodies of those who died in support of Franco's crusade were exhumed after the end of the civil war and their tombstones were engraved with the phrase *Caídos por Dios por España* (Those who fell for God and Spain). By contrast, those who died from the Republican side were demonized and humiliated by Francoist discourse and had to make do with an unmarked grave. The social historian Helen Graham (2004: 324) expertly explains how fears about the past interacted with the rise of the Pact of Forgetting around the time of the democratic transition:

The "pact of silence" was needed not only because of the Francoist elites, but also because of the wide complicity of "ordinary Spaniards" in the repression – not only the civilian militia, or local priests across Spain, but hundreds of thousands of people who for political reasons and many other sorts of reasons, had responded to the regime's enthusiastic encouragement to denounce their neighbors, acquaintances and often even family members – denunciations for which no corroboration was either sought or required. So it was widespread social fear that underlay the "pact of silence": the fears of those who were complicit, the fear and guilt of the families and heirs of those who denounced and murdered, as well as of those who were denounced and murdered. Fear, in short, of the consequences of reopening old wounds that the social and cultural policies of Francoism had, decade on decade, expressly and explicitly prevented from healing.

The passage of time was another important factor in the rise of a societal consensus on "forgetting." Most Spaniards who lived through the transition to democracy in the mid-1970s were born after the end of the civil war. The country's political leaders, while deeply influenced by the memory of the war, were the children of those who had fought the war and thus had played no role in the war itself. Not surprisingly, the scholarship on the historical memory in Spain makes note of a "generational memory gap" (Gálvez Biesca 2006: 27) between those who actually lived the war and those who experienced its consequences. These same studies also make note of a "lack of transition of memory" from those who experienced the trauma of the war to their children and grandchildren. Other studies suggest that around the time of the transition to democracy there was "a high level of ignorance about the facts of the war" among the general public (Davis 2005: 865), a consequence not only of the manipulation of the memory of the civil war by the Franco regime but also of people's uneasiness in speaking about the war.

The dramatic economic boom of the late 1960s also encouraged a culture of distancing oneself from the past in a variety of complementary ways. On the one hand, social and economic progress gave rise to a consumerist society obsessed with upward social mobility. This directly implied a certain propensity toward setting the unpleasantness of the past aside. As noted by Michael Richards (2004: 88):

There was a great contrast between the enormous hardship of the early post-civil war years and the consumerism of the 1960s, which preceded the transition. This contributed to the relegation of the past as a subject of concern to most people and, at a personal level, there were good psychological reasons for trying to forget the sheer awfulness of the war and its aftermath.

Table 8.2   Public perceptions of Franco's legacy, 1985–2000 (%)

Response	1985	1987	1995	2000
Positive	17.7	16.7	11.2	10.4
Negative	27.3	31.6	34	37.4
Both positive and negative	46.2	44.6	48.9	46.4
Don't know	8.5	7.1	5.9	5.8

Source: Adapted from Aguilar and Humlebaek (2002)

On the other hand, the association of the dictatorship with unprecedented order and economic prosperity created very ambivalent attitudes about the past within the general public during the democratic transition and its aftermath. Table 8.2 shows that the public's collective memory of the Francoist era is certainly complex, with almost half of the public acknowledging "both positive and negative" aspects to the dictatorship. The consistency over almost the entire post-Franco era of this mixed verdict has led some to argue that "the relatively low negative evaluation of the Franco period" helps explain "the absence during the transition of social movements demanding policies of retroactive justice" (Aguilar and Humlebaek 2002: 132).

Finally, there is the issue of the collective memory of the civil war that developed during the late Franco period, shaped by both the authoritarian state and its democratic opposition. Official vehicles of state culture (films, documentaries, textbooks, and a variety of civic organizations) underscored the high price that the nation had paid for the political excesses of the interwar years, together with a determination not to repeat them ever again. This was the central theme of the 1959 state-sponsored film *El camino de la paz* (The Path to Peace), Franco's official telling of the story of the civil war. Oddly enough, the "never again" theme was also adopted by the "mid-century generation," the very influential anti-Franco intelligentsia that emerged during the 1950s and 1960s, comprised of dissident artists, writers, filmmakers, and thinkers. Working from a position of safety and, in some cases, privilege (some of them were the children of the winners of the civil war), the members of the mid-century generation were very influential in shaping popular attitudes about how the civil war was to be remembered during the years leading to the transition to democracy.[3]

Rather than taking sides and placing blame, the narrative of the civil war constructed by the dissident intelligentsia saw this event as an act of collective madness with devastating consequences for future generations, irrespective of their social status and ideological differences. As remarked by a cultural critic, the work of the mid-century generation regards the civil war "as an abstract moral outrage, a wild orgy of blood-letting, whose appalling effects are visited upon a whole generation of innocent children, irrespective of social and class differences" (Jordan 1995: 246). This reading of the civil war all but obscured the facts that the civil war was fought for very specific political and economic reasons, that the postwar period had disproportionate negative consequences for the losing side of the war, and that the winning side destroyed a democratic government and drove the nation into civil war and decades of dictatorship.

Nonetheless, the argument about collective responsibility and shared guilt facilitated by the members of the mid-century generation provided a useful approach for handling the past around the notion of forgive and forget, a point compellingly conveyed in their work. The early work of novelists such as Juan Goytisolo and Ana María Matute portrays children whose lives are irreparably damaged by the horrors of the war. Children are also a central focus of the end-of-the-dictatorship films of the early 1970s. Inspired by the masters of postwar Italian cinema (De Sica and Rossellini, in particular), they contrasted sharply with the nationalistic epics favored by the Compañía Industrial de Film Español (CIFESA), the state-owned film company, and the frivolous comedies that dominated Spanish commercial film-making after 1959. The "new" Spanish cinema aimed at dealing with such themes as the suppression of memory and the consequences of political repression – albeit often obliquely, due to the nature of the Francoist repression (until 1976, the state required that all scripts be scrutinized by state-approved inspectors). The indisputable master of such films is Carlos Saura, whose work dramatizes the twilight of the Francoist era. In some of his best-known films, such as *Ana y los lobos* (1972), *La prima Angélica* (1973), and *Cría Cuervos* (1975) – prototypes of the "children of Franco" films – Saura skillfully uses child characters to convey the costs of the Francoist dictatorship, but also offer a glimpse of hope about the coming democratic future (Evans 1995: 307).

THE RETURN OF THE PAST

The past exploded as an issue in Spanish politics in the late 1990s with the emergence of the movement for the recovery of the historical memory. Its catalyst was General Pinochet's arrest in October 16, 1998 while on a private visit to Britain. Prior to his visit, a warrant for his arrest had been issued by Spanish authorities in a Valencia court on charges related to the death of Spanish citizens living in Chile in the years that followed Pinochet's assault on Chilean democracy in 1973. Ironically, the same judge who issued the warrant for Pinochet's arrest, Baltasar Garzón, was a prominent member of the judiciary during the first Socialist administration (1982–6). The party was a supporter of the amnesty agreement of 1977, and at the time of the Pinochet indictment had refused to allow any investigation into Spain's own past.

Predictably, Pinochet's arrest triggered charges of hypocrisy throughout South America and complaints by the Chileans that Spain had no business involving itself in the affairs of Chile's dictatorial past while refusing to confront its own. "Mind your own affairs" and "let the Chilean people deal with Pinochet" were the common reactions of ordinary Chileans to Pinochet's arrest in Europe, even by those desperate to see the former dictator pay for his crimes. Such charges touched a chord in Spain, where they generated a lively debate about the willingness of the country's judicial apparatus to go after a foreign dictator while being reluctant to examine the turbulent legacy of its own dictator. Writing in *El País* (April 22, 2001), former prime minister Felipe González, whose own administration refused to delve into the crimes of the Franco era, acknowledged his discomfort and embarrassment on seeing Spain demanding from other countries in South America what it did not dare demand of itself.

The debate over the Pinochet affair, and the obvious parallels between Spanish and Chilean history (especially the fall of a left-wing democratic government as a consequence of a right-wing coup in Spain in 1936 and in Chile in 1973, followed by a prolonged period of authoritarian rule), awakened what until then had been a dormant issue: the obvious limitations of the Spanish democratic transition in dealing with Franco's legacy of repression. Much of this debate, as some have pointed out (Davis 2005: 869), had "some kind of psychological transference factor at work – the impulse to do to Pinochet what was not done to Franco." The Spanish public overwhelmingly supported the Pinochet indictment and many private citizens became involved in helping the exile Chilean community in Spain gather the testimony used by the Spanish judges to prosecute Pinochet. In a way, it was as if the Spaniards were wishing to punish Pinochet for the crimes committed by Franco, a point conveyed by numerous editorials and op-ed pages, such as one by the noted Spanish political commentator Francisco Umbral. He keenly observed that "for the Spanish people, the Pinochet arrest is the vicarious dream of a historical impossibility, that of Franco being arrested in bed" (Davis 2005: 868). There was much historical symbolism in this projection by the Spanish public, since Pinochet, who fashioned himself as the "Franco of South America" was the only foreign head of state to attend Franco's funeral.

Adding fuel to the debate about the political memory in Spain were a number of anniversaries that converged in the early 2000s: the twenty-fifth anniversary of Franco's death in 2000; the twentieth anniversary of the failed military coup attempt in 2001; the twenty-fifth anniversary of the first elections of the post-Franco era and of the legalization of the Spanish Communist Party in 2002; and the twenty-fifth anniversary of the new constitution in 2003. Many perceived the observation of these anniversaries by the government and the media as reflecting a "selective and ahistorical interpretation" of events (Blakeley 2005: 46). In particular, media treatment of these anniversaries, especially of Franco's death, had a distinctly celebratory, forward-looking spin, described by critics as "the myth of re-foundation of the Spanish state" designed to sever "the spatial and temporal links of modern Spanish society with its Francoist and 'transitional' past" (Solís 2003: 61).

The title of the special supplement from El País (November 19, 2000), Spain's paper of record, devoted to the twentieth anniversary of Franco's death is particularly revealing: Aquella remota dictadura (that remote dictatorship).[4] In it some of Spain's leading intellectuals ponder the nation's trajectory since 1975 and the state of the memory of Franco and his regime. According to Javier Pradera, Spain has undergone "a profound transformation." "Nothing remains of substance of the Francoist repressive apparatus, having been replaced by a democratic state comparable to the other members of the European Union." Jesús Rodríguez makes note of "the twenty five years that feel like a century." Franco is "a ghost," "a distant, ugly, stranger to the lives of the young." Luis Carandell makes reference to the norms and values of Francoist Spain as "things that make us laugh." "Franco no longer hurts," writes Arcadi Espada.

As would be expected, the regional–nationalist press had a perspective on Franco and the post-Franco era that stood in pointed contrast to the celebratory discourse offered by the national press led by El País. The Catalan daily Avui, in its own supplement observing 25 years of Franco's passing, emphasized "Spain's unresolved and uncompleted transition" and "a Spanish state still bogged down in its past" (Solís

2003). Unlike *El País*, *Avui* sees the transition to democracy that followed Franco's death not as an epic closure but rather as a work in progress. An editorial of November 20, 2000 titled "Presence and Residues of Francoism" makes specific reference to the material legacy of the Franco regime still on display in Catalonia, such as Barcelona's military museum, "A museum that hails Franco and his victorious troops and that pays homage to the rebels that destroyed the legal and democratic system."

Breaking the silence

It was in this climate of a resensitized environment about the memory of the past triggered by the Pinochet affair that civil society organizations willing to pierce through the wall of silence imposed by the post-transition political order began to emerge in Spain. Principal among them is the Asociación para la Recuperación de la Memoria Histórica (ARMH), an organization formed in 2000 by Emilio Silva, a journalist whose successful search for the clandestine grave of his grandfather, who was shot to death together with 12 other men in October 1936 by Franco's army in the province of León, put him in contact with many other relatives of victims of Franco's fascist insurgency.[5] The organization is primarily devoted to the exhumation of unmarked civil war graves of people summarily executed by the insurgents.[6] It estimates the existence of some 30,000 such graves in Spain. Other organizations were soon created, such as the Forum for Memory, the Association of War Children, the Association of Ex-Political Prisoners, and the Association of the Descendants of the Spanish Exile. By 2004, it is estimated that the movement for the recovery of the historical memory had birthed over 160 associations working at the national, regional, and provincial levels (Gálvez Biesca 2006: 34).

Aiding in the rise of the ARMH and its sister organizations (and legitimating their work) was a much-reconfigured international environment. When the Spanish transition to democracy unfolded, an international legal framework for dealing with legacies such as those of the Franco regime was still in its infancy. By the late 1990s, however, a "cosmopolitan liberal consensus on transitional justice" had already been consolidated, which provided legal mechanisms and precedents for dealing with the legacy of human rights abuses left behind by the Franco regime (Golob 2003). Among the ARMH's principal achievements is having the United Nations include Spain in its list of countries that have yet to resolve the issue of state crimes and repression. In November 2002, the United Nations Working Group on Enforced or Involuntary Disappearances urged the Spanish government to undertake investigations about the fate of the killings of Republicans following the end of the civil war and exhumations of known graves of the remains of the disappeared. The case made by the ARMH to the United Nations called for the Spanish government to pay for the exhumation of the bodies, to give them a proper burial, and to establish a commission to investigate the facts surrounding the fate of those who disappeared during the war.

The ARMH did not wait for the government to respond to the United Nations resolution to start digging up graves in Spain. In September 2000, the organization made national headlines with the exhumation of 13 bodies from a mass civil war grave located in the province of León.[7] By 2006, the ARMH had exhumed some 40 gravesites containing 520 bodies and the story of mass excavations had begun to garner international headlines (Elkin 2006: 42). Much of the attention has been devoted to the ongoing saga of the search for the body of Federico García Lorca, Spain's most celebrated poet and playwright of the twentieth century, and the most famous victim of the Spanish Civil War. Lorca was shot by a Nationalist militia in August 1936 (presumably because of his homosexuality and family connections to the Socialist mayor of the city of Granada) and his body was unceremoniously dumped in a trench in the vicinity of the village of Viznar, outside Granada.

Some of the exhumations speak volumes about the savagery of the killings executed by the Nationalist army. Many of the bodies show that the victims were tortured before being shot in the head and that they were buried in hurriedly dug graves by the roadside or in remote rural fields. Even the burial itself was an act of revenge for the Francoist army. Most of the exhumed bodies reveal that they were buried face down – an insult according to Catholic tradition – an action that was in keeping with Franco's view of the Republicans as "unbelievers" and "godless Communists" (Elkin 2006: 39). Also central to the work of the ARMH is collecting oral histories from survivors of Franco's repression and from relatives and friends of those killed by the Nationalist insurgency. These stories suggest that a good number of the dead were not soldiers from the Republican army but rather ordinary people killed after the end of the war suspected of aiding the *huídos*, the Republicans who chose to take to the hills rather than surrender to Franco, and subsequently the *maquis*, the Spanish exiles who played a prominent role in the French Resistance to fascism and who began to enter Spain in the hopes of toppling Franco after the end of World War II. Both groups staged sporadic attacks on the Franco regime until their successful eradication by the mid-1940s. While some of the victims were gunned down by Franco's infamous "escuadra negra" (black squadron) during the war, others simply vanished while being taken from their homes for a *paseo* (stroll) by the state police. These stories recall more recent experiences of torture and murder from Videla's Argentina and Pinochet's Chile that occasioned the "disappearance" of thousands during the South American dirty wars of the 1970s and 1980s.

Most shocking to the general public, however, were the stories about the fear that many of the relatives of the victims still feel about revealing what they know about the graves. Many confessed discovering the graves shortly after the killings took place and keeping in hiding details of their precise location for more than 60 years. Others confess that for years they had paid anonymous visits to the graves to clean them or to simply lay flowers on them. An article in *El País* (August 6, 2002) with the macabre title of "The Earth Returns its Dead" tells the poignant tale of an 87-year-old woman giving her son a map of where her two brothers were buried after being shot by Franco's army in 1937, for fear that she would die before their bodies were exhumed.

Also telling are the reports about the pain that many have suffered from not being at liberty to discuss the fate of their loved ones while stories about the gruesome findings of truth commissions in Central America, Argentina, and other countries filled the Spanish and international media. Franco's victims quoted by the BBC (July 18, 2000) complain, "They go on about other countries but nothing about us: we have suffered much more and longer." *Newsweek*'s Mike Elkin (2006: 43) reports how Spaniards touched by Franco's violence coped with such memories: "the children and siblings of victims learned how to not talk about it, as if it were a stain on their families. They learned to live with the burden." Such tales suggest that while the collective memory about the past in Spain had in fact entered into some kind of societal amnesia, personal memories had remained remarkably vivid.

The work of the ARMH coincided with rising popular interest in historical subjects, as suggested by the record crowds drawn by a 2002 exhibition in Madrid that examined the history of the world of exile created by the civil war and the Franco dictatorship, and a wave of bestsellers which dissected relatively unexamined subjects about the civil war and the Franco era. These included *Los años difíciles* (The Difficult Years), edited by Carlos Elordi, which examines personal documents of ordinary Spaniards in wartime Spain, such as the letters written by prisoners to their relatives before being executed; Isaías Lafuente's *Esclavos de la patria* (Slaves of the Fatherland) (2002), a study of Franco's labor camps; and *Los niños perdidos del franquismo* (The Lost Children of Francoism) (2002) by Ricard Vinyes and others, which details the lives of children from Republican families stolen by Francoist officials or sent overseas to Russia and parts of Latin America to spare them the suffering of the war.

In the absence of national policy on the issue of how to deal with the past and the public's demands to see something done about this, several regional governments began to take matters into their own hands. In 2002, the regional government of Asturias authorized funds for the search, exhumation, and reburial of mass graves, an important step since the largest number of them is believed to exist in this region. The following year, the Catalan government authorized its own search. Between 2003 and 2005, the regional governments of Catalonia, Extremadura, Asturias, the Basque Country, Navarra, and Andalusia created commissions to study the condition of the victims of the civil war and the Franco regime, and to recommend ways to address the civil and human rights abuses of these eras. On April 17, 2005 the city of Madrid, without authorization from the central government, removed the statue of General Franco at San Juan de la Cruz plaza at Nuevos Ministerios, the last remaining one in the capital city. This secret operation – executed under the cover of night and under the pretext of renovating the plaza on which the statue resided – ended a debate that had raged for years between the central government and the regional one over who had ownership of the statue, how to dispose of it, and what to do with it once it had been removed from its original location.

Once it gained popular support, the movement for the recovery of the historical memory eventually found sponsors within the nation's political leadership. Hoping to score some points against the ruling right-wing government, the left-wing parties, after dragging their feet on this issue for years, began to press for accountability on a whole host of matters dealing with the past. The Socialist party sponsored a 2002 parliamentary declaration that denounced Franco's 1936 uprising as anti-democratic, in many respects the opening salvo in the current debate over the past. That same year the parliament approved unanimously a resolution sponsored by Izquierda Unida (IU), a party to the left of the Socialist party, recognizing "the tragedy of Franco's slaves." After the end of the civil war, political prisoners were utilized by the state as forced labor for the purposes of building monuments to the regime such as *El Valle de los Caídos*, but also to build public works such as dams and canals, prisons, viaducts, railway lines, and factories. Prisoners were usually hired out to work for private companies, with the state keeping about 75 percent of their wage.

In 2003 IU used the commemoration of the twenty-fifth anniversary of the 1978 constitution to "prevent forgetfulness and poor memory," as articulated by one of the organizers. The party convened a gathering of survivors of Franco's prison camps and participants in the International Brigades, the all-volunteer army that fought Franco alongside the Republican army, including the American Lincoln Battalion. Now in their eighties and nineties, the honorees were given a tour of the Congress, were handed copies of the Spanish constitution, and heard laudatory speeches from politicians about the sacrifices they had made for the Spanish nation.[8] The Communist party, which like the Socialist party was a willing collaborator in the pact of silence, has recently opened "offices of historical memory" in its regional branches to promote debate and dialogue about the past.

A counter-movement

Ensuring that the debate over the past in Spain would become an incendiary one was the government's handling of both Pinochet's arrest and the civil society movement to "recover" the past that it spawned. During its years in office (1996–2004), the conservative Popular Party (PP) refused to support any policy or plan that would upset the post-transition pact of silence, on grounds that the nation had greatly benefited from it. While the Spanish public overwhelmingly endorsed Pinochet's arrest, the government of Prime Minister José María Aznar wished that the case would simply go away. It declared his government neutral on the prosecution of Pinochet and endeavored diplomatically to undermine the right of Spanish courts to legislate universal jurisprudence. This opened the Aznar government to charges that it was protecting Pinochet, a sensitive charge to be sure, given the PP's close historic links to the Franco regime.

The government of Aznar also worked hard to impede the work of the ARHM, even though the group made it clear that it did not seek vengeance or retribution, but only assistance to identify the unmarked graves from both sides of the civil war and give them a proper burial. "Of course the government recognizes the rights of families to privately re-bury their dead but we see no point in reopening old wounds that afflicted Spanish society," observed a PP member of the Spanish parliament to the BBC (July 18, 2002). A more disdainful attitude toward the work of the ARMH was delivered by Manuel Fraga, a senior PP elder and former president of the Galician regional government, when he proclaimed at the party's 2003 national convention, "We have had enough of unburying the dead" (Gálvez Biesca 2006: 31). This refusal of the government to aid the work of the ARMH struck many Spaniards as hypocritical. Franco had exhumed the bodies of Nationalists following the end of the civil war. And the Aznar government had already paid millions to exhume and repatriate from Russia the corpses of several Spanish volunteers from the battalion sent by Franco (the Blue Division) to support Nazi troops during World War II as a symbol of his support for Adolf Hitler.

Aznar also declined the request by the ARMH to open the military archives that house the records of the disappeared, their personal belongings, and in many cases their last letters and messages to their relatives. These records have never been opened to the public. The government also declined requests from the regional government of Catalonia to transfer to the region documents pertaining to the hunting of Catalans by the Franco regime during and after the civil war, currently resting in the General Archives of the Civil War in Salamanca. The government argued that these documents, which had been looted by Francoist officials from Catalonia, were an integral part of the archives and that separating them from the rest of the collection would amount to an offense against Spanish history. The government also vehemently opposed the removal of monuments to Franco and his associates from public spaces. In some cases the government ordered them back to the original location after they had been removed by local authorities.

The Aznar government also fought the parties of the left in their attempt to examine the crimes and abuses of the Franco regime. Although the PP agreed to the 2002 resolution condemning the 1936 coup, it did so only after it had secured a commitment from the Socialist party not to ever again raise the issue of the past in the parliament. Following this agreement, the PSOE withdrew its call for the organization of a truth commission as requested by local groups and the United Nations. The government also agreed to honor the "slaves" of the Franco dictatorship, but it did not accept compensation as demanded by the motion. Aznar declined to attend a 2003 parliamentary ceremony convened by the parties of the left to honor former political prisoners, members of the Republican exile, anti-Franco guerilla members, and representatives of the International Brigades, as part of the twenty-fifth anniversary of the constitution. In explaining Aznar's actions, Luis de Grandes, the PP's parliamentary spokesman, mocked the 2003 reunion as a "mothball revival" intended by the left to incite old resentments (*Guardian*, December 1, 2003).

As a counter-strategy to the work of the ARMH, the PP launched its own memory project devoted to restoring Spain's Francoist past. The government provided a grant to the Francisco Franco Foundation intended to recast the memory of the dictatorship by highlighting the peace and prosperity that Franco had brought to the country. In towns and cities controlled by the PP, the party sought to restore the names of streets once bearing names associated with the Franco dictatorship. The PP also lent its support to groups and individuals from the right who question the validity of what was being "recovered." One of the most popular journalist-historians in Spain today is Pío Moa, the author of a recent series of bestseller books, the most popular being *Los mitos de la guerra civil Española* (The Myths of the Spanish Civil War (2006)), which offers controversial interpretations of Spanish history, especially the civil war. In his books, Moa pointedly questions the generally accepted view that Franco overthrew democracy in Spain in 1936. He also questions the extent to which Spain's interwar government was in fact democratic, given its radical policies. Finally, Moa maintains that the advent of the Franco regime saved Spain from revolution and chaos, that it prevented the fragmentation of the nation along ethnic and linguistic lines, and that the policies of the Franco regime created the foundation for today's successful democracy.

Legislating the Recovery of Memory

Since coming to power in 2004, the Zapatero administration has made recovering Spain's political memory a legislative priority. Zapatero authorized 1.3 million euros for the exhumation and reburial of the estimated 30,000 unnamed civil war graves of individuals killed by Franco's Nationalist army. He also commissioned a group of military experts to adjudicate the dispute over the Catalan records housed at the state's civil war archives. They saw no objection to the Catalan governments request for their return to Catalonia, as long as conditions for their preservation were provided. Zapatero also created an inter-ministerial commission chaired by his deputy prime minister, Teresa Fernández de la Vega, and modeled after similar commissions established by several regional governments, to examine the situation of the victims of the civil war and the Franco era. Established by royal decree in June 2004, its main task was to lay the political–legal groundwork for the "Law of Historical Memory," which was approved by the Spanish Congress in October 2007.

In contrast to other national efforts designed to bring about "truth and reconciliation," especially those of South America, South Africa, and post-communist Europe, whose emphasis is on "fact-finding" and "accountability" (see Kritz 1996), the Spanish law focuses on compensatory schemes and attempts to recover the historical memory. This is in keeping with the intent of the law as stipulated in its preamble: "To recognize and expand the rights of those victimized by the prosecution or violence of the Civil War and the Dictatorship, for political or ideological reasons; to promote the recuperation of personal and family memory; and to adopt measures destined to suppress elements of division among the citizenry with the goal of promoting cohesion and solidarity across the different generations of Spaniards around constitutional principles, values, and liberties." To that end, the law calls for the creation of a committee of five "wise men" to document every claim of abuse from either side of the civil war and to adjudicate the appropriate reparation, including monetary compensation and the restoration of Spanish citizenship. The law also calls for "the retirement of shields, plaques and statues and other commemorations to the Spanish Civil War that exalt one of the warring bands or that can be identified with the regime installed in Spain after the end of the war." Organizations that refuse to comply with the law run the risk of losing public support for their activities. Moreover, the law introduces procedures for overturning sentences handed down by Francoist tribunals and criminalizes pro-Franco demonstrations at *El Valle de los Caídos*. It state that "acts of a political nature or that exalt the civil war, its protagonists, or Francoism will not be allowed to be carried out in any part of the grounds."

It is easy to read Zapatero's "memory" policies as an act of political opportunism. But there is more at play behind his actions. Much has been made of the fact that his grandfather, Captain Juan Rodríguez Lozano, was shot by a Francoist firing squad for refusing to join the rebellion against the Republican government. Less noticed is the fact that Zapatero is part of a new generation of politicians not beholden to the national compromises of the democratic transition. Shattering the foundations of the Pact of Forgetting is part of what he calls the "unfinished business" of the democratic transition, a task his administration contends that Spanish democracy is strong enough to face. Carmen Calvo, Spain's Minister of Culture, has observed that "after 30 years, Spanish society is mature enough to engage in a conversation about what really happened" (*Time*, November 13, 2005). Such attitudes are being fueled not only by the fact that the Pinochet affair shattered the silence upon the past imposed by the democratic transition, but also by the demographic changes sweeping through the political class and the country at large. Most of the country's leaders, beginning with Zapatero himself, only 43 years old at the time of his election to prime minister, do not share the fear that in 1977 kept the public from wanting to confront the past. "We are the first generation to approach the past without fear or trauma," notes the political scientist Paloma Aguilar (*Time*, November 13, 2005).

Judging by the tone of the parliamentary debates that the Law of Historical Memory generated, it appears that Zapatero has walked directly on to a minefield. The PP is crying foul and accusing Zapatero of breaking his earlier compromise to let bygones be bygones. During the deliberations of the law, Manuel Atencia, the PP's spokesman, described the law as "a grave error" (*El País,* December 12, 2006). According to Atencia, "the badly-named historical memory is an attempt by the government to use history in a partisan way. For the PP the key word is reconciliation not memory." Even harsher were the words of PP leaders in justifying why they were voting against most of the provisions of the law. During the final vote, Jorge Fernandez Díaz, another PP leader, branded the law as "sectarian," "a final blow to the consensus born with the transition" (EFE, October 18, 2007). Echoing the common charge that Zapatero's policies are reviving the "two Spains," Fernández Díaz added that: "One of the two Spains once again freezes our heart."

Many on the left are also unhappy with Zapatero's effort to confront the past, which they have denounced as a half-baked effort. Esquerra Republicana de Catalunya (ERC) actually voted against the law on grounds that its provisions "fail to end the Spanish system of impunity installed with the transition" (*El País*, October 31, 2007), because, among other things, it does not authorize the opening of Franco's archives. The IU opposed the compromise in the law that will allow some Francoist monuments to remain in their existing location provided that they possess artistic or cultural value. Such exclusions prompted the IU leader Gaspar Llamazares to complain, "We have recently passed laws in this country that ban sexist and racist advertising but we cannot prohibit the glorification of Spanish fascism" (*El País*, August 25, 2006).

International human rights organizations have also criticized Spain's "memory law." Amnesty International, Human Rights Watch, and the International Commission of Jurists have described the law as "disappointing," since its provisions fall short of established standards of international transitional justice (*El País*, March 23, 2007). In meetings with the Spanish government, representatives of these organizations have highlighted several deficiencies in the law, including the protection it offers to the identity of the perpetrators of state-sponsored violence, the restrictions placed upon who has access to the archives of the Franco regime, the lack of acknowledgment of responsibility on the part of the state for human rights abuses committed against society, which means that in Spain it is unlikely that anyone will ever face charges of crimes against humanity. These shortcomings in the eyes of the international human rights organizations prevent the truth from emerging and treat the victims of human rights abuses as "passive elements." Wilder Tyler, director of the legal department of Human Rights Watch, in an interview with *El País* (March 23, 2007), has called upon Spain to remedy the shortcomings in the Law of Historical Memory by invoking the country's role as a model for other new democracies and its efforts to bring about transitional justice in other countries, especially in South America: "Spain is an obligatory reference to many countries. It has been in the process of democratic transition. I do not understand why Spain does not apply the same standards of justice and reparation that it demands of other countries."

Not surprisingly, the new law has not settled the past. Human rights groups are demanding that *El Valle de los Caídos* be transformed into a research center intended to highlight the horrors of the civil war and the Franco regime. Jaume Bosch of the Catalan Green party, which spearheaded the idea of transforming "the Valley" into a "center for interpretation," argues: "Auschwitz has been converted into a learning center; Argentina has turned its torture prisons into places for explanation. Too many years have passed for us to simply leave the Valley as the Franco regime left it" (*Time*, November 13, 2005). Others are demanding that the remains of Franco and José Antonio Primo de Rivera (the founder of the Falange) be removed from the site. At the very least, they contend that the site should include information that places this Francoist monument within some kind of historical perspective about the nature of the Franco regime, especially in light of the fact that many of the visitors to the monument are tourists without much knowledge of Spanish history. To be sure, any attempt to "reconsider" *El Valle* is likely to raise the ire of the sectors of Spanish society that still venerate Franco. Witness their reaction to Zapatero's proposed ban on tributes to Franco at the monument. Radical right-wing groups have targeted PSOE legislators, including one whose house was vandalized. *El Valle no se toca* (The Valley is not to be touched) was the warning painted on the legislator's front door.

Equally troublesome is the demand of several groups that the Spanish Catholic Church and the Vatican issue an apology to the Spanish people for their support of Franco's nationalist uprising. This issue is potentially explosive, for it brings to light many of the actions of the Republicans toward the Catholic Church during the civil war. The Second Republic was famous for its anti-clerical policies (Republican authorities stripped the Church of its property and other assets) and the Republican army was responsible for many unspeakable acts against the Church. We may never know the extent of the violence perpetrated by the Republicans against the Church during the years of civil war, but numerous monasteries, convents, and churches were raided and profaned, and hundreds (perhaps thousands) of priests murdered and nuns raped. In remembrance of these events, in 2001 Pope John Paul II beatified 233 Catholics as martyrs murdered by Republicans in the civil war. An additional 500 Catholics were beatified by the Vatican in October 2007 to coincide with the passage of the Law of Historical Memory.

CONCLUSION

It is unlikely that the fight over the past will prove a destabilizing factor in Spanish politics. Spain has undertaken to confront its painful past with the luxury of having a set of fully consolidated democratic institutions. Moreover, notwithstanding the acrimony that Zapatero's proposed Law of Historical Memory has created, it is interesting to note that no one is questioning the blanket pardon granted to those accused of political crimes during the transition. Tellingly, nobody in Spain is calling for a repeal of the 1977 Law of Political Amnesty, the linchpin of the Pact of Forgetting. This suggests at least two things. The first is that the intention of the movement for the recovery of the historical memory is about setting the historical record straight rather than punishing anyone for any particular action. This point is best expressed by the historian

Javier Tussell, who just before passing away in 2005 remarked, "In Spain there is a willingness for amnesty not amnesia" (Elkin 2006: 43).

The second point is the tacit recognition that the decision to "forget" the past was probably the best approach for Spain in dealing with its difficult and painful past at the time of the democratic transition, something readily admitted even by those currently fronting the effort to recover the past. "The pact of silence was necessary for the transition to democracy," observes José Maria Pedreña, head of the Forum for Memory (*Time*, November 13, 2005). Carlos Castresana Fernández, the Spanish public prosecutor in charge of Pinochet's indictment, and one of Spain's best-known human rights activists, notes that "the years of democratic transition were spent in a permanent state of necessity that forced the least bad of bad options, which culminated in the untruthful process that gave us back our freedom" (*El País*, July 16, 2007). This recognition by Spanish human rights activists that setting the past aside was a necessary step on the road toward a stable democracy is especially revealing because it stands in almost shocking contrast to the very influential transitional justice paradigm promoted by the international human rights community, which contends, in a nutshell, that "embarking on the process of reconciliation" is a prerequisite for democratization (Boraine 2006: 20). Its popularity has made "confronting the past" around the time of the democratic transition all the rage in democratizing societies.[9]

However attractive and compelling, this conflation of democratization and reconciliation is broadly challenged by the Spanish experience.[10] It is clear that democracy was consolidated in Spain decades before the nation undertook to reconcile with its past. Real reconciliation appears only to have begun in recent years with the launching of the recovery of history movement. Ironically, democratic consolidation was facilitated in Spain in large measure because the political elite purposely privileged democratization over reconciliation. Choosing not to confront the past during the transition to democracy, Spain was spared the destabilizing effects of putting the old regime on trial. The South American experience pointedly reveals the perils that this can pose to a fragile democracy. In Argentina, the government was compelled to end the military trials that got under way in the late 1980s after they proved destabilizing to the new democratic regime by generating multiple military rebellions. In Chile, the democratic government that followed the Pinochet regime quickly introduced legislation to end ongoing trials and preclude future ones after the military took to the streets of Santiago in the so-called *Bionazo*, a show of force named after beret-wearing soldiers.

Another insight revealed by the Spanish experience is the need for a more expansive understanding of what "transitional justice" entails. The emphasis on documenting the truth, restoring dignity to victims, and seeking closure on human rights abuses is certainly well placed, but it may be rendered meaningless unless it is accompanied by an effort to strengthen judicial institutions as well by empowering them to act independently from the government. It is ironic that Spain, which by all accounts violated all the conventional wisdom of the transitional justice paradigm during its transition to democracy, is probably the most successful new democracy in institutionalizing the rule of law and in strengthening the judicial apparatus. Whenever the military has misbehaved, as in 1981, when military rebels launched an attempted coup, or in 1986–9, when the military employed extra-judicial means for fighting ETA, it has been severely punished. The Pinochet indictment is perhaps the most telling example of the maturity and independence of the Spanish judiciary. The case was launched and prosecuted against the wishes of the government.

The final lesson taught by the Spanish experience relates to the employment of political pacts in the process of democratization: they come with a price, a point often overlooked in much of the praise that this type of political strategy has received by "transitologists." Broadly speaking, political pacts are praised by democratization scholars for the capacity they possess for introducing democracy in as non-confrontational a manner as possible. But it important to recognize that political pacts have hidden costs and undesirable side-effects, however justified and well intended their purpose. The Pact of Forgetting had the unintended consequence of perpetuating the repression of the Franco regime well into the democratic period. Those forced to keep silent for the duration of Franco's authoritarian regime were obliged to do the same under the new democratic regime. Fortunately, political pacts need not live in perpetuity. They can be renegotiated and even discarded once they have outlived their purpose.

9

ZAPATERO'S SPAIN: A SECOND TRANSITION

To his enemies from the right, Prime Minister José Luis Rodríguez Zapatero is a naïve and reckless politician whose policies are endangering the political stability that Spain has enjoyed in the post-Franco era. Their nickname for him says it all: "Bambi." To his supporters from the left, Zapatero is the great reformer, the man who will rid Spain of the last vestiges of "Old Spain," from machismo, to homophobia, to the last monument to Francoism. These radically divergent opinions of Zapatero are mirrored in characterizations of his administrations on both sides of the Atlantic as "a second transition," a metaphor intended to suggest "a new phase of democratic development" (*Economist*, June 24, 2004), as well as "a new era of dire omens" (Woodworth 2005: 69). In either case, the point being stressed is the same one: the revolution that Zapatero has brought to Spanish politics.

Claiming that "I don't want to be a great leader, I want to be a good democrat," (*Time*, September 19, 2004), Zapatero has broadly reshaped Spanish politics. Since entering office as a consequence of the controversial March 14, 2004 elections, his administration has implemented policies that not long ago would have brought the country close to a constitutional crisis or at the very least a highly destabilizing point. Along the way, Zapatero has dramatically upset the political order that consolidated in the post-Franco era. Not surprisingly, relations between the nation's two major parties – the socialist PSOE and the conservative PP – have never been more contentious (*El País*, July 18, 2005). Indeed, talks about the return of the dreaded phenomenon of *La crispación*, the heightened state of political polarization that the nation lived in through the interwar years, and which led to a devastating civil war, have haunted Zapatero's government almost from its inception.

This concluding chapter assesses the policies of the Zapatero era. Much of the discussion is centered on examining whether the painstakingly crafted "post-transition settlement" that emerged in the wake of Franco's death in 1975, which places a high premium on political consensus and compromise, and which is largely credited with the political stability of the last three decades, has been shattered as a consequence of Zapatero's policies. This is the central charge of the right against the Zapatero administration, accusations that are echoed in some quarters of the international community, the United States most prominently. The chapter begins with an overview of Zapatero's rise to power and continues with a summary of his policy record. It leaves little doubt about the attack he has unleashed on the political and social order that consolidated after Franco. Yet, the right's complaint that the Zapatero administration has destroyed the post-transition settlement does not stand up to rigorous scrutiny.

On the one hand, it conveniently ignores the fact that the post-transition settlement basically unraveled under the last four years of the Aznar administration (2000–4), when the nation experienced a strong tilt to the right. It also overlooks the PP's own contributions to the political polarization of the Zapatero era, especially the party's politicization of the terrorist attack of March 11, 2004. On the other hand, the PP's criticism of Zapatero fails to take into account the support that the general public has offered to many of his policy initiatives. As seen shortly, in some of the most controversial areas of policy making that Zapatero has ventured into, he has followed rather than led public opinion. This reflects a clear desire among the public for a more liberal and open democracy than that created after Franco's death in 1975. More generally, the reaction of the right to Zapatero's policy initiatives reflects very different perceptions of the political bargains that were secured following Franco's death. For the right, the post-Franco democratic settlement was the final destination for the nation; for Zapatero, by contrast, this was a point of departure.

THE RISE OF A RADICAL DEMOCRAT

On April 17, 2004, at the time of his inauguration as Spain's fifth prime minister in the post-Franco period, few could have anticipated the changes in store for the country. After all, a Socialist administration was hardly a novelty for Spain; the country had been governed by the PSOE from 1982 to 1996. Notwithstanding the massive corruption scandals that eventually put an end to what is often referred to as "the golden years" of Spanish socialism, that earlier run at the helm of the government suggested a clear recipe for long-term electoral success: conservative economic policies mixed with a cautious progressivism that did not antagonize either the right or its allies in society, the Catholic Church most clearly. Zapatero adopted the first part of the equation and boldly tossed the second half to the wind. Much of his political program, as will be seen shortly, has driven a stake through the very heart of the compromises that the left made with both the right and the Catholic Church at the time of the transition to democracy. It corresponds to a political philosophy that he has termed "Citizen Socialism," which advances "near pacifism in foreign policy, expanding civil rights, and a preference for following rather than guiding the will of the people" (*International Herald Tribune*, December 5, 2006).

Zapatero's family background is often cited as the genesis of his political orientations. According to his biographer, his family taught him to be "tolerant, thoughtful, prudent and austere" (Campillo Madrigal 2004: 294). Looming large over his upbringing was the memory of his grandfather, Captain Juan Rodríguez Lozano, who was shot by a Francoist firing squad for refusing to join the rebellion against the Republican government in 1936. Zapatero himself has revealed that his interest in politics was piqued at age 18 by reading the handwritten testament that his grandfather wrote just 24 hours prior to his execution. In this document, Captain Rodríguez Lozano asked his family to forgive those who were about to execute him and to clear his name at the appropriate time. It concludes with his creed, which Zapatero recited in the conclusion of his 2004 inaugural speech to the Spanish Congress: "An infinite yearning for peace, love of good and the betterment of those less fortunate."[1]

Good fortune marked Zapatero's meteoric rise to power; he was 26 years old when first elected to the Spanish Congress (the youngest member ever), representing the province of León, and 43 by the time of his presidential inauguration. The crisis that befell the PSOE after the 1996 elections provided the opportunity for Zapatero to gain control of the party. He announced his intention to run for General Secretary of the PSOE after the party's disastrous performance in the 2000 general election. That year, for the first time in the post-transition era, a conservative party gained an absolute majority of parliamentary seats. Given the overall state of disarray of the PSOE, to say nothing of the disappointment with its existing leadership, Zapatero's youth and inspiring political message proved clearly appealing to the party's members. By 2000, he had emerged as the new face of Spanish socialism, leading Nueva Via (new route), a political movement devoted to "a democratic socialism that would allow the PSOE to recover its credibility and the citizens' trust" (Campillo Madrigal 2004: 234). The average age of the group was 40.

As seen in chapter 4, Zapatero was not the projected winner of the March 14, 2004 general elections. Although he ran a competent campaign that emphasized his opposition to Spain's participation in the American-led invasion of Iraq, a popular position with the general public, most Spaniards regarded him as unprepared for the job of leader of the nation. But the terrorist attack on Atocha station on March 11, 2004, which left 192 people dead and over 2,500 injured, significantly altered the political dynamics of the election by essentially destroying the credibility of Zapatero's opposition. The outgoing prime minister, José María Aznar, and his anointed successor, Mariano Rajoy, fearing that the electorate would see the attack on Atocha as linked to Spain's participation in the war in Iraq, put the blame on the local terrorist organization ETA in the face of compelling evidence pointing to radical Islamic groups. Zapatero capitalized on the government's mismanagement of "M-11" while energizing the Socialist base, giving the PSOE an unexpected, comfortable victory over the PP.

Turning politics upside down

Zapatero's mandate, as he has argued repeatedly, is to accomplish the "unfinished business" of the democratic transition, a task he contends that Spanish democracy is strong enough to face. Nothing suggests this better than the support he has lent to the effort to "recover" Spain's historical memory, a direct affront to the *Pacto del Olvido* (the Pact of Forgetting), the explicit intra-elite agreement forged by the national parties following Franco's death to bury the past. As seen previously (chapter 8), prior to 2004, no government in Spain, either from the right or the left, had made revisiting the past a component of its legislative program. Other initiatives undertaken by Zapatero have brought nothing short of a social revolution with important implications for education, women's rights, and family law. Reforms in these areas have inevitably entailed a confrontation with the Spanish Catholic Church, which historically has had a big (if not decisive) say in these matters.

Within the first 24 months of his administration, Zapatero abolished the practice of displaying religious symbols in public places, such as crucifixes in prisons, courthouses, and military buildings, which he deemed a violation of the divide between church and state. He shelved a Church-backed law passed by the previous administration that called for compulsory religious instruction in public schools. Instead, he proposed optional religious offerings that integrate religion into the curriculum as a cultural topic in the teaching of such subjects as art, history, politics, and music. He also curtailed longstanding subsidies to private schools, a huge deal considering that approximately one-third of all Spanish children receive primary instruction at private institutions, the vast majority of them run by the Catholic Church. Zapatero relaxed abortion laws by allowing abortions to be performed during the first 12 weeks of pregnancy and liberalized divorce with the introduction of a "fast-track" model. Couples in Spain are no longer required to explain their reasons for wanting a divorce or to complete a mandatory separation before concluding the marriage. A two-year mandatory period was reduced to just ten days. Zapatero also authorized stem cell research using embryos created for fertility treatment but which are no longer wanted by their owners. These policies prompted the Vatican to accuse Zapatero of pushing an anti-Catholic legislative agenda driven by "lay fundamentalism and agnostic totalitarianism" (Inter-Press News Agency, April 13, 2007).

A self-described "radical feminist," Zapatero has advanced an ambitious agenda of women's rights in a country famous for having invented macho culture. He appointed women to 50 percent of cabinet posts, the highest percentage in any government in Europe, including education, health, agriculture, housing, environment, and public works. To top things up, he also appointed a female to the second highest post in government, the deputy prime ministership. Zapatero declared domestic violence against women, which he described as "Spain's worst shame and an unacceptable evil" (*El Mundo*, April 23, 2004), his top priority after terrorism, a point symbolically marked within hours of being sworn in as Spain's new prime minister with a hospital visit to a woman who had been burned and beaten by her husband, together with visits to the victims of the March 11, 2004 terrorist attack on Madrid's Atocha station.[2] The first bill Zapatero sent to the national parliament, just one week into his administration, was a controversial new law aimed at curtailing domestic violence.[3] It imposes stiffer sentences on male perpetrators of domestic violence than on females, in response to the argument advanced by Spanish feminists that males are responsible for the majority of crimes of passion, which result in dozens of murders of females in Spain every year. The government also set up special courts to deal with complaints from women claiming physical and/or psychological abuse and has increased by 90 percent the number of police officers trained to deal with matters of domestic violence.

The 2007 Law for Equality between Women and Men seeks to open new opportunities for women in government and the business world, in a country where, according to the Instituto de la Mujer (Women's Institute), a government-sponsored think tank, women sit on less than 5 percent of corporate boards and overall earn 30 percent less than their male counterparts. It will be required of political parties that at least 40 percent of their lists of candidates running for office in national and local elections be female. It grants paternity leave to fathers for up to three weeks and extends maternity leave for mothers up to 13 weeks in cases of premature births. The law also gives preferential treatment in awarding government contracts to firms with the highest percentages of female executives. Yet to come is a change in the law that would allow women the right to ascend to the throne of the Spanish monarchy. The current law stipulates that the first-born male always takes precedence in the line of succession to the crown, even if he has an older sister. This change is seen as especially complex, since it requires amending the 1978 constitution.

Redefining marriage

In the eyes of conservative politicians and the Catholic Church, Zapatero outdid himself in tearing apart Spain's social fabric by signing into law on April 22, 2005 the creation of same-sex marriages, making Spain the first Catholic-majority country and only the third country in Europe after the Netherlands and Belgium to allow such marriages. The law that legalized gay marriage in Spain is especially expansive and includes provisions, such as adoption rights, not found in similar legislation enacted in other European states or in Massachusetts, the only American state to have legalized same-sex marriages. Highlights of the law, as summarized by Castresana (2005: 134), include the right to custody over the couple's children, legal adoption, separation and divorce, residency, Spanish citizenship when one of the partners is a foreigner, and the right not to bear witness against a partner indicted in criminal processes. In essence, according to Castresana, "any comparison between heterosexual and homosexual marriages will now find them undifferentiated."

Predictably, the gay marriage law provoked a nasty backlash from the Catholic Church. The Archbishop of Madrid, Cardinal Antonio Maria Rouco Varela, complained that Zapatero's actions had "turned Madrid into Sodom and Gomorrah" (*Washington Post*, April 11, 2005), a point echoed by the larger Catholic establishment. The Spanish Conference of Bishops noted that the new law on same-sex marriage "introduced a dangerous and disruptive element into the institution of marriage, and thereby into our just social order" (*New York Times*, April 21, 2004). Seeking to prevent the legalization of same-sex marriages, the Catholic Church joined forces with the PP, which in a last-minute attempt to stop its passage through the parliament proposed instead the creation of "civil unions." Encouraged by the Vatican and the Spanish Bishops' Conference, PP mayors in cities across Spain also threatened the government with civil disobedience by refusing to wed same-sex couples. Working in tandem, the Church and the PP managed an unusual feat: sending conservatives onto the streets en masse. Hoping to change the terms of the parliamentary debate, the PP and the Catholic Church organized massive demonstrations across the country, including one in Madrid that drew some 600,000 protestors, the largest mass demonstration in Spain since the one against the military coup of February 1981.

The gay marriage law also triggered a showdown with the Vatican, which over the years has witnessed with great concern Spain's transition from the most devout Catholic country in Europe under Franco to one of its most secular under Zapatero. Vatican authorities denounced the Socialist government's policy on marriage as "profoundly negative and destructive of family and society" (*New York Times*, April 21, 2004). It did not help that Zapatero responded in kind. Much was made by the Vatican of Zapatero's decision to skip the mass that Pope Benedict XVI gave in Valencia, on July 10, 2006, in observation of the fifth World Meeting of Families, which was attended by 1.6 million people. A Vatican official complained that even Fidel Castro, whom the Church had excommunicated in 1962, attended mass when Pope John Paul II visited Havana in 1998. Adding insult to injury, it was revealed that the Zapatero administration had funded a conference for gay, bisexual, and transgender families, also held in Valencia, to coincide with the Pope's visit to the city.

Tackling immigration

Zapatero has also undertaken policies intended to tackle the problem of immigration, a relatively new but already very important issue in Spanish politics. According to an October 2005 poll by the Spanish radio network Cadena Ser, 54 percent of Spaniards regard immigration as the matter of greatest concern to them, outranking such perennial issues as terrorism and unemployment. The prominence of immigration in people's consciousness reflects the dramatic spike in the number of legal and especially illegal immigrants entering the country in the last two decades (see chapter 7). Public concern about immigration is also fueled by the sensationalized manner in which the subject is covered by the media. National newspapers include a section on "the immigration problem," which keeps track of the number of illegal immigrants apprehended by the police. On television, the Spanish public is fed an almost daily diet of images of people attempting to enter the country illegally. Especially gripping are the stories featuring the often tragic journey of the *pateras*, rubber rafts teeming with illegal immigrants arriving at multiple points along Spain's shores.

Zapatero's efforts on the immigration front have centered on revamping the *Ley de Extranjería* (Law on Foreigners), which came into effect on July 1, 1985, to comply with regulations imposed by the EU, which Spain joined on January 1, 1986. The focus of this law was on strengthening governmental powers over the resident illegal population (such as the right to deport anyone convicted of illicit activities) rather than tightening border control. By contrast, Zapatero's overhaul of immigration legislation has aimed at regularizing the status of the so-called *sin papeles* (without papers). The law has a carrot and a stick. For those willing to come out of the shadow of illegality, the Zapatero government has promised amnesty and the path toward full Spanish citizenship. Those choosing not to register, however, face the threat of deportation. By 2007, Spain's amnesty policy had led to the legalization of over 1 million illegal migrants who could prove that they were employed (*Business Week*, May 21, 2007).

Although these policies have been supported by most sectors of Spanish society, including the media, the Catholic Church, organized labor, the nation's employers' lobby, and most opposition parties, the PP leadership has denounced Zapatero's immigration initiatives as an "open-door" policy. It labeled them foolhardy, since they would probably invite further illegal immigration into the country. In a play aimed at capitalizing on rising Islamophobia in Spain, PP leaders also contended that the new immigration plan could place the nation in peril by providing fresh recruits to radical Islamic organizations located in Spain.

Expanding regional autonomy

Zapatero has also trodden boldly into the treacherous waters of the politics of regional autonomy. Upon entering office, he faced a crisis in the Basque Country, where the local parliament approved in December 2004 the so-called "Ibarretxe Plan," which called for a new Basque "status of free association with Spain." Zapatero argued that this action, which in his view amounted to a unilateral act of independence, was unconstitutional, a position supported by the majority of parliamentarians, who overwhelmingly rejected the Basque proposal in the Cortes in January 2005. But Zapatero has actively supported extending new powers to the more moderate and politically astute Catalan government, which critics on the right argue may have the outcome Zapatero most fears about the Basque Country: the eventual secession of Catalonia from Spain. In June 18, 2006, with the support of the Zapatero government, Catalan voters approved a sweeping overhaul of their autonomy charter with Madrid, with the final tally of the vote indicating that 74 percent supported it and 21 percent were against it, with the rest choosing not to respond.

Catalonia's new compact of regional governance, hatched in consultation between the Zapatero government and the Catalan Socialist party, the regional branch of the national PSOE, which presently governs Catalonia, refers to the region as a "nation" rather than a "nationality." It also contends that the region's powers of self-government emanate from the Catalan people rather than the Spanish constitution and grants Catalonia more control over such issues as tax collection, immigration policy, and judicial affairs. These changes were opposed by the PP on grounds that they represent the first step toward outright independence for the Catalans and might encourage other regions to seek similar privileges. "This is a time bomb," declared the PP leader Mariano Rajoy, adding that Catalonia's new autonomy compact "is the beginning of the end of the State Spaniards drew in 1978" (*International Herald Tribune*, March 30, 2006). He has promised to fight these new provisions in the Spanish courts.

Some of the fiercest opposition to the Catalan plan, however, came from within the Socialist party and the Zapatero administration itself. José Bono, the Defense Minister, resigned from his post in protest at the Catalan plan for greater autonomy once Zapatero made it clear that the government intended to support it. Alfonso Guerra, a prominent elder within the PSOE, criticized the plan for creating a "polarizing climate along regional lines reminiscent of the last days of the Soviet Union" (*New York Times*, June 19, 2006). Rather predictably, the most strenuous reaction came from the armed forces, which historically have violently opposed giving any degree of autonomy to the regions. Two military officers who suggested that the military was ready to quell the demands of the Catalans for more autonomy were promptly relieved of their responsibilities. Perhaps due to the expressions of discontent from within the Zapatero government, the extension of greater autonomy powers to the Catalans has caused the most significant drop in Zapatero's approval ratings since his election. A key concern of the general public, especially Socialist voters outside of Catalonia, is the way in which the plan will weaken the capacity of the central state to share the nation's wealth with the less developed parts of the country.

Zapatero appears unfazed by the opposition that his support for regional rights has occasioned. He declared himself to be very pleased with the Catalan vote and expressed his desire that other regions would take up his offer to discuss ways of enhancing their own statutes of autonomy with Madrid. "With this new statute, the identity of Catalonia will be better recognized. It will have better instruments for administering self-government, and it will preserve the rich pluralism that is inherent to Catalan society," Zapatero asserted after the Catalan vote (*New York Times*, June 19, 2006). Central to his reasoning is that extending greater regional autonomy is the only effective way to keep restive regions such as Catalonia within Spanish borders. He appears to have got his wish. On February 18, 2007, the residents of Andalusia, Spain's most populous region, voted for a new autonomy compact that will, among other things, grant the region administrative control of the water resources of the region and a larger portion of its tax revenue than before. Unlike the revision of Catalonia's compact, however, the national parliament swiftly approved Andalusia's new compact, since it did not involve any discussion of nationality.

Fighting terrorism

As would be expected, it is Zapatero's approach to the highly sensitive issue of terrorism that has elicited the loudest criticism. Upon entering office, Zapatero issued ETA an invitation for talks on the condition that its leaders agree to abandon their armed struggle against the state. This offer immediately drew fire from the PP, since it violated the longstanding policy of not entering into dialogue with organizations that espouse terrorism. Indeed, this understanding had been at the heart of the PP–PSOE anti-terrorist pact of the late 1990s. In the view of the PP, talks with ETA were tantamount to "betraying the dead," a reference to the nearly 1,000 deaths attributed to ETA since it embraced a strategy of terrorism in the late 1960s (*El País*, January 16, 2007). Negotiations with ETA, however, appear to have only embarrassed the government and given the opposition more ammunition for attacking Zapatero.

After agreeing to a cease-fire in March 2006, a prerequisite for negotiations with the government, ETA renewed its killing campaign on December 2006, leaving the Zapatero government vulnerable to charges of being naïve in its approach to handling ETA. "Are we not better off now with a permanent cease-fire or when we had bombs and explosions? This time next year, we will be better off than we are today," remarked Zapatero in his end-of-the-year press conference on December 28, 2006, just days before ETA detonated a massive bomb at Madrid's Barajas airport that killed two immigrants from Ecuador and caused tens of millions of dollars of damage (*El País*, December 31, 2006). Following the return of ETA terrorism and heavy criticisms from the PP, Zapatero ended talks with ETA, declaring that "with violence there is no negotiation, any type of dialogue" (*El País*, December 31, 2006). He also apologized to the nation for his earlier optimistic remarks and proposed the creation of a new anti-terrorist pact that would incorporate not only the nation's leading parties but also organizations from civil society, for the purpose of creating "a great democratic consensus" in the fight against terrorism (*El País*, January 16, 2007).

Zapatero has also drawn the ire of both the left and the right for his approach to dealing with the growing threat posed by radical Islamic terrorists, a situation underscored by the very events that aided in his election to the presidency in 2004. This threat had been escalating for years before the tragic events of March 11, 2004. Islamic designs on Spain are a staple in the agenda of many radical Islamic organizations, including Osama bin Ladin's al Qaeda terrorist network; they are central to redeeming the tragedy of "al-Andalus," the Christian conquest of the Muslims' stronghold in southern Spain by the Spanish crown in 1492. By the early 1990s, al Qaeda itself was already well established in Spain as a training ground for Islamic terrorists. And, as stated by *El País* (May 9, 2004), news that an attack on Spain by radical Islamic terrorists was imminent, due to Spain's involvement in the wars in Iraq and Afghanistan, had been widely reported in the Spanish media prior to 2004.

In the wake of the terrorist attack of March 11, 2004, Zapatero has worked to strengthen the state's security apparatus and its ability to monitor the movement of radical Islamic extremists within Spain. This has been greatly facilitated by the creation of the National Center for Intelligence Coordination. It brings together the police, the Civil Guard and the National Intelligence Service under one roof with the purpose of facilitating the sharing of information. Small mosques, which generally do not register with the state, are one of the main targets of this new security scheme. In an interview with *El País* (May 2, 2004), Minister of the Interior José Antonio Alonso argued that "We need to get a legal situation in which we can control the Imams in small mosques since that is where Islamic fundamentalism of the kind that kills people is disseminated." Such actions have led to complaints, at home and abroad, of the willingness of the government to abridge civil rights in the fight against terrorism (see, especially, Human Rights Watch 2005).

Zapatero has also taken steps to initiate a dialogue with Islamic organizations in Spain, in the hope of creating what he has termed an "Alliance of Civilizations." This project, presented by Zapatero at the United Nations in September 2004, draws upon Spain's history of *convivencia*, a period during the Middle Ages when Christians, Jews, and Muslims peacefully co-existed in the Iberian Peninsula. It aims to counter the post-9/11 conventional wisdom that a clash of civilizations is inevitable between the West and the Islamic world, by promoting mutual understanding and respect for diversity and multiculturalism. As Zapatero explained to his UN audience: "This alliance would have as its fundamental objective to deepen political, cultural and education relations between those who represent the so-called Western world and, in this historic moment, the area of Arab and Muslim countries" (BBC News Online, September 22, 2004).

Many foreign governments, including the United States, and international organizations have praised Zapatero's big ideas about an alliance of civilizations as an enlightened approach to help ease growing polarization in the world. At home, however, Zapatero's opposition has roundly criticized them in language that borders on the hysterical. Former prime minister Aznar dismissed them as "an enormous absurdity," while Rajoy, when head of the PP, described them as suggestive of Zapatero's "astronomical ignorance, manifest irresponsibility or supine idiocy" (Woodworth 2005: 73). Furthermore, PP leaders consider the proposal "an embarrassing abandonment of efforts in the face of terrorism, as it does not advocate policing measures and an urgent democratic change in Arab and Muslim countries" (Barreñada 2006: 101).

A new foreign policy direction

Zapatero has also brought a radical change in the direction of Spain's foreign policy, often resulting in direct confrontation with the United States. Declaring the American war in Iraq "a disaster" and the ensuing occupation of that country "an even greater disaster," Zapatero abruptly pulled the Spanish troops out of Iraq (BBC News Online, March 15, 2004). In doing so, he dramatically reversed the country's foreign policy, which under Aznar had gained a decidedly pro-American and anti-European orientation. "I want Europe to see us again as pro-European," he told Cadena Ser (March 15, 2004) in announcing his decision to withdraw Spain from the coalition of nations represented in Iraq. "Spain is going to see eye to eye with Europe," he added, a remark intended to suggest that Madrid was now on board with Paris and Berlin in their opposition to Washington's policy on Iraq.

To underscore his "Europeanist" credentials, Zapatero made Spanish approval of the new EU constitution a priority. He launched an expensive "Being First in Europe" campaign designed to make Spain the first nation to ratify by national referendum the EU constitution with decidedly mixed results. On February 20, 2005 the Spanish people overwhelmingly approved the text of the constitution with 77 percent in favor and 17 percent against, but the turnout was embarrassingly low: 42 percent. This was the second lowest vote for any EU referendum by a member state, and the lowest of the previous three referendums held in Spain since the democratic transition (the December 1976 referendum on moving forward with democratic reforms; the December 1978 referendum on the new Spanish constitution; and the March 1986 referendum on whether or not to pull the country out of NATO). The opposition blamed the low turnout on the government's decision to rush a vote on the constitution. "This vote is a failure for the person who convened it," maintained Miguel Ángel Acebes, Secretary General of the PP (El País, February 21, 2005). Zapatero explained the high abstention rate as a sign of approval. "Since no party had called for abstention no one can derive any conclusion from the abstention rate" (El País, February 21, 2005). Independent observers point to the overall lack of knowledge among the general public of what was in the constitution – according to polls, nine out of ten people had little idea what was in the text (BBC News Online, February 29, 2005) – and voters' fatigue. The vote on the European constitution was the fourth time that the voters had been asked to go to the polls in less than 24 months, following the regional elections of May 25, 2003, the general elections of March 14, 2004, and the European elections of June 13, 2004.

Zapatero has also shown a not-so-subtle strain of anti-Americanism. This was in full display on October 12, 2004, as part of the celebrations of Spain's "National Day," which also serves as a day of celebration of Columbus's "discovery" of the Americas under the sponsorship of the Spanish crown, and recognition of the service to the nation of the armed forces. Zapatero's Ministry of Defense disinvited the delegation of American marines that had taken part in the military parade along Madrid's main boulevard since the terrorist attacks of September 11, 2001. In place of the Americans, Zapatero invited 48 soldiers from a French regiment in recognition of the sixtieth anniversary of the liberation of Paris from the Nazis, who marched alongside veterans from both sides of the Spanish Civil War. They were joined by relatives of victims of violence, including those killed by Basque separatists and the terrorist attack on Madrid's Atocha train station, and Spanish journalists killed in war zones. Explaining the absence of the Americans, Defense Minister José Bono said that he had decided not to invite the Americans because "it is a national holiday, not a US holiday" (Associated Press, October 12, 2004). He added: "What does not continue is subordination and getting down on our knees for any foreign government, whichever it may be."

Zapatero also embraced a new approach to relations with Latin America, much to the annoyance of Washington. In May 25, 2005, on a visit to Mexico, he declared that "the times of looking only to the northern half of the Americas are over; Latin America should be our biggest priority" (EFE, May 25, 2005). This pursuit has led Zapatero to embrace many left-leaning governments in Latin America previously shunned by the Aznar administration. In a move that displeased Washington a great deal, Zapatero sold ten C-295 transport planes and four coastal patrol corvettes worth $1.7 billion (1.3 billion euros) to the Venezuelan government of Hugo Chávez, whose "Bolivarian" revolution put Venezuela on the Bush administration's list of "rogue" states. Zapatero also relaxed the sanctions against Cuba that the European Union had placed on the Caribbean island as a consequence of Fidel Castro's imprisonment of 75 dissidents in 2005. Zapatero contended that the EU strategy of sanctions against Castro was "the worst possible for improving the fate of dissidents and prisoners of conscience" (COHA 2005). Zapatero has also developed a close relationship with two other left-wing leaders of Latin America: Brazil's Luiz Inácio "Lula" Da Silva and Argentina's Nestor Kirchner, to whom he has promised to back a proposed Mercosur (Southern Common Market)–EU free trade agreement that could break the current stalemate over the proposed alternative to the American-backed Free Trade Area of the Americas (FTAA). In an effort to placate the United States and the EU, and to counter criticisms that his Latin American policy is entirely one-sided, Zapatero has lent his support to Colombia's *Ley de Justicia y Paz* (Justice and Peace Law), a law enacted by the Colombian government to cope with the endless war between the government and left-wing guerilla movements, which human rights organizations have criticized for "creating a legal limbo where human rights will be immune to prosecution" (COHA 2005).

A CASUALTY OF ZAPATERO'S POLICIES?

The charge that Zapatero has violated the code of political behavior enshrined in the post-transition settlement is a common complaint from the right. As expressed by the conservative leader Ignacio Astarloa, "Zapatero is destroying the consensus that we have created during the democracy. He takes democracy for granted and he takes social and political stability for granted" (*New York Times*, December 15, 2006). This argument is often wedded to the highly polarizing charge that Zapatero is dividing Spain in two, an accusation rich in resonance with the notion of the "Two Spains" perpetually at war with each other (see chapter 1). A typical comment is that of Emilio Lamo de Espinoza, of the conservative research think tank Elcano Royal Institute, who has been quoted as saying that Zapatero "is governing with half of Spain, but against almost the entire other half. That is risky" (*New York Times*, December 13, 2006). Similar arguments are being heard abroad. A US analyst writes (Ho 2005: 31):

The central problem surrounding many of Zapatero's reforms is speed. Zapatero is simply moving too fast in his attempt to establish a "New Spain." In a way, his provisions for Spain thus far have been rather short-sighted. Given the frequency and new nature of his policies, it seems Zapatero is driven, at least partially, to simply differentiate himself from the previous administration as much as possible. Nevertheless, Zapatero must look at the bigger picture of Spain's future and learn to compromise with opposition parties.

Notwithstanding the obviously controversial nature of Zapatero's policies, there is something disingenuous in the criticism from the right. Aznar "left Spain more deeply divided than at any time since the Franco dictatorship," observes the political commentator Paddy Woodworth (2004: 8). An abundance of evidence sustains this claim. The PP was the first governing party to undermine the foundations of the post-transition settlement. Well before Zapatero's takeover of the government, the PP had already violated all of the provisions of the settlement, especially during its last four years in office (2000–4), when the party enjoyed a parliamentary majority. As seen previously (chapter 4), it was Aznar's project of "Constitutional Patriotism" that resuscitated the past as a political issue, with its plan to rewrite Spanish history and his refusal to entertain even the most modest of demands from advocates of the movement for the recovery of the historical memory, to say nothing of his financing of the activities of the Francisco Franco Foundation. Aznar's attempt to inject religious instruction into the primary school curriculum came dangerously close to violating the separation of church and state.

Political consensus also took a hit under Aznar. In contrast to his predecessors, Aznar put very little value on consultation with the opposition. Reflecting an attitude described by some as "democratic fundamentalism," Aznar believed "that those who were not with him were against him and came close to saying that those who were against him could not be democrats" (Woodworth 2004: 8). Perhaps nothing reveals this better than his decision to take Spain to war in Iraq without any debate in the national parliament. It was eight months after the start of the war that Aznar saw fit to address the Spanish parliament on this issue as part of a day of mourning over the death of seven Spanish intelligence officers killed in Iraq. Telling also was his treatment of the nationalist regions. His government outlawed HB, the political branch of ETA, thereby depriving the state of an intermediary with the terrorist organization. More moderate political organizations were treated harshly as well, a consequence of Aznar's belief that autonomous regions had already pushed the limits of what would be tolerated by the central state. From 2001 forward, Aznar basically stopped talking to Basque premier Juan José Ibarretxe, even though he controls the most important political institution in the Basque region. This hard-line stance became more pronounced and offensive as the 2004 campaign came to a close. The PP unleashed an attack on nationalist parties in Catalonia and the Basque Country which, judging from the results of the elections in both regions, only succeeded in turning off moderate nationalist voters. In February 2004, the PP accused the PNV of supporting ETA terrorist activities and the ERC of having talked with and conspired with ETA (Chari 2004: 961). Neither charge had any validity.

The right-wing argument that Zapatero has destroyed the post-transition settlement – especially the emphasis on consensus on public policy – also ignores much of the evidence that actually underscores the very important role that consensus has played in public policy under the Zapatero administration. It is remarkable that Zapatero has managed to reshape many aspects of Spanish society while lacking a majority of the votes in the national parliament or even a formal coalition government. In the 2004 elections, the PSOE obtained 164 seats in the 350-seat Congress of Deputies, while the PP, the leading opposition party, obtained 148. This suggests that the Zapatero government has had to work with other political parties to get its agenda approved by the Spanish Congress, something it has apparently succeeded in doing, given the relatively comfortable margins that have accompanied the enactment of some of Zapatero's most controversial policies. Indeed, on the basis of many of these votes, the PP is the odd man in Spanish politics, out of step with the majority of the parliamentary parties.

The law that legalized same-sex marriage was approved by a vote of 187–147 in the Congress of Deputies, with the opposition coming primarily from the PP. The new Catalan autonomy compact was approved by a vote of 189–154, with the opposition coming almost exclusively from the PP. All the political parties, save the PP and the ERC, supported the Law of Historical Memory; and in the case of the ERC, it rejected the law because it did not go far enough. The Law of Equality between Women and Men was approved 192–0, with the majority of the PP delegation (119) voting to abstain. More significant is that every party represented in the Congress supported this law except for the PP.

Finally, the argument that Zapatero is shattering the post-Francoist political consensus ignores the obvious desire of the Spanish electorate for a more open and indeed democratic society than the one envisioned by the founding fathers of Spanish democracy in the late 1970s. Every "radical" policy implemented by Zapatero (the withdrawal of Spanish troops from Iraq, the recovering of the historical memory, same-sex marriage and gender equality in government and the workplace) was a campaign promise made to the electorate during the 2004 elections.[4] Moreover, the bulk of Zapatero's agenda is very much in synch with the public's wishes. This hardly offers support to the right's image of Zapatero as a one-man crusade out to radicalize Spain.

Indeed, on a variety of issues it appears that Zapatero is responding to the wishes of the electorate rather than forcing his political views upon them, a point often overlooked by his critics. A June 2004 poll by the Madrid newspaper *El Mundo* showed that 80.3 percent of the public supported Zapatero's decision to withdraw the Spanish troops from Iraq. For all the cries of radicalism that greeted Zapatero's endorsement of same-sex marriages, this actually entailed very little political risk. With public opinion showing two out of every three Spaniards in favor of the new law, the damage that anti-gay demonstrations could inflict on the government was very limited (*El País*, June 19, 2005). The same can be said of Zapatero's attempt to diminish the role of the Catholic Church in public life. The June 2004 survey by *El Mundo* showed that 53.3 percent of the public approved of the government's decision to remove compulsory religious education from the public schools.

It is also worth noting that it is not just the left that finds the constitutionality of the state's subsidies of Church activities a violation of the separation of church and state. And even some within the Catholic Church itself would like to see changes in the way in which the Church operates. A notable critic of the Spanish Catholic hierarchy is the theologian Enrique Miret Magdalena of the John XXIII Association of Men and Women Theologians, who argues that the Church should divorce itself completely from the state as a way of safeguarding its independence from the state and of enhancing its credibility with the public and other organizations in civil society. In response to the seemingly endless debate over whether the state should finance religious instruction, Miret Magdalena has contended that "Religious instruction should be paid for by the faithful themselves, as a demonstration of their faith and of their interest in receiving such education for themselves and their children" (Inter-Press News Agency, April 13, 2007).

Zapatero's willingness to confront the past is another telling example of him reflecting the wishes of the citizenry rather than imposing his will or that of his party upon the nation. Not only are his policies in this area in keeping with the existing international consensus on "transitional justice" that has consolidated in the last decade, but they also take their cues from Spanish regional governance (Kritz 1995). As seen in chapter 8, in the absence of national policy on the issue of how to deal with the past, regional governments began to take matters into their own hands years before the central government began to legislate on this issue. It was the regional governments, led by those of Catalonia and the Basque Country, that first condemned Franco's 1936 insurrection as an illegitimate attack upon a popularly elected government. Regional governments also took the lead in financing the exhumation of civil war casualties; the same for the investigations into the fate of the victims of Franco's repression and the attempt to remove Francoist monuments from public view. Indeed, a solid argument can be made that on the issue of the historical memory, the national government under the Zapatero administration is basically catching up with the regions.

More revealing yet, despite all the political controversy and rancor that has greeted Zapatero's policies, the public has remained on the whole supportive of his performance in office. Throughout much of 2004–5, Zapatero's performance was rated as "good" or "very good" by 60 percent of the Spanish public.[5] His popularity then experienced a marked decline in early 2006, falling to about 40 percent, a consequence of ETA's decision to break its last cease-fire with the bombing at Barajas airport. This act was widely read by the public as a failure of Zapatero's policy to engage the terrorist organization in negotiations with the government. But even at 40 percent approval, Zapatero's rating ranked significantly higher than the 20 percent approval registered by Rajoy, the leader of the opposition.

CONCLUSION

Time will tell what political price Zapatero will pay for his daring gamble to stake his government on an ambitious attempt to revamp the country's social and political structures.[6] But as he concludes his first term of office (2004–8), certainly one of the most eventful in Spain's still-young democracy, important lessons about Spanish politics can already be discerned. Arguably the most compelling is that Spanish democracy no longer depends for its stability or its survival upon the special political protections born with the democratic transition. Zapatero's willingness to undo some of the foundational agreements upon which democracy was established in Spain, such as the denial of the past, while undertaking a significant expansion of civil and political rights, demonstrates the maturity of Spanish democracy. The fact that these radical changes to the political status quo have been accepted with such ease by Spanish society speaks volumes about the strength of democracy in Spain. Ironically, the radicalism of Zapatero's "second transition" policies could not have been so easily sustained were it not for the political stability that Spain gained from its very conservative democratic transition. The decades of cautious and pragmatic political leadership that followed the demise of Francoism created a yearning among the Spanish public for bold and imaginative political reforms (powerfully suggested by Zapatero's own rise to power), while at the same time giving new democratic institutions the capacity needed to undertake those reforms.

NOTES

Chapter 1 A Post-Transition Settlement

1 According to the Barcelona newspaper *La Vanguardia* (August 25, 2006), two other statues of General Franco remain in public view: one in the town square of the seaside city of Santander and the other one in Melilla, a Spanish outpost in northern Africa.

2 For a revealing photographic essay of Franco's material legacy on display across Spain, see "La caza del monumento fascista, recopilación de símbolos, calles, etc. . . . en todo el Estado," available at www.foroporlamemoria.info/simbolos_franquistas.php.

3 This information was provided to the author by the PSOE's public affairs office.

4 The argument that the success of democracy in Spain is owed to a political settlement echoes other elite-centered approaches for understanding Spanish democratization (see Share 1986; Gunther 1992; Linz and Stepan 1989, 1996). Alternative approaches emphasize either the favorable international context in which democracy was introduced in Spain, especially the role of the European Union (see Whitehead 1996), or the role of popular organizations, and civil society more generally, in undermining the legitimacy of the Franco regime (see Foweraker 1989).

5 *Pacto del Olvido* and *Pacto del Silencio* are unofficial terms created by scholars to suggest the informal but willful intention of the Spanish political class to bury the past. Interestingly enough, these mostly negative terms are a relatively recent invention that reflects a shift in scholarly perception about how the Spaniards dealt with the past during the transition. Initially welcomed as a uniformly positive step toward democratization, the decision to deal with the past by simply not dealing with it is at the present time seen through more critical lenses (see Blakeley 2005; Davis 2005; Humlebaek 2007; Encarnación forthcoming).

6 This hands-off approach by the central state with respect to Franco's material legacy explains why much of it is found in the capital city of Madrid and in the traditionally conservative rural parts of the country. By contrast, in regions with a strong nationalist tradition and/or in bastions of republicanism, such as Catalonia and the Basque Country, memorials to the Franco regime are relatively rare.

7 "Cava" is the champagne-like drink produced in the vineyards of Catalonia.

8 According to Diamond and Platter (1996: ix), between 1974 and 1990 some 30 countries made the transition to democracy. An additional three dozen countries – primarily in central

and eastern Europe, the former Soviet Union, and Africa – transitioned to democracy in the subsequent five years. Together with Portugal and Greece, Spain inaugurated this global democratic revolution in the mid-1970s.

9   The idea of "The Two Spains" is usually associated with the poetry of Antonio Machado, a leading member of the Generation of '98, a group of intellectuals who contemplated Spain's descent into chaos and decay following the Spanish-American War of 1898. A line in one of his poems makes reference to two Spains, "one that dies and one that yawns." The concept of two Spains, however, predates Machado. References to it are found in the nineteenth century and even earlier, including the often-quoted phrase of the satirist Mariano José de Larra: "Here lies half of Spain. It died of the other half."

10 For a broad discussion of this and other myths about the national character of Spain, see Caro Baroja (1970).

11 Bizarrely, during the 1960s the Spanish tourism office employed the phrase "Spain is Different" to promote foreign travel to Spain.

12 This tally of ETA's terrorist activities comes from the Spanish Ministry of the Interior. It does not include ETA's most recent attacks, such as the December 30, 2006 bombing of a parking lot at Madrid's Barajas airport, which killed two Ecuadorian immigrants, and the December 1, 2007 shooting of two Guardia Civil officers in the French city of Bayonne, which left one dead and the other one in a coma.

Chapter 2   Politics and the Lessons of History

1   The many excellent texts that cover Spanish history in the nineteenth and twentieth centuries are too numerous to list here. A concise account upon which this chapter is based is Herr (1971).

2   These characterizations of the Primo de Rivera dictatorship owe much to the personality of the dictator, especially his Andalusian roots, and passion for drinking and womanizing. He also succeeded in seducing nascent labor organizations with his social policies, such as the expansion of housing and medical services for the workers. This led the socialist UGT leadership to agree to form part of the regime-sponsored *comites paritarios* (parity committees). They allowed Spanish workers the opportunity to negotiate wage policy with representatives from the Ministry of Labor and national employers' confederations.

3   Owing to its importance in Spain's history, especially in the years leading to the civil war, Spanish anarchism has inspired a vast literature. For a treatment of the rise in popularity of anarchist ideologies in Spain, see Esenwein (1989). For a view of the role of anarchist organizations during the Second Republic and the Spanish Civil War, especially the CNT, see Malefakis (1970). For an analysis of the internal workings of anarchist organizations, see Bookchin (1977).

4   The Generation of '98 includes writers born between 1864 and 1875. It includes such prominent figures as Miguel de Unamuno, Pío Baroja, Antonio Machado, and Ramón del Valle-Inclán. They restored Spain's intellectual and literary prominence even as the country was in outright decline.

5   For more extensive accounts of the politics of the Second Republic, see Jackson (1965), Linz (1979), and Payne (1993). A brief but very illuminating text from which this analysis draws is Blinkhorn (1988).

6   The data in this section are drawn from Gunther, Montero, and Botella (2004: 30).

7   As would be expected, the Spanish Civil War has generated a vast and diverse literature. Perhaps the best-known general volume is Thomas (1977). Of the many memoirs and eyewitness accounts of the Spanish Civil War available in English, few match the intensity and insight of George Orwell's 1952 classic, *Homage to Catalonia*.

8   Accounting for the number of deaths linked to the civil war in Spain has proved notoriously difficult. Jackson's estimate of 580,000 casualties breaks downs as follows: 100,000 battlefield deaths; 10,000 in air raids; 50,000 of disease and malnutrition during the war; 20,000 Republican zone "paseos" (strolls) and political reprisals; 200,000 wartime Nationalist "paseos" and political reprisals; and 200,000 "red" prisoner deaths through execution or disease, 1939–43. A more recent account by Preston (1990: 41–2) estimates that some 300,000 Spaniards died in direct combat and that 440,000 people (mostly Republicans) went into exile, of whom 10,000 died in Nazi concentration camps. Preston estimates that some 400,000 people spent time in Franco's prisons and labor camps, victims of Franco's 1939 Law of Political Responsibilities. Either scenario puts the level of violence and repression in Spain well above that of other countries victimized by a right-wing authoritarian regime, such as Argentina, Brazil, Uruguay, and Chile. By way of contrast, in Argentina, which between 1976 and 1983 suffered the most violent military regime ever installed in a South American country, the number of documented casualties calculated by the country's National Commission on Disappeared Persons (CONADEP) is 8,961.

9   The most comprehensive treatment of the history and policies of the Franco regime is Payne (1987). Biographies of Franco available in English include Trythall (1970), Fusi (1987), and Preston (1994).

10 For a broader overview of economic policy under Franco, see Anderson (1970) and Gunther (1980). A very concise text from which this chapter draws is Harrison (1993).

11 Unless otherwise noted, the statistics for this section come from de Riquer I Permanyer (1995: 262–5).

Chapter 3   The Primacy of Democratic Crafting

1   The notion of "democratic consolidation," as this author has argued (Encarnación 2002), remains highly contested and open to multiple interpretations. The most influential interpretation is that offered by Linz and Stepan (1996), which aptly enough is based on the Spanish experience. It contends that democracies attain consolidation when the following conditions are met: (1) no significant national, social, economic, political, or institutional actors spend significant resources attempting to achieve the objective of a non-democratic regime; (2) a strong majority of public opinion holds the belief that democratic procedures and institutions are the most appropriate way to govern; and (3) governmental and non-governmental forces alike become subject to, and habituat to, the resolution of conflict within the specific laws sanctioned by the new democratic process (see Linz and Stepan 1996: 6).

2   This contention echoes the "transitology" literature, which emphasizes the agency embedded in the strategic interactions of political actors, who are believed to be capable of affecting the process of democratization in both beneficial and detrimental ways (Rustow 1970; O'Donnell and Schmitter 1986; Di Palma 1990; Higley and Gunther 1992). This is hardly surprising since the Spanish political experience of the post-Franco era is generally credited with "reviving" this literature and giving it the currency that it presently enjoys among democratization students.

3   The role of King Juan Carlos in the transition to democracy in Spain is generally underplayed. Yet, as suggested by this analysis, his numerous, timely interventions on behalf of the establishment of Spanish democracy cannot be ignored. An excellent profile of the King and his role during the democratic transition is Powell (1996).

4   As reported by Aguilar (2001: 98), the Second Republic called politicians from the Primo de Rivera dictatorship to account for their political excesses, as Franco did with the Republicans, and the Primo de Rivera authorities did with the leaders of the Restoration regime.

It is further noted that one of the first measures adopted by the leaders of the Second Republic was to condemn the King for high treason.

5   Chapter 7 includes a broader discussion of the content of the Moncloa pacts.

6   The names of those who signed the Moncloa pacts attest to the extraordinary political inclusiveness of this agreement: Adolfo Suárez and Leopoldo Sotelo representing the government and the UCD, Felipe González of the Spanish Socialist party (PSOE), Joan Reventós i Carner of the Socialist Convergence of Catalonia (CSC), Josep Ma. Triginer of the Socialist Party of Catalonia (PSC), Manuel Fraga Iribarne of the Popular Alliance (AP), Enrique Tierno Galván of the Socialist Popular Party (PSP), Juan Ajuriaguerra of the Basque Nationalist Party (PNV), Miguel Roca of Catalonia's Convergència i Unió (CiU), and Santiago Carrillo of the Spanish Communist Party (PCE).

7   Author's interview with Mr Calvo Sotelo (Madrid: November 11, 1993).

8   The Basque Nationalist Party (PNV) eventually withdrew its support from the constitutional committee. Thus, it is generally assumed that the Basques were not represented in the early deliberations of the constitution. This "exclusion" eventually led the party to abstain from the parliamentary vote on the constitution and to call for an abstention of Basque voters from the constitutional referendum. That said, as Gunther (2007: 17) notes, the PNV leader has publicly stated that "his party had gotten almost everything it had asked for in the course of the negotiations."

9   According to the *Christian Science Monitor* (October 1, 2004), the subvention given by the state to the Catholic Church to finance its educational, cultural, and ecclesiastical activities stands at €3.6 billion ($4.3 billion) for 2004. The bulk of this money comes through what is called "tax assignment," which gives taxpayers the option of allocating a percentage of their income tax burden to the Church.

10   The flag underwent a makeover in 1981–2, when the Francoist coat of arms (which featured symbols used by the Catholic kings in the fifteenth century and the Falange) was replaced with the royal crown and the emblem of the Bourbon royal family.

11   Freedom House rates each country on a freedom scale according to the extent to which political and civil rights are respected, with 1 representing the highest level of respect and 7 the least. "Political rights" is equated with such things as a significant range of voters' choice and political leaders being able to openly compete and be elected to positions of power in government. "Civil rights" concerns the protection of religious, ethnic, economic, and personal freedoms, as well as freedom of the press, belief, and association. Countries whose combined score for respect for civil and political rights averages 1 to 3.3 are deemed "free" (read "fully democratic"), those averaging 3 to 3.5 are deemed "partly free," and those with an average rating of 5.5 to 7 are deemed "not free." Data from Freedom House used in this section comes from Freedom House, "Freedom in the World: The Annual Survey of Political Rights and Civil Liberties," available at www.freedomhouse.org/uploads/Chart83File137.pdf/.

12   For a broader comparative discussion of pact making in Spain and South America, see Encarnación (2005).

Chapter 4   From Contention to Moderation: Party Politics

1   For a detailed overview of the PCE during its clandestine years, see Hermet (1972); for the party's role during the transition to democracy, see Mujal-León (1983, 1985).

2   A reflection of its status as Spain's oldest party and the dominant party since the transition, the literature on the PSOE is quite extensive. For a comprehensive history of the party, see Gillespie (1989). The party's trajectory during the democratic transition is covered by Share (1989), Gunther (1986a), and Maravall (1985). Méndez-Lago (2005) examines the party after its 1996 electoral defeat.

3   Ironically, the PSOE emerged from the Franco dictatorship proclaiming a Marxist economic agenda that was more radical than the one promoted by the PCE. During the 1977 campaign, the PSOE's platform called for the immediate nationalization of banking and utilities, while the PCE generally avoided any reference to this subject (Mujal-León 1985: 162). The PSOE was also more inclined than the PCE to use mass mobilization strategies and rhetoric during the electoral contests of 1977 and 1979. This was an attempt to copy the early success of the Communists, even as the Communists themselves were abandoning such strategies in an attempt to be seen as more moderate than the PSOE.

4   Author's interview with Mr Calvo Sotelo, Madrid, 1994.

5   The scandals of the Socialist era of the 1980s and early 1990s account for Spain's rise in the European ratings of Transparency International's Corruption Perception Index. This study uses a scale from 0 to 10 (with 0 indicating the lowest level of corruption and 10 the highest) to measure corruption levels around the world. Spain's rating for 1995 (4.35) put the country in the company of Italy and Greece, two countries widely regarded as the most corrupt within the EU. Since the mid-1990s, the corruption picture in Spain has changed significantly. The 2006 survey gives Spain a 6.8 rating, placing the country in the middle among EU countries. See *Transparency International Corruption Perceptions Index* (2006). Available at www.transparency.org.

6   For a broader view of the history of the PP, see Baón (2001).

7   Another memorable gaffe was Gerald Ford's 1975 visit to Madrid, just months before Franco's death. As recounted by Maxwell (1991: 39), the visit by the American president left Spaniards wondering what was the point of the visit other than to give the impression that "a big friend was rallying around."

Chapter 5   The Dark Side of Success? A Civil Society Deficit

1   Tocqueville, a nineteenth-century French political theorist, is widely regarded as the patron saint of civil society. *Democracy in America*, a chronicle of his travels throughout New England in the early 1800s, characterizes voluntary associations as the key to a successful democratic public life. This claim has been taken up in recent years by a new generation of "neo-Tocquevilleans" (see Putnam 1993; Diamond 1999; Encarnación 2006).

2   Following common political science usage, the term "civil society" in this chapter refers to the "third sector" of society (after the state and the market) that brings together ordinary citizens for the purpose of advancing mutual goals and interests. This social sphere includes but is not limited to collective actors such as organized labor, civic institutions, recreational associations, and religious groupings (see Encarnación 2001b).

3   Notable among these "reformist currents" were a new law of associations (1964) that allowed for the formation of all kinds of voluntary associations, as long as they were not of a political nature, and a new press law (1966) that lifted some censorship controls and replaced them with fines and sanctions.

4   On the Spanish labor movement during the transition to democracy, see Maravall (1978); Pérez-Díaz (1980); Zufiaur (1985); Balfour (1989); Fishman (1990); Encarnación (2001a).

5   So closely was the Communist party associated with the societal struggle against Francoism that, according to one scholar, participation in its anti-Franco activities "made membership or collaboration with the Communist party almost a necessary rite of passage for the new generation of Spaniards coming onto the political scene" (Gunther 1986b: 92).

6   Author's interview with former Prime Minister Leopoldo Calvo Sotelo, Madrid, 1994.

7   It is also interesting to point out that countries which did not experience a "pacted" or negotiated transition, such as Argentina and Portugal, have also been cited for having a civil

society deficit, at least when measured by the density of associational ties (see Encarnación 2003: index).

8   According to survey data (Centro de Investigaciones Sociológicas 2004), although a clear majority of Spaniards think of themselves as Catholics (80 percent), only 18 percent of them attend mass on a regular basis.

9   For a broader view on the Catholic Church and politics in Spain, see Linz (1984), Payne (1984), and Martínez-Torrón (2006).

Chapter 6   A Nation of Nations: Decentralizing the State

1   This reference to Ford's work is found in Chislett (2002: 71). Chislett also references a 24-country survey by UNESCO (2000) which concluded that a higher percentage of Spaniards identified more with their province than with their country (46% compared with the average of 28%) and only 25% of respondents agreed with the statement that they wanted to be a citizen of their country against an average of 47%.

2   The term "historic" usually applies to those regions that prior to 1977 had been successful in securing some degree of autonomy from the central government.

3   The Basque Country encompasses approximately 160 square kilometers spread over both sides of the Spanish/French border with a combined population of 3 million people, 2.7 million of whom reside on the Spanish side. North of the border, the Basque Country comprises the French provinces of Soule, Labourd, and Basse Navarre; south of the border it encompasses the Spanish provinces of Ávala, Vizcaya, Guipúzcoa, and Navarra. Navarra, however, is contested Basque territory. The Basques regard this region as part of their traditional territory. The "Navarros" themselves, who currently comprise their own autonomous community, are not in accord with that interpretation. The 1979 autonomy statute of the Basque Country, however, does provide for the possibility of the eventual incorporation of Navarra into the Basque community, presuming that the "Navarros" themselves support it.

4   For complete histories of ETA and analyses of its effects on Basque politics and society, see Collins (1988), Garmedia (1995), and Clark (1990).

5   The destruction of Guernica is memorialized in Picasso's *Guernica*, his most famous and controversial painting. An icon of contemporary Spanish politics, *Guernica* was painted for the Spanish Pavilion at the 1937 Paris International Exhibition to raise funds for the struggling Second Republic, and subsequently traveled the world advertising the plight of Spain under Franco. The painting made its way to Spain in 1981 (after many years at the Museum of Modern Art in New York) in keeping with Picasso's wishes that the painting be donated to the Spanish state after the restoration of democracy.

6   The region of Catalonia incorporates the provinces of Barcelona, Girona, Lleida, and Tarragona.

7   Separatist terrorism, however, has not been a stranger in Catalonia. Basque terrorists have been active in Barcelona for years, and Catalan separatist groups, most notably Terra Lliure (Free Land), active between 1979 and 1995, have resorted to planting bombs in public places and shooting political opponents in their campaign for an independent Catalonia.

8   The Kingdon of Aragón was comprised of Aragón, Catalonia, Valencia, and Majorca. Of the four Hispanic kingdoms that existed at the end of the sixteenth century (Castile, Aragón, Portugal, and Navarra), Aragón was the second largest in land mass (after Castile) and the third in the size of the population.

9   The Basque statute of autonomy was passed at the height of the civil war in 1937, when the region was half-occupied by Franco's Nationalist army. The Galicians had voted on their autonomy referendum before the Basques in 1936, just a few weeks before the start of the war, but were less successful in advancing their autonomy project because the region was under Francoist control from the onset of the war.

10 An exception to this general assertion was the autonomous community of Andalusia, which was the fourth one created through the fast-track model.

11 Spain's autonomous communities are (names are given in Spanish) Andalucía, Aragón, Asturias, Baleares, Canarias, Cantabria, Castilla-La Mancha, Castilla-León, Cataluña, Extremadura, Galicia, Madrid, Murcia, Navarra, País Vasco, Rioja, and Valencia.

12 The Euskobarómetro data are available at www.ehu.es/cpvweb. They are also cited in Mata (2005).

Chapter 7   Growing Pains: Modernizing the Economy

1 According to this report from the *Economist*, the Spanish economy may already be larger than Italy's if the "black economy" is incorporated into the equation. The Italians count it, the Spaniards do not.

2 Employment statistics in Spain are notoriously unreliable. This one and others used in this chapter come from the Instituto Nacional del Empleo and the Secretaría de Estado y Comercio.

3 For purposes of consistency, this chapter uses the name European Economic Community (EEC) rather than the present and more common European Union (EU). EEC was the official name of the body at the time of Spain's incorporation. It is also the name found in much of the literature on the political economy of Spanish democratization.

4 Between 1950 and 1973 there was a rough balance between the number of workers leaving Spain and those returning, with the latter higher by only 11,930; but between 1970 and 1984, the excess of workers returning to Spain had increased to 309,892 (Folgado Blanco 1984).

5 The "active" female population in Spain was 3,852,6000, but by 1989 it had swollen to 5,109,200 (Bresser Pereira et al. 1993: 128).

6 Histories of the INI are only available in Spanish. See Aceña Martín and Comín (1991).

7 *The 2007 Index of Economic Freedom* (Washington, DC: The Heritage Foundation and Dow Jones & Company, Inc., 2007), available at www.heritage.org/index.

8 According to estimates from the World Bank (2002), 22.6 percent of Spanish GDP was produced by the informal economy, tying Spain and Portugal for fourth highest within the EU, after Greece, Italy, and Belgium (see http://rru.worldbank.org/documents/paperslinks/informal_economy.pdf).

9 Author's interview with Mr Fuentes Quintana (Madrid: February 28, 1994).

10 See "Programa de saneamiento y reforma económica," in *Los Pactos de la Moncloa* (Madrid: Servicio Central de Publicaciones de la Secretaría General Técnica de la Presidencia del Gobierno, 1977).

11 Only one national union, the CNT, the historic anarchist syndicate from the Republican era, sought to mobilize the workers against the Moncloa pacts, with little if any success, a testament to its marginal status in contemporary Spanish politics.

12 Author's interview (Madrid: February 11, 1994).

13 Available at www.migrationpolicy.org.

14 Much of the infamy surrounding the Washington Consensus comes from the collapse of Argentina's economy in September 2001, which until then had been the primary laboratory for testing its policy propositions about economic reform and democratization.

Chapter 8   Awakened Ghosts: Memory and Politics

1 This chapter is based on Encarnación (forthcoming).

2 Even though the movement for the recovery of historical memory is widely thought of as having been launched in 2000, it is important to recognize the considerable academic

scholarship that preceded it. For an excellent review of this literature, see Gálvez Biesca (2006). It is also important to recognize the very difficult and at times hostile environment in which this literature developed during the 1980s and 1990s, when neither the political class nor society at large appeared especially interested in delving into the past.

3 This background about the mid-century generation has led some to contend that their work reflects not only that of a generation traumatized by the legacy of the civil war, but also that of a generation burdened with a tremendous sense of "class guilt." From this perspective, their work should be seen as "the expression of an anxiety for responsibility in order to correct the errors of the older generation" (their parents) and to account for that generation's apparent indifference to the social and political inequities arising from Franco's victory (Jordan 1995: 246–7).

4 The quotations from El País and Avui cited in this section are taken from Solís (2003).

5 It is important to note that, although ARMH gets the credit for having launched the movement for the recovery of historical memory, this organization was preceded by several that toiled in semi-obscurity for years, including the oldest of them all, the Association of Ex-prisoners of Catalonia (created in 1976 although not legalized until the 1980s), the Association and Archive of War and Exile, the Society of History and Justice of Andalusia, and the Friends of the International Brigades.

6 This and other information comes from the Association for the Recovery of Historical Memory, Second Declaration of the ARMH before the UN Working Group on Forced Disappearances, 2002; available at www.memoriahistorica.org.

7 Some reports indicate that this was not the first instance of exhumations in the post-Franco period. Clandestine exhumation of civil war graves executed by the relatives of the victims began to take place soon after Franco's death but ended abruptly following the attempted military coup of February 23, 1981 (see Gálvez Biesca 2006: 33).

8 The members of the International Brigades were granted Spanish citizenship in 1996, a promise made by the Republican government in 1938.

9 Since the early 1980s, there have been approximately 27 such commissions in places as diverse as Argentina, Sierra Leone, and Liberia. National governments have organized most of them with the rest created by the United Nations and non-governmental organizations (NGOs).

10 Interestingly enough, history shows that forgetting has in fact been a sound choice for some of the world's most successful democracies. As Garton Ash (1998: 35) reminds us, "much of postwar West European democracy was constructed on a foundation of forgetting." He notes that the postwar French Republic was built "upon more or less a policy of supplanting the painful memory of collaboration in Vichy and occupied France with De Gaulle's unifying national myth of a single, eternally resistant France." Kurt Waldheim's Austria was "restyled as the innocent victim of Nazi aggression." In West Germany, in the 1950s, "determined efforts were made to ignore the Nazi past."

Chapter 9   Zapatero's Spain: A Second Transition

1 Available at www.la-moncloa.es/Presidente/Discursodeinvestidura/default.htm.

2 According to government statistics from the Instituto de la Mujer, on average one woman dies per week at the hands of her partner or ex-partner in Spain. The issue of domestic violence gained prominence in national politics during the 2004 political campaign. In the four months before the election, 19 women and 14 children were killed as a consequence of domestic abuse, including a woman burned to death with her children who had repeatedly asked for police protection.

3   The constitutionality and rationality of this law is currently being challenged by, interestingly enough, other feminists who argue that penalizing one sex over the other one does not serve the cause of diminishing violence against women and may in fact have counterproductive results (see *El País*, August 20, 2005).

4   It is often remarked that Zapatero made these promises because he did not expect to win the elections.

5   The polling data cited here are extrapolated from a variety of sources, including the newspaper *El Mundo* and the databank of the Centro de Investigaciones Sociológicas (CIS).

6   As this book was going to press, Spain held the tenth national elections of the post-Franco era on March 9, 2008. The socialist party, led by Zapatero, prevailed with 43.64 percent of the vote, versus 40.11 percent for the conservative PP. In the new parliament, the PSOE will have 169 seats, 5 more than in the previous one, and 7 short of an absolute majority. This victory was a vindication of sorts for Zapatero, whose 2004 election was demeaned by the PP as an accident stemming from the political fallout of the March 11, 2004 terrorist bombings. Zapatero has pledged "to govern better and with less polarization."

REFERENCES

Acena Martín, Pablo and Francisco Comin (1991). *INI: 50 años de industrialización en España*. Madrid: Espase Calpe.

Agüero, Felipe (1995). "Democratic Consolidation and the Military in Southern Europe and South America," in Richard Gunther, P. Nikiforos Diamandouros, and Hans-Jürgen Puhle, eds., *The Politics of Democratic Consolidation: Southern Europe in Comparative Perspective*. Baltimore, Md: Johns Hopkins University Press.

Aguilar, Paloma (2001). "Justice, Politics and Memory in the Spanish Transition," in Alexandra Barahona de Brito, Carmen González, and Paloma Aguilar, eds., *The Politics of Memory*. Oxford: Oxford University Press.

Aguilar, Paloma (2002). *Memory and Amnesia: The Role of the Spanish Civil War in the Transition to Democracy*, translated by Mark Oakley. New York: Berghahn.

Aguilar, Paloma and Carsten Humlebaek (2002). "Collective Memory and National Identity in the Spanish Democracy." *History and Memory* 14 (1/2): 121–44.

Almond, Gabriel and Sidney Verba (1963). *The Civic Culture: Political Attitudes and Democracy in Five Nations*. Princeton, NJ: Princeton University Press.

Alted, Alicia (1995). "Cultural Control," in Helen Graham and Jo Labanyi, eds., *Spanish Cultural Studies: An Introduction*. New York: Oxford University Press.

Amnesty International (2003). "The Lethal Cost of Freedom of Expression in the Basque Country," Press Release, February 11.

Amodia, José (1976). *Franco's Political Legacies: From Fascism to Façade Democracy*. London: Penguin.

Anderson, Charles (1970). *The Political Economy of Modern Spain: Policy-Making in an Authoritarian Regime*. Madison: University of Wisconsin Press.

Balfour, Sebastian (1989). *Dictatorship, Workers and the City: Labour in Greater Barcelona since 1939*. Oxford: Oxford University Press.

Balfour, Sebastian (2005). "The Reinvention of Spanish Conservatism: The Popular Party," in Sebastian Balfour, ed., *The Politics of Contemporary Spain*. London: Routledge.

Banfield, Edward (1958). *The Moral Basis of a Backward Society*. Glencoe, Ill.: Free Press.

Baón, Rogelio (2001). *Historia del Partido Popular: Del Franquismo a la Refundación*. Madrid: Ibersaf.

Barreñada, Isaías (2006). "Alliance of Civilizations, Spanish Public Diplomacy, and Cosmopolitan Proposal," *Mediterranean Politics* 11 (1): 99–104.

Beevor, Antony (1982). *The Spanish Civil War.* London: Penguin.

Bermeo, Nancy (1990). "The Politics of Public Enterprise in Portugal, Spain and Greece," in Ezra Suleiman and John Waterbury, eds., *The Political Economy of Public Sector Reform and Privatization.* Boulder, Colo.: Westview Press.

Bermeo, Nancy (1992). "Democracy and the Lessons of Dictatorship," *Comparative Politics* 24 (3): 271–91.

Bermeo, Nancy (1994). "Sacrifice, Sequence and Strength in Successful Dual Transitions: Lessons from Spain," *Journal of Politics* 56: 601–27.

Bermeo, Nancy (2000). "What's Working in Southern Europe?" in Nancy Bermeo, ed., *Unemployment in Southern Europe: Coping with the Consequences.* London: Frank Cass.

Bermeo, Nancy (2003). *Ordinary People in Extraordinary Times: The Citizenry and the Breakdown of Democracy.* Princeton, NJ: Princeton University Press.

Bermeo, Nancy with José García-Durán (1994). "Spain: Dual Transition Implemented by Two Parties," in Stephan Haggard and Steven B. Webb (eds.), *Voting for Reform: Democracy, Political Liberalization, and Economic Adjustment.* New York: Oxford University Press.

Betz, Hans-Georg (1995). *Radical Right-wing Populism in Western Europe.* New York: St. Martin's Press.

Blakeley, Georgina (2005). "Digging Up Spain's Past: Consequences of Truth and Reconciliation," *Democratization* 12: 44–83.

Blinkhorn, Martin (1988). *Democracy and Civil War in Spain.* London: Routledge.

Bookchin, Murray (1977). *The Spanish Anarchists: The Heroic Years, 1868–1936.* New York: Free Life Editions.

Boraine, Alexander L. (2006). "Transitional Justice: A Holistic Interpretation," *Journal of International Affairs* 60 (1): 17–27.

Boyd, Carolyn (1997). *Historia Patria: Politics, History, and National Identity in Spain, 1875–1975.* Princeton, NJ: Princeton University Press.

Brasslof, A. (1998). *Religion and Politics in Spain: The Spanish Church in Transition, 1962–1996.* London: Macmillan.

Brooksbank Jones, Anny (1995). "Work, Women, and the Family: A Critical Perspective," in Helen Graham and Jo Labanyi, eds., *Spanish Cultural Studies: An Introduction.* New York: Oxford University Press.

Burgess, Katrina (2000). "Unemployment and Union Strategies in Spain," in Nancy Bermeo, ed., *Unemployment in Southern Europe: Coping with the Consequences.* London: Frank Cass.

Campillo Madrigal, Óscar (2004). *Zapatero: Presidente a la primera.* Madrid: Esfera de los Libros.

Capo Giol, Jordi (1981). "Estrategias para un sistema de partidos," *Revistas de Estudios Políticos* 23: 153–67.

Caro Baroja, Julio (1970). *El mito del carácter nacional.* Madrid: Seminarios y Ediciones.

Carrillo, Santiago (1965). *Después de Franco, Qué?* Paris: Ediciones Sociales.

Casquete, Jesús (2006). "The Power of Demonstrations," *Social Movement Studies* 5 (1): 45–60.

Castresana, Carlos (2005). "Gay Marriage in Spain," *Peace Review* 17: 131–6.

Centro de Investigaciones Sociológicas (2004). *Estimación de Voto*, Estudio No. 2555. Enero-Febrero.

Chari, Raj S. (2004). "The 2004 Spanish Election: Terrorism as a Catalyst for Change?," *West European Politics* 7 (5): 956–63.

Chislett, William (2002). *The Internationalization of the Spanish Economy.* Madrid: Real Instituto Elcano.

Clark, Robert P. (1990). *The Basque Insurgents*. Madison: University of Wisconsin Press.

Collins, Roger (1988). *The Basques*. Oxford: Blackwell.

Comisiones Obreras (1989). *De los pactos de la Moncloa al ASE*. Madrid C.S. de Comisiones Obreras.

Conversi, Daniele (1997). *The Basques, the Catalans and Spain: Alternative Routes to Nationalist Mobilization*. London: Hurst.

Conversi, Daniele (2002). "The Smooth Transition: Spain's 1978 Constitution and the Nationalities Question," *National Identities* 4 (3): 223–44.

Costa, Josep (2003). "Catalan Linguistic Policy: Liberal or Illiberal?," *Nations and Nationalism* 9 (3): 413–32.

Council on Hemispheric Affairs (2005). "Spain's Zapatero Emerges as a Bold New Foreign Policy Factor in Latin America." Press Release.

Coverdale, John F. (1985). "Regional Nationalism and the Elections in the Basque Country," in Howard R. Penniman and Eusebio Mujal-León, eds., *Spain at the Polls, 1977, 1979, and 1982*. Durham, NC: Duke University Press.

Crameri, Kathryn (2000). "Banal Catalanism?," *National Identities* 2 (2): 145–57.

Davis, Madeleine (2005). "Is Spain Recovering its Memory? Breaking the Pacto del Olvido," *Human Rights Quarterly* 27: 858–80.

de Riquer I Permanyer, Borja (1995). "Social and Economic Change in a Climate of Political Immobilism," in Helen Graham and Jo Labanyi, eds., *Spanish Cultural Studies: An Introduction*. New York: Oxford University Press.

Diamond, Larry (1999). *Developing Democracy: Toward Consolidation*. Baltimore, Md.: Johns Hopkins University Press.

Diamond, Larry and Larry Plattner, eds., (1996). *The Global Resurgence of Democracy*. Baltimore, Md: Johns Hopkins University Press.

Di Palma, Giuseppe (1990). *To Craft Democracies: An Essay on Democratic Transitions*. Berkeley, CA: University of California Press.

Dowling, Andrew (2001). "The Reconstruction of Political Catalanism 1939–75," *International Journal of Iberian Studies* 14 (1): 17–25.

Eastwell, Roger (2000). "The Re-birth of the Extreme Right in Western Europe?," *Parliamentary Affairs* 53: 407–25.

Elkin, Mike (2006). "Opening Franco's Graves," *Archeology* (September/October): 38–43.

Ellwood, Sheelagh (1995). "The Moving Image of the Franco Regime," in Helen Graham and Jo Labanyi, eds., *Spanish Cultural Studies: An Introduction*. New York: Oxford University Press.

Elordi, Carlos (1996). "El Largo invierno del 76," in Santos Juliá, Javier Pradera, and Joaquín Prieto, eds., *Memoria de la transición*. Madrid: Ediciones El País.

Elorza, Antonio (1995). "Regional Autonomy and Cultural Policy," in Helen Graham and Jo Labanyi, eds., *Spanish Cultural Studies: An Introduction*. New York: Oxford University Press.

Encarnación, Omar G. (1997). "Social Concertation in Democratic and Market Transitions: Comparative Lessons from Spain," *Comparative Political Studies* 30 (4): 387–419.

Encarnación, Omar G. (1999). "Federalism and the Paradox of Corporatism," *West European Politics* 22 (2): 90–115.

Encarnación, Omar G. (2000). "Beyond Transitions: The Politics of Democratic Consolidation," *Comparative Politics* 32 (2): 479–98.

Encarnación, Omar G. (2001a). "Labor and Pacted Democracy: Post-Franco Spain in Comparative Perspective," *Comparative Politics* 33 (2): 337–55.

Encarnación, Omar G. (2001b). "Civil Society and the Consolidation of Democracy in Spain," *Political Science Quarterly* 116 (1): 53–79.

Encarnación, Omar G. (2003). *The Myth of Civil Society: Social Capital and Democratic Consolidation in Spain and Brazil*. New York: Palgrave Macmillan.

Encarnación, Omar G. (2004). "The Politics of Immigration: Why Spain is Different," *Mediterranean Quarterly* 15 (4): 167–85.

Encarnación, Omar G. (2005). "Do Political Pacts Freeze Democracy? Lessons from Spain and South America," *West European Politics* 28 (1): 182–203.

Encarnación, Omar G. (2006). "Civil Society Reconsidered," *Comparative Politics* 38 (3): 357–76.

Encarnación, Omar G. (2007). "Democracy and Dirty Wars in Spain," *Human Rights Quarterly* 29 (4): 950–72.

Encarnación, Omar G. (forthcoming). "Reconciliation after Democratization: Coping with the Past in Spain," *Political Science Quarterly*.

Esenwein, G. R. (1989). *Anarchist Ideology and the Working Class Movement in Spain, 1868–1898*. Berkeley: University of California Press.

European Industrial Relations Observatory (2003). *Trade Union Membership Online*. Available at: www.eiro.eurofound.eu.int/2004/03/update/tn0403105u.html).

Evans, Peter (1995). "Back to the Future: Cinema and Democracy," in Helen Graham and Jo Labanyi, eds., *Spanish Cultural Studies: An Introduction*. New York: Oxford University Press.

Farrell, Mary (2005). "Spain in the New European Union," in Sebastian Balfour, ed., *The Politics of Contemporary Spain*. London: Routledge.

Fernández, Josep-Anton (1995). "Becoming Normal: Cultural Production and Cultural Policy in Catalonia," in Helen Graham and Jo Labanyi, eds., *Spanish Cultural Studies: An Introduction*. Oxford: Oxford University Press.

Fishman, Robert (1990a). "Rethinking State and Regime: Southern Europe's Transition to Democracy," *World Politics* 42 (3): 422–40.

Fishman, Robert (1990b). *Working Class Organizations and the Return to Democracy in Spain*. Ithaca, NY: Cornell University Press.

Fishman, Robert (2003). "Shaping, not Making, Democracy: The European Union and the Post-authoritarian Political Transformation of Spain and Portugal," in Sebastián Royo and Paul Christopher Manuel, eds., *Spain and Portugal in the European Union: The First Fifteen Years*. London: Frank Cass.

Fishman, Robert (2007). "On Being a Weberian (After Spain's March 11–14): Notes on the Continuing Relevance of Weber's Methodological Approach," in Laurence McFalls, ed., *Max Weber's "Objectivity" Reconsidered*. Toronto: University of Toronto Press.

Folgado Blanco, José (1984). *Concertación Social y Política Presupuestaria*, Dissertation, Universidad Autónoma de Madrid.

Foweraker, Joe (1987). "Corporatist Strategies and the Transition to Democracy in Spain," *Comparative Politics* 20 (1): 57–72.

Foweraker, Joe (1989). *Making Democracy in Spain*. Cambridge: Cambridge University Press.

Friedman, Max Paul and Padric Kenney, eds. (2005). *Partisan Histories: The Past in Contemporary Global Politics*. New York: Palgrave.

Fuentes Quintana, Enrique (1980). "Economía y política en la transición democrática española: fundamentos y enseñanzas de una experiencia," *Pensamiento Iberoamericano* 1: 143–59.

Fukuyama, Francis (1995). *Trust: The Social Virtues and the Creation of Prosperity*. New York: Free Press.

Fusi, Juan Pablo (1987). *Franco: A Biography*, translated by Felipe Fernández-Armesto. New York: Harper & Row.

Gálvez Biesca, Sergio (2006). "El proceso de la recuperación de la 'memoria histórica' en España: Una aproximación a los movimientos sociales por la memoria," *International Journal of Iberian Studies* 19 (1): 25–7.

Garmedia, José M. (1995). *Historia de ETA*. San Sebastián: R&B Ediciones.

Garton Ash, Timothy (1998). "The Truth about Dictatorship," *The New York Review of Books* (February 19): 35–40.

Gillespie, Richard (1989). *The Spanish Socialist Party: A History of Factionalism*. Oxford: Clarendon Press.

Gilmore, David (1985). *The Transformation of Spain*. London: Quartet.

Gimeno Martínez, Javier (2006). "Designing Symbols: The Logos of Spanish Autonomous Communities (1977–1991)," *Journal of Spanish Cultural Studies* 7 (1): 51–74.

Golob, Stephanie (2003). "Forced to be Free: Globalized Justice, Pacted Democracy and the Pinochet Affair," *Democratization* 9 (2): 21–42.

González Cuevas, Pedro Carlos (2000). *Historia de la derechas españolas: De la ilustración a nuestros días*. Madrid: Biblioteca Nueva.

Graham, Helen (1995). "Gender and the State: Women in the 1940s," in Helen Graham and Jo Labanyi, eds., *Spanish Cultural Studies: An Introduction*. Oxford: Oxford University Press.

Graham, Helen (2004). "The Spanish Civil War: 1936–2003," *Science and Society* 68 (3): 313–28.

Gunther, Richard (1980). *Public Policy in a No-party State: Spanish Planning and Budgeting in the Twilight of the Franquis Era*. Berkeley: University of California Press.

Gunther, Richard (1986a). "The Parties in Opposition," in Stanley Payne, ed., *The Politics of Democratic Spain*. Chicago, Ill.: Chicago Council on Foreign Relations.

Gunther, Richard (1986b). "The Spanish Socialist Party: From Clandestine Opposition to Party Government," in Stanley Payne, ed., *The Politics of Democratic Spain*. Chicago, Ill.: Chicago Council on Foreign Relations.

Gunther, Richard (1992). "Spain: The Very Model of the Modern Elite Settlement," in John Higley and Richard Gunther, eds., *Elites and Democratic Consolidation in Latin America and Southern Europe*. Cambridge: Cambridge University Press.

Gunther, Richard (2007). "The Spanish Model Revisited," paper presented at the conference "New Perpectives on the Spanish Transition to Democracy," King's College London, May 18–19.

Gunther, Richard, José María Montero, and Joan Botella (2004). *Democracy in Modern Spain*. New Haven, Conn.: Yale University Press.

Gunther, Richard, Giacomo Sani, and Goldie Shabad (1980). "Party Strategies and Mass Cleavages in the 1979 Spanish Parliamentary Election," paper presented at the 1980 Annual Meeting of the American Political Science Association, Washington, DC.

Hagopian, Frances (1992). "The Compromised Consolidation: The Political Class in the Brazilian Transition," in Guillermo O'Donnell and J. Samuel Valenzuela, eds., *Issues in Democratic Consolidation: The New South American Democracies in Comparative Perspective*. Notre Dame, Ind.: University of Notre Dame Press.

Hamann, Kerstin (2005). "Third Way Conservatism? The Popular Party and Labour Relations in Spain," *International Journal of Iberian Studies* 18: (2): 67–82.

Harrison, Joseph (1993). *The Spanish Economy: From the Civil War to the European Community*. London: Macmillan.

Harrison, Joseph (2006). *Economic Crisis and Democratic Consolidation in Spain, 1976–1982*, Working Papers in Economic History, Universidad Carlos III de Madrid.

Hermet, Guy. (1972). *Los comunistas en España*. Madrid: Ruedo Ibérico.

Herr, Richard (1971). *An Historical Essay on Modern Spain*. Berkeley: University of California Press.

Herzberger, David K. (1991). "Narrating the Past: History and the Novel of Memory in Post-War Spain," *PMLA* 106 (1): 34–45.

Higley, John and Richard Gunther, eds. (1992). *Elites and Democratic Consolidation in Latin America and Southern Europe*. Cambridge: Cambridge University Press.

Hipsher, Patricia L. (1996). "Democratization and the Decline of Urban Social Movements in Chile and Spain," *Comparative Politics* 27: 273–97.

Ho, Norman (2005). "Spain No More? The Zapatero Administration and Declining Spanish Identity," *Harvard International Review* 27 (3): 28–31.

Hopkin, Jonathan (1999). *Party Formation and Democratic Transition in Spain: The Creation and Collapse of the Union of the Democratic Centre*. London: Macmillan.

Howard, Marc Morje (2003). *The Weakness of Civil Society in Post-Communist Europe*. Baltimore, Md.: Johns Hopkins University Press.

Human Rights Watch (2005). *Setting an Example? Counter-terrorism Measures in Spain*. HRW 17 (1). Available at: www.hrw.org/reports/2005/spain0105/.

Humlebaek, Carsten (2007). "Revisiting the so-called 'Pacto del Olvido,'" paper presented at the conference "New Perspectives on the Spanish Transition," King's College London, May 16–18.

Huneeus, Carlos (1985). *La Unión de Centro Democrático y la transición a la democracia en España*. Madrid: Centro de Investigaciones Sociológicas.

Huntington, Samuel (1991). *The Third Wave: Democratization in the Late Twentieth Century*. Norman: University of Oklahoma Press.

Inglehart, Ronald (1997). *Modernization and Post-modernization: Cultural, Economic and Political Change in 43 Societies*. Princeton, NJ: Princeton University Press.

Jackson, Gabriel (1965). *The Spanish Republic and the Civil War, 1931–1939*. Princeton, NJ: Princeton University Press.

Jordan, Barry (1995). "The Emergence of a Dissident Intelligentsia," in Helen Graham and Jo Labanyi, eds., *Spanish Cultural Studies: An Introduction*. New York: Oxford University Press.

Karl, Terry L. (1987). "Petroleum and Political Pacts: The Transition to Democracy in Venezuela," *Latin American Research Review* 22 (1): 63–94.

Kennedy, Paul (2001). "Spain's 'Third Wave'? The Spanish Socialist Party's Utilization of European Integration," *Journal of Southern Europe and the Balkans* 3 (1): 48–59.

Kissane, Bill and Nick Sitter (2005). "Civil Wars, Party Politics and the Consolidation of Regimes in Twentieth Century Europe," *Democratization* 2 (2): 183–201.

Kritz, Neil J., ed. (1995). *Transitional Justice: How Democracies Reckon with Former Regimes*. Washington, DC: United States Institute of Peace Press.

La Caixa (2000). *Del real al euro: una historia de la peseta* (Barcelona: Fundación La Caixa).

Lijphart, Arend (1968). *The Politics of Accommodation*. Berkeley: University of California Press.

Linz, Juan (1970). "An Authoritarian Regime: Spain," in Erik Allardt and Stein Rokkan, eds., *Mass Politics*. New York: Free Press.

Linz, Juan (1973). "Early State-building and Late Peripheral Nationalisms Against the State: The Case of Spain," in S. N. Eisenstadt and Stein Rokkan, eds., *Building States and Nations*. Beverly Hills, Calif.: Sage.

Linz, Juan (1979). "Europe's Southern Frontier: Evolving Towards What?," *Daedalus* 128 (Winter): 179–209.

Linz, Juan (1981). "A Century of Politics and Interests in Spain," in Suzanne Berger, ed., *Organizing Interests in Western Europe*. Cambridge: Cambridge University Press.

Linz, Juan (1984). "Church and State in Spain from the Civil War to the Return of Democracy," *Daedalus* 120 (Summer): 159–78.

Linz, Juan and Alfred Stepan (1989). "Political Crafting of Democratic Consolidation or Destruction: European and South American Comparisons," in Robert A. Pastor, ed., *Democracy in the Americas*. New York: Holmes and Meir.

Linz, Juan and Alfred Stepan (1996). *Problems of Democratic Transition and Consolidation*. Baltimore, Md.: Johns Hopkins University Press.

Lipset, Seymour M. (1959). "Some Social Requisites of Democracy: Economic Development and Political Legitimacy," *American Political Science Review* 53: 69–105.

López-Claro, Augusto (1988). *The Search for Efficiency in the Adjustment Process: Spain in the 1980s*. Washington, DC: International Monetary Fund.

López Pina, Antonio (1985). "Shaping the Constitution," in Howard R. Penniman and Eusebio Mujal-León, eds., *Spain at the Polls, 1977, 1979, and 1982*. Durham, NC: Duke University Press.

López-Pintor, Rafael (1985). "The October 1982 Elections and the Evolution of the Spanish Party System," in Howard R. Penniman and Eusebio Mujal-León, eds., *Spain at the Polls, 1977, 1979, and 1982*. Durham, NC: Duke University Press.

MacDonald, Ross and Monica Bernardo (2006). "The Politics of Victimhood: Historical Memory and Peace in Spain and the Basque Region," *Journal of International Affairs* 60 (1): 173–90.

McDonough, Peter, Samuel Barnes, and Antonio López Pina (1998). *The Cultural Dynamics of Democratization in Spain*. Ithaca, NY: Cornell University Press.

McElrath, Roger G. (1989). *Trade Unions and the Industrial Relations Climate in Spain*. Philadelphia: Multinational Industrial Relations Series, Wharton School, University of Pennsylvania.

Malefakis, Edward (1970). *Agrarian Reform and Peasant Revolution in Spain*. New Haven, Conn.: Yale University Press.

Malefakis, Edward (1995). "Contours of Southern European History," in Richard Gunther, P. Nikiforos Diamandouros, and Hans-Jürgen Puhle, eds., *The Politics of Democratic Consolidation: Southern Europe in Comparative Perspective*. Baltimore, Md.: Johns Hopkins University Press.

Maravall, José M. (1978). *Dictatorship and Dissent: Workers and Students in Franco's Spain*. London: Tavistock.

Maravall, José M. (1982). *The Transition to Democracy in Spain*. London: Croom Helm.

Maravall, José M. (1985). "The Socialist Alternative: The Policies and Electorate of the PSOE," in Howard R. Penniman and Eusebio M. Mujal-León (eds.), *Spain at the Polls, 1977, 1979, and 1982*. Durham, NC: Duke University Press.

Maravall, José M. (1997). *Regimes, Politics and Markets, Democratization and Economic Change in Southern and Eastern Europe*. Oxford: Oxford University Press.

Maravall, José M. and Julián Santamaría (1986). "Political Change in Spain and the Prospects for Democracy," in Guillermo O'Donnell, Philippe Schmitter, and Laurence Whitehead, eds., *Transitions from Authoritarian Rule*. Baltimore, Md.: Johns Hopkins University Press.

Marsal, Juan F. and Javier Roiz (1985). "Catalan Nationalism and the Spanish Elections," in Howard R. Penniman and Eusebio Mujal-León, eds., *Spain at the Polls, 1977, 1979, and 1982*. Durham, NC: Duke University Press.

Martin, Benjamin (1990). *The Agony of Modernization: Labor and Industrialization in Spain*. Ithaca, NY: Cornell University Press.

Martín-Cortés, Irene (2003). "Political Parties and Interest in Politics in Greece and Spain. Where are the 'still enchanted' citizens?," paper presented at the ECPR workshop "Changes in Political Involvement: Disenchantment, Mobilization and Electoral Turnout," Edinburgh, Scotland.

Martín-Cortés, Irene (2007). "Disenchantment and Political Culture in Spain and Greece," paper presented at the conference "New Perspectives on the Spanish Transition to Democracy," King's College London, May 17–18.

Martínez, Robert (1993). *Business and Democracy in Spain*. Westport, Conn.: Praeger.

Martínez-Torrón, Javier (2006). "Religious Freedom and Democratic Change in Spain," *Brigham Young University Law Review* (3): 777–809.

Mata, José Manuel (2005). "Terrorism and Nationalist Conflict: The Weakness of Democracy in the Basque Country," in Sebastian Balfour, ed., *The Politics of Contemporary Spain*. London: Routledge.

Maxwell, Kenneth (1986). "Spain and Portugal: A Comparative Perspective," in Stanley Payne, ed., *The Politics of Democratic Spain*. Chicago, Ill.: Chicago Council on Foreign Affairs.

Maxwell, Kenneth (1991). "Spain's Transition to Democracy: A Model for Eastern Europe?," *Proceedings of the Academy of Political Science* 38 (1): 35–49.

Meisler, Stanley (1977). "Spain's New Democracy," *Foreign Affairs* 56 (1): 190–208.

Méndez-Lago, Mónica (2005). "The Socialist Party in Government and Opposition," in Sebastian Balfour, ed., *The Politics of Contemporary Spain*. London: Routledge.

Michener, James (1968). *Iberia*. New York: Random House.

Migration Policy Institute (2003). *Spain: Country Profile*. Washington, DC. Available at http://www.migrationinformation.org/Resources/Spain.cfm.

Morlino, Leonardo and José R. Montero (1995). "Legitimacy and Democracy in Southern Europe," in Richard Gunther, P. Nikiforos Diamandouros, and Hans-Jürgen Puhle, eds., *The Politics of Democratic Consolidation: Southern Europe in Comparative Perspective*. Baltimore, Md.: Johns Hopkins University Press.

Morse, M. Richard (1964). "The Heritage of Latin America," in Louis Hartz, ed., *The Founding of New Societies*. New York: Harcourt Brace Jovanovich.

Mujal-León, Eusebio (1983). *Communism and Political Change in Spain*. Bloomington: Indiana University Press.

Mujal-León, Eusebio (1985). "The Spanish Communists and the Search for Electoral Space," in Howard R. Penniman and Eusebio M. Mujal-León, eds., *Spain at the Polls, 1977, 1979, and 1982*. Durham, NC: Duke University Press.

Muro, Diego (2005). "Nationalism and Nostalgia: The Case of Radical Basque Nationalism," *Nations and Nationalisms* 11 (4): 571–89.

Muro, Diego (2008). *Ethnicity and Violence: The Case of Radical Basque Nationalism*. London: Routledge.

Nam, Taehyun (2007). "Rough Days in Democracies: Comparing Protests in Democracies," *European Journal of Political Research* 46: 97–120.

Núñez Seixas, Xose Manoel (2005). "Conservative Spanish Nationalism since the Early 1990s," in Sebastian Balfour, ed., *The Politics of Contemporary Spain*. London: Routledge.

O'Donnell, Guillermo (1996). "Delegative Democracy," in Larry Diamond and Marc Plattner, eds., *The Global Resurgence of Democracy*. Baltimore, Md.: Johns Hopkins University Press.

O'Donnell, Guillermo and Philippe Schmitter (1986). *Transitions from Authoritarian Rule: Tentative Conclusions about Uncertain Democracies*. Baltimore, Md.: Johns Hopkins University Press.

Ortega y Gasset, José (1963). *Obras Completas*. Madrid: Revista de Occidente.

Páez, Dario, Nekane Basabe, Silvia Ubillos, and José Luis González-Castro (2007). "Social Sharing, Participation in Demonstrations, Emotional Climate, and Coping with Collective Violence after the March 11th Madrid Bombings," *Journal of Social Issues* 63: 323–37.

Payne, Stanley (1961). *Falange: A History of Spanish Fascism*. Stanford, Calif.: Stanford University Press.

Payne, Stanley (1970). *The Spanish Revolution*. New York: Norton.

Payne, Stanley (1984). *Spanish Catholicism*. Madison: University of Wisconsin Press.

Payne, Stanley (1985). "Representative Government in Spain," in Howard R. Penniman and Eusebio Mujal-León, eds., *Spain at the Polls, 1977, 1979, and 1982*. Durham, NC: Duke University Press.

Payne, Stanley (1986a). "Introduction," in Stanley Payne, ed., *The Politics of Democratic Spain*. Chicago, Ill.: Chicago Council on Foreign Affairs.

Payne, Stanley (1986b). "Conclusion," in Stanley Payne, ed., *The Politics of Democratic Spain*. Chicago, Ill.: Chicago Council on Foreign Affairs.

Payne, Stanley (1987). *The Franco Regime*. Madison: University of Wisconsin Press.

Payne, Stanley (1993). *Spain's First Democracy: The Second Republic, 1931–1936*. Madison: University of Wisconsin Press.

Payne, Stanley (2004). *The Spanish Civil War, the Soviet Union and Communism*. New Haven, Conn.: Yale University Press.

Peces-Barba, Gregorio (1988). *La elaboración de la Constitución de 1978*. Madrid: Centro de Estudios Constitucionales.

Pereira, Luiz Bresser, Adam Przeworski, and José María Maravall (1993). *Economic Reforms in New Democracies: A Social-democratic Approach*. New York: Cambridge University Press.

Pérez-Díaz, Victor (1980). *Clase Obrera, orden social y conciencia de clase*. Madrid: Fundación del Instituto National de Industria.

Pérez-Díaz, Victor (1986). "Economic Policies and Social Pacts in Spain during the Transition: The Two Faces of Neo-corporatism," *European Sociological Review* 21 (1): 1–19.

Pérez-Díaz, Victor (1990). *The Emergence of Democratic Spain and the "Invention" of a Democratic Tradition*. Estudio/Working Paper 1990/1. Madrid: Instituto Juan March.

Pérez-Díaz, Victor (1993). *La Primacía de la sociedad civil: el proceso de formación de la España democrática*. Madrid: Editorial Alianza.

Powell, Charles (1996). *Juan Carlos: Self-made Monarch*. London: Macmillan.

Preston, Paul (1990). *The Politics of Revenge: Fascism and the Military in Twentieth Century Spain*. London: Unwin Hayman.

Preston, Paul (1994). *Franco: A Biography*. New York: Basic Books.

Preston, Paul (1995). "The Urban and Rural Guerrilla of the 1940s," in Helen Graham and Jo Labanyi, eds., *Spanish Cultural Studies: An Introduction*. New York: Oxford University Press.

Pridham, Geoffrey (1995). "The International Context of Democratic Consolidation: Southern Europe in Comparative Perspective," in Richard Gunther, P. Nikiforos Diamandouros, and Hans-Jürgen Puhle, eds., *The Politics of Democratic Consolidation: Southern Europe in Comparative Perspective*. Baltimore, Md.: Johns Hopkins University Press.

Przeworski, Adam (1991). *Democracy and the Market*. New York: Cambridge University Press.

Putnam, Robert (1993). *Making Democracy Work: Civic Traditions in Modern Italy*. Princeton, NJ: Princeton University Press.

Requena, Miguel and Jorge Benedicto (1988). *Relaciones interpersonales: Actitudes y valores en la España de los ochenta*. Madrid: Centro de Investigaciones Sociológicas.

Requena Santos, Félix (1994). "Redes de amistad, felicidad y familia," *Revista Española de Investigaciones Sociológicas* 66: 73–89.

Richards, Michael (2004). "Between Memory and History: Social Relationships and Ways of Remembering the Spanish Civil War," *International Journal of Iberian Studies* 19 (1): 85–94.

Richards, Mike (1995). "The Material Reality of State Power," in Helen Graham and Jo Labanyi, eds., *Spanish Cultural Studies: An Introduction*. New York: Oxford University Press.

Roldán Ros, Juan (1985). "The Media and the Elections," in Howard R. Penniman and Eusebio Mujal-León, eds., *Spain at the Polls, 1977, 1979, and 1982*. Durham, NC: Duke University Press.

Roller, Elisa (2002). When Does Language Become Exclusivist? Linguistic Politics in Catalonia," *National Identities* 4 (3): 273–89.

Rostow, W. Walt (1960). *The Stages of Economic Growth*. New York: Cambridge University Press.

Royo, Sebastián (2000). *From Social Democracy to Neo-liberalism: The Consequences of Party Hegemony in Spain, 1992–1996*. New York: St. Martin's Press.

Royo, Sebastián (2006). "Beyond Confrontation: The Resurgence of Social Bargaining in Spain in the 1990s," *Comparative Political Studies* 39 (8): 969–95.

Royo, Sebastián (2007). "The Spanish Economy after 21 Years of EU Membership," *Newsletter of Iberian Politics* 2 (1): 1–9.

Rustow, Dankwart (1970). "Transitions to Democracy," *Comparative Politics* 2 (3): 337–65.

Sammers, Michael (2001). "Here to Work: Undocumented Immigration into the United States and Western Europe," *SAIS Review* 21 (Winter–Spring): 131–45.

Shabad, Goldie (1986). "After Autonomy: The Dynamics of Regionalism in Spain," in Stanley Payne, ed., *The Politics of Democratic Spain*. Chicago, Ill.: Council of Foreign Affairs.

Share, Donald (1986). *The Making of Spanish Democracy*. New York: Praeger.

Share, Donald (1989). *Dilemmas of Social Democracy: The Spanish Socialist Workers' Party in the 1980s*. Westport, Conn.: Greenwood Press.

Smith, W. Rand (2000). "Unemployment and the Left Coalition in France and Spain," in Nancy Bermeo, ed., *Unemployment in Southern Europe: Coping with the Consequences*. London: Frank Cass.

Solís, Fernando León (2003). "The Transition(s) to Democracy and Discourses of Memory," *International Journal of Iberian Studies* 16 (1): 49–63.

Tarrow, Sidney (1994). *Power in Movement*. New York: Cambridge University Press.

Thomas, Hugh (1977). *The Spanish Civil War*. London: Penguin.

Tocqueville, Alexis de (1969). *Democracy in America*. Garden City, NY: Anchor Books.

Trythall, J. W. D. (1970). *El Caudillo: The Political Biography of Franco*. New York: McGraw-Hill.

Tusell Gómez, Javier (1985). "The Democratic Center and Christian Democracy in 1977 and 1979," in Howard R. Penniman and Eusebio Mujal-León, eds., *Spain at the Polls: 1977, 1979, and 1982*. Durham, NC: Duke University Press.

UNESCO (2000). *World Culture Report*. Paris.

Visser, Jelle (1990). "In Search of Inclusive Unionism," *Bulletin of Comparative Labor Relations* 18: 173–4.

Wert Ortega, José Ignacio (1985). "The Transition from Below," in Howard Penniman and Eusebio Mujal-León, eds., *Spain at the Polls, 1977, 1979, and 1982*. Durham, NC: Duke University Press.

Whitehead, Laurence (1996). *The International Dimensions of Democratization*. New York: Oxford University Press.

Wiarda, Howard (1973). "Toward a Framework for the Study of Political Change in the Iberic–Latin Tradition: The Corporative Model", *World Politics* 25: 206–35.

Wiarda, Howard (2000). "Spain 2000: A Normal Country?," *Mediterranean Quarterly* 11 (3): 30–61.

Williamson, John (1994). *The Political Economy of Policy Reform*. Washington, DC: Institute of International Economics.

Woodworth, Paddy (2004). "Spain Changes Course," *World Policy Journal* 21 (2): 7–24.

Woodworth, Paddy (2005). "Spain's 'Second Transition,'" *World Policy Journal* 22 (3): 69–80.

Zakaria, Fareed (2003). *The Future of Freedom: Illiberal Democracy at Home and Abroad.* New York: Norton.

Zaverucha, Jorge (1993). "The Degree of Military Political Autonomy during the Spanish, Argentine and Brazilian Transitions," *Journal of Latin American Studies* 25 (2): 283–99.

Zufiaur, José María (1985). "El sindicalismo español en la transición y la crisis," *Papeles de Economía Española* 22: 202–34.

INDEX